A MATURE FAITH

Louvain Theological and Pastoral Monographs is a publishing venture whose purpose is to provide those involved in pastoral ministry throughout the world with studies inspired by Louvain's long tradition of theological excellence within the Roman Catholic tradition. The volumes selected for publication in the series are expected to express some of today's finest reflection on current theology and pastoral practice.

LOUVAIN THEOLOGICAL & PASTORAL MONOGRAPHS
—————— 25 ——————

A MATURE FAITH

Daniël J. Louw

PEETERS PRESS
LOUVAIN

41328227

10-28-02

© 1999, Peeters, Bondgenotenlaan 153, 3000 Leuven, Belgium

ISBN 90-429-0686-3 (Peeters Leuven)
D. 1998/0602/303

"What a piece of work is man! How noble in reason! how infinite in faculties! in form and moving, how express and admirable! in action, how like an angel! in apprehension, how like a god! the beauty of the world! the paragon of animals! And yet, to me, what is this quintessence of dust?"

(Act II, Scene II)

"What is a man,
If his chief good and market of his time
Be but to sleep and feed? a beast, no more."

(Act IV, Scene V)

(William Shakespeare: *Hamlet, Prince of Denmark*
[Middlesex: Spring Books, 1968[11]])

"What is a man that you are mindful of him,
the son of man that you care for him?
You made him a little lower than the heavenly beings
and crowned him with glory and honor."

(Psalm 8:4-5)

A MATURE FAITH SPIRITUAL DIRECTION AND ANTHROPOLOGY IN A THEOLOGY OF PASTORAL CARE AND COUNSELING

TABLE OF CONTENTS

INTRODUCTION

Our interest in the design of an anthropology for pastoral care stems mainly from the fact that pastoral counseling deals primarily with existential, relational and contextual problems. Hence our attempt to link life issues to an understanding of God which can help parishioners and other people to make decisions regarding the purposefulness of their lives and to take responsibility for the questions put forth by suffering and pain. It could be argued that the need for an anthropology in pastoral care stems from theodicy and the experience in pastoral ministry that exposure to suffering poses two main questions: "Who am I?" (What is meant by humanity and personal identity? What is the significance of our human life?); and: "Who is God?" (the appropriateness of different God-images within different contexts and their significance to our human misery).

These two questions compel pastoral care to undertake a paradigm shift, moving from the traditional "soul care" to a much broader undertaking: "faith care within the contextuality of life care." Furthermore, these contribute to what can be called a "hermeneutics of pastoral care." Hermeneutics then refers to the understanding of different narratives and life stories within the existential reality of pain, suffering, anxiety, guilt and despair, as well as our human need for meaning, hope, liberation, care and compassion. Although the scope of pastoral care is much broader than the realm of suffering, suffering poignantly exposes two important dimensions of our being: the dimension of *identity* (who am I?) and the *transcendent* dimension of our human existence (what is meant by human destiny, the ultimate concern, and how do these concepts link with the concept, "God"?). A hermeneutics of pastoral care is therefore engaged in the challenge to link the significance of human life to an understanding of God which enhances meaning *in* suffering. A pastoral anthropology should therefore try to meet the challenge of how to reflect on God while simultaneously contributing to a more just and caring human society.

However, it must be admitted that the interest in a theological anthropology has been caused by other factors too. In his book, *Anthropologie in Theologischer Perspektive*, W. Pannenberg points out that contemporary philosophical issues urge one to reflect on a theological anthropology.[1] To be frank, postmodernity's quest for human identity within relativity, plurality, globalization and a fragmented society, forces one to reflect anew on the issue of being human.

According to Pannenberg the main reason for such a reflection is that Christian theology is engaged in the question regarding the salvation of human beings ("die Heilsfrage des Menschen").[2] Healing and wholeness are not only on the agenda of postmodernity. It is predominantly a question for the Christian faith.

Furthermore, theological issues such as the notion of the suffering God (*theologia crucis*) and the incarnation, force pastoral theology to reflect on the meaning of human identity. Pannenberg identifies this motif (incarnation) as the main theological reason for reflection on the doctrine of persons.[3]

The danger in a pastoral anthropology is to become so spellbound by our being human (the issue of personal identity) and the contemporary quest for justice and humanity (anthropocentrism)

[1] See W. Pannenberg, *Anthropologie in Theologischer Perspektive* (1983), p. 12.
[2] *Ibid.*, p. 12.
[3] *Ibid.*, p. 13.

that the relationship with God becomes irrelevant. The danger is to become so psychological and contextualized that the notion of God is just a pious afterthought. To avoid this danger, the categories "mature faith" and "spiritual direction" have been introduced as an indication that our reflection tries to combine the quest for humanity and meaning with the problem of metaphorical and hermeneutical theology: the naming of God and the influence of God-images on our self-understanding and identity.

Another danger in a design of a pastoral anthropology is that all attention is given to God, while our quest for identity and humanity is being ignored. One must admit that, although a Christian anthropology is theonomous, it should not become so God-centered that the danger of "theocentrism" lurks. A biblical approach is not there to "safeguard" God, but to disclose our human identity *before* God (*coram Deo*). It should focus on the salvation of human beings in order to restore their humanity within the network of relationships as well as within the contextuality of environmental issues. In this regard Hall's assertion is most helpful: "A religious tradition whose very *Theos* is other-centered cannot be described adequately as a theocentric tradition."[4] The God of the biblical faith is fundamentally creation-oriented (geocentric) and human-oriented (anthropocentric). "To the God-orientation of repentant humanity there corresponds a human-orientation of the gracious God."[5] This the reason why I pay attention to creaturehood: realism in a pastoral anthropology (1.4); the interplay between faith and personality (2.5); the nature of mental health (adulthood) (2.6); identity and growth (2.7); maturity and the interplay of values and virtues (2.8); and an attempt to probe into the possibility of a psychological interpretation of scriptural texts.

[4] D. J. Hall, *Professing the Faith* (1993), p. 346.
[5] *Ibid.*, p. 346.

The point I want to make is that a theonomous approach should focus hermeneutically on the meaning of God-images in order to disclose a better understanding of what human identity is about. A pastoral theology should thus take seriously our human quest for meaning.

My attempt to design a pastoral anthropology from the perspective of pneumatology is not to ignore Christology and the implication of, for example, soteriology for a human self-understanding. The thrust of my argument is that if one is indeed liberated for creaturehood, this affirmation should not be merely in terms of our "creatureliness," but in terms of the "charismatic character" of our being *with* God, *in* Christ, *within* creation: the gifts of the Spirit as the enrichment of creaturehood and the empowerment of our being human.

Another reason for a pastoral anthropology is the praxis of ministry. It is, to a certain extent, a functional reason. Pastoral ministry is not only about faith and God. It is indeed about the significance of human relations within contexts. This is the reason why our approach for a pastoral anthropology can be described as a "functional anthropology," *i.e.*, an anthropology which does not solely focus on the nature of human beings, but on their conduct and function as well. Furthermore, by "functional anthropology" is meant the relevancy of the Christian faith with regard to identity, maturity and burning existential issues such as anxiety, guilt and despair.

When designing an anthropology, the challenge for a pastoral theology is how to relate Christology (justification) to pneumatology (sanctification) and, further, how to apply this to the process of developing identity and maturity. What then is the impact of salvation[6] on human development and virtues? What contribution

---

[6] Salvation gives pastoral care a unique identity. See R. Sons, *Seelsorge zwischen Bibel und Psychotherapie* (1995), p. 110: "Bleibt die Psychotherapie auf den Bereich psychischer oder auch medizinischer Heilung begrenzt, so sprengt die Seelsorge diesen Rahmen, indem sie das Heil des Menschen zu ihrem Proprium erklärt." Pastoral care should operate with both the constitutive character

can be made by pastoral care to foster personal growth in order to help the human psyche to cope better with life? We even toy with the idea whether a pneumatological stance in pastoral anthropology could lead to the design of a "psychology of grace"; *i.e.*, a model in which salvation is interpreted in a more integrative model for human wholeness.

Pastoral care and pastoral theology are those disciplines within a practical theology which are engaged with what traditionally has been called *cura animarum* — the care of souls. As part of practical theology, pastoral care deals with God's involvement with our being human and our spiritual journey through life. Essentially, it is engaged with the human search for meaning and our quest for significance, purposefulness and humanity,

As a theological discipline, pastoral care focuses on the meaning of such concepts as care, help and comfort from the perspective of the Christian faith. It deals with the process of communicating the Gospel and the encounter and discourse between God and persons. This encounter is based on the notion of stewardship and the covenantal partnership between God and human beings.

In the past, pastoral care commuted between either a *theological reduction* (our basic problem is sin — one is in need of redemption) or a *psychological reduction* (our basic problem is blocked, inner potentialities — one is in need of self-realization). What had been understood by pastoral care was often more psychotherapy within a Christian context than spiritual direction or *cura animarum*.

A *bipolar approach* in pastoral care is an attempt to work with the principle of mutuality and correlation. God *and* human beings,

---

of the Word and the describing character of a psychotherapeutic process of communicating. "Handelt es sich bei der Seelsorge um ein 'konstituierendes' Wort, so ergeht in der Psychotherapie ein 'konstatierendes' Wort. Geht es hier om die Stiftung eines neuen Verhältnisses, nämlich des Gottesverhältnisses, so geht es dort um Beschreibung eines Selbstverhältnisses" (p. 176).

theology *and* psychology, pastoral care *and* the human sciences should, therefore, not operate separately, opposing one another, but more in terms of a integrative approach. Nevertheless, pastoral care should maintain its distinctive character, namely as *cura animarum*, *i.e.,* the care for people's spiritual needs. Our assumption is that care is a theological issue and should be interpreted in terms of an *eschatological perspective*.[7]

By "eschatology" is not meant a doctrine regarding the "end" of time and history. Eschatology is connected to the notion of salvation (Heil) and refers to the essential quality and status of our new being in Christ.[8] An eschatological perspective interprets human beings in terms of the event of Christ's death and resurrection. It reckons with the new *aeon*. Recreation determines the direction and destination of creation. The implication of such an eschatological approach in theology is that reality is assessed in terms of the already and not yet of God's coming Kingdom. Grace defines the essence of our being and the character of humanity. Spiritual direction is then viewed as the outcome of a dynamic and vital hope which encompasses more than visual perception. It reckons with the transcendent dimension of the Christian faith, *i.e.,* the faithfulness of God.

[7] K. M. Woschitz (*De Homine* [1984]) gives a thorough description of different perspectives on our being human. His finding is that in Christian theology the perspective of faith dominates. "Im Glauben an das offenbarende Wort weiss sich der Mensch gleichsam von 'oben' gedeutet und erleuchtet sowie vom Soll des Glaubens beansprucht. Die christliche Existenzweise ist Glaubensexistenz und der Glaube ein geschichtliches 'Prinzip,' d.i. das, woher, worin und woraufhin sich das Leben vollzieht. Er hat sein geschichtliches Unterpfand in Jezus Christus" (p. 283).

[8] "Christliche Eschatologie hat jedoch mit solchem apokalyptischen 'Endlösungen' nichts zu tun denn ihr Thema ist gar nicht 'das Ende,' sondern vielmehr die Neuschöpfung aller Dinge. Christliche Eschatologie ist die erinnerte Hoffnung der Auferweckung des gekreuzigten Christus und spricht darum von neuen Anfangen im tödlichen Ende" (J. Moltmann, "Theologie im Projekt der Moderne" [1995], p. 12).

A metaphorical and hermeneutical approach

Because of the influence of metaphorical theology, pastoral care should be interpreted more and more in a hermeneutical paradigm than in a kerygmatic or homiletic paradigm. It becomes clear that the pastoral encounter is not merely about proclamation and admonition. Pastoral care is about communication, trying to establish a relationship of trust and empathy through listening skills. But, as a theological science, pastoral care is more than communication. At stake is the discourse of the Gospel and the narrative of salvation. Pastoral care should therefore maintain its theological character. In order to do this, a pastoral hermeneutics of care and counseling should deal with the naming of God and religious experiences which refer to spirituality and the ultimate.

A hermeneutics of pastoral care deals with the interpretation of the presence of God within human relationships and social contexts. It also tries to interpret existential issues from the perspective of the Christian faith. Central to a hermeneutical approach in pastoral care is dealing with different metaphors which reveal God's compassion and care. Hence the importance of God-images and the interpretation of experiences of faith. In short, a pastoral hermeneutics of care and counseling is about religious experiences which give an indication of believers' perception of God and their interpretation of the significance of their existence; hence the quest for spirituality in a pastoral strategy for counselling. The outcome of such a focus on spirituality should hopefully shed some new light on the very important issue of the interplay between a Christian faith and the current quest for human rights and humanity.

Traditionally, the different functions of pastoral care have been described as: *healing, sustaining, guiding, reconciliation* and *nurturing*. Within the framework of a hermeneutics of pastoral care, a sixth one must be added: *interpretation* and *diagnosis/assessment*.

Hence the challenge to a pastoral hermeneutics to deal with metaphors which portray God. Such a portrayal in pastoral theology must not be understood in terms of a dogmatic model (to systematize information about God in a rational way), but to understand God in relation to contextual issues and suffering (to interpret crises and problematic/painful events with the aid of experiences of faith which refer to God).

When employing a metaphorical approach in pastoral theology, one should be aware of the underlying assumption that all reference to God is indirect. "No words or phrases refer directly to God, for God-language can refer only through the detour of a description that probably belongs elsewhere."[9] Metaphors refer to a non-literal, indirect and figurative way of speech without denying the reality and the ontological quality of that which they denote.

Hick makes a distinction between metaphorical and literal speech. The latter refers to meaning in a lexicographical sense. "Metaphorical" is derived from the Greek *metaphorein*, to transfer. There is a transfer of meaning — the unknown is explained in terms of the known. One term is illuminated by attaching to it some of the associations of another, so that the metaphor is "that trope, or figure of speech, in which we speak of one thing in terms suggestive of another."[10] Hick further argues that metaphors serve to promote communication and a sense of community.

Theology may be defined in many ways. The most famous definition, without doubt, is that of Anselm of Canterbury: *fides quaerens intellectum*, faith seeking understanding. Within the current demand for dialogue and communication, theology should be

---

[9] See S. McFague, *Models of God* (1987), p. 34.

[10] See J. Soskice, *Metaphor and Religious Language* (Oxford: Clarendon Press [1985]), p. 54, cited in Hick, *The Metaphor of God Incarnate* (1993), p. 99.

supplemented by the notion of: *fides quaerens verbum,* faith seeking ways of saying, or more precisely, ways of discoursing.[11]

Theology needs both: understanding and communication. But then, understanding is not the *intellectus* of speculative rationality, but that understanding which entails different experiences of God. Understanding is a process of contextual interpretation, not of rational explanation.

Theological and pastoral communication is more than merely interpreting and denoting messages. Pastoral communication entails communion, fellowship,[12] *i.e.,* that kind of communication where people can experience the presence of God as a space for intimacy and unconditional love. And that is exactly what spiritual direction in pastoral care is about. It focuses on our human disposition. But, by doing so, human behavior and human acts become increasingly important. This is the reason for a third supplementation: theology is indeed practical and is seeking ways of "appropriate doing." Meaningful and just actions become important. Theology must therefore be supplemented by the following formula: *fides quaerens actum* — faith seeking ways of appropriate/just doing/action.

Correlation and the existential concern

Pastoral care, as a theological discipline, could be defined in terms of Tracy's description of theology as "the discipline that articulates

---

[11] See M. Viau, *Perspectives on Practical Theologies and Methodologies* (1997), p. 4.

[12] L. Benze (*Die Kirche als Kommunikation* [1996], p. 2) describes the inner structure of the church in terms of communication. "Kirche als jene Semiogenese." Without communication, the church loses its identity. "Nimmt man die Kommunikation aus der christlichen Theologie heraus, bleibt kein einziges Dogma, überhaupt nichts."

mutually critical correlations between the meaning and truth of an interpretation of the Christian faith and the meaning and truth of an interpretation of the contemporary situation."[13] Both practical and pastoral theology are involved in a communication process which should result in concrete and meaningful *actions of faith* (*fides quaerens actum*). The challenge to pastoral theology thus is to develop an anthropological theory for human transformation and direction which reckons with existential contexts. It should also try to assess the existential value of God-images and deal with the interplay between God-images and our human self-understanding.

The implication of our argument for designing a theological anthropology is that the naming of God in pastoral care is essentially an existential concern. Very aptly Braaten remarks as follows: "The question of God arises out of the human quest for meaning; it is, thus a structural dimension of human existence. Statements and symbols about God function to answer questions concerning the nature and destiny of human existence."[14] Pastoral theology is not a theology "from above," but a theology "from below." Braaten[15] calls it the existential locus of God-language.

Although he is a sociologist, P. L. Berger pleaded in his now famous book, *A Rumor of Angels*,[16] for that kind of awareness of transcendency which can contribute to joyful play — the human being as *humo ludens*. "In openness to the signals of transcendence the true proportions of our experience are rediscovered. This is the comic relief of redemption; it makes it possible for us to laugh and to play with a new fullness."[17]

---

[13] See D. Tracy, "The Foundations of Practical Theology" (1983), p. 62.

[14] See C. E. Braaten, "The Problem of God-language Today," *Our Naming of God* (1989), p. 20.

[15] *Ibid.*, p. 19.

[16] See P. L. Berger, *A Rumor of Angels* (1969), p. 121.

[17] *Ibid.*, p. 75.

A pastoral hermeneutics which is concerned with spiritual direction is an attempt to rediscover "signals of transcendence" which create hope and joy on an extential level. This attempt should deal with the overall new theological agenda posed by postmodernity: "... how can the Christian faith be made intelligible amid an emerging postmodern consciousness that, although driven by a thirst for both individual and cosmic wholeness, still affirms and extends such modern themes as evolutionary progress, future consciousness, and individual freedom?"[18]

What then should *wholeness* and *healing* entail when they are assessed in terms of the perspective of spiritual direction and a Christian understanding of persons (anthropology)?

A relational model

Closely linked to the issue of wholeness and healing is *the naming of God* which Tracy calls an understanding of God in relational terms, without rendering God a conceptual prisoner of a new intellectual system of totality with no real moment of infinity allowing God to be God.[19] How should one perceive God within a postmodern society? What is the link between our naming of God and spiritual direction?[20]

It must be admitted that the concept "anthropology," and the notion of a "doctrine of persons" are, as such, foreign to Scripture. The latter deals with different perspectives on our being human. It

---

[18] See T. Peters, *God - the World's Future* (1992), p. 6.

[19] See D. Tracy, *On Naming the Present* (1994), p. 41.

[20] "Eine theologische Anthropologie geht von der These aus, dass der Mensch sich selbst in seinem Ursprung, Wesen und Ziel von Gott her verstehen und sich in seinem Handeln an Gottes geoffenbarten Willen orientieren muss" (H. Köhler, *Theologische Anthropologie* [1967], p. 9).

does not unfold a systematic description of the nature of human beings. By "a pastoral anthropology" is not meant such a systematic description or theological theory. Its purpose is to reflect on the significance of our relationship with God and its possible consequences for interpreting humanity.

The implication of a relational model is that it deals with the notion of interconnectedness and the systemic nature of the human environment. "It declares that in the Christian understanding the most significant thing to be said about being, is that it is integrated — whole, interconnected, not fragmented, but delicately interrelated, ecological, relational."[21] A relational model implies that being, in all its aspects and manifestations, is relational. This is what Hall calls "the ontology of communion."[22] This means that the meaning question is linked to the ontological assumption of the interrelatedness — the integrity — of all that is. "It means, further, that the ethic which emanates from this system of meaning is directed toward the restoration of broken relationships. To state it once more in a single theorem: For the tradition of Jerusalem *being* means *being-with*."[23] An ontology of communion and an understanding of humanity as cohumanity should, therefore, inevitably result in what I want to call "an anthropology of responsibility": *respondeo ergo sum*.

The classic point of departure for a theological anthropology is always the notion: our creatureliness (creaturehood) and its connection to the concept, "the image of God." The latter should not be ignored. However, our starting point is the Old Testament's notion of *nefešj* (spiritual life) and the Pauline expression, the human being as a spiritual being, *pneuma*. *Pneuma* then refers to our spiritual relationship with God and to the new being in Christ.

---

[21] D. J. Hall, *Professing the Faith* (1993), p. 317.

[22] *Ibid.*, p. 304.

[23] *Ibid.*, p. 321.

Christian spirituality should, therefore, reflect the eschatological stance of human beings, *i.e.,* our being recreated in the image of Christ and baptized in the Spirit. *Pneuma* refers to the transformation from "death" to "life" (resurrection) (Rom 6:4[24]). We have been justified by faith (Rom 5:1) and should now live a life guided by the Spirit of God. We have been saved in hope (Rom 8:24-25). Spiritual direction should thus explore the connection between hope and our being a "spiritual person."

Assumptions and basic issues

Our basic assumption is that the distinctiveness of pastoral care resides in the fact that two of its main objectives are spiritual growth and the development of a mature faith.

Another assumption is that the assessment of God-images in spiritual direction should not derail, becoming a mere cognitive analysis. Very aptly, H. Andriessen warns against such a danger in spiritual direction.[25] According to Andriessen, the danger in spiritual direction is to interpret God in cognitive categories, when the focus should be on experiences of faith which entail imagination, reflection, emotion, and contextuality. Andriessen advocates a spiritual direction which deals with internalized rather than formalized experiences of God.[26]

---

[24] *The Holy Bible* (New International Version) (New York: New York International Bible Society, 1978[7]), was used as reference throughout this work.

[25] See H. Andriessen, *Oorspronkelijk Bestaan* (1996), pp. 54-55.

[26] "Hoe dit ook zij, van geestelijke begeleiding wordt verhoopt dat men erdoor geholpen wordt zich van het Godsbeeld dat men heeft verinnerlijkt, bewust worden. Men kan ook zeggen: dat men leert beseffen hoe men op grond van zijn geschiedenis en ontwikkeling geleerd heeft met God om te gaan" (*Ibid.,* p. 55).

These assumptions are linked to the following three basic issues which are at stake in a doctrine of human being.

• *Human identity and vocation.* A Christian anthropology should help people to affirm their being and develop a realistic understanding of themselves. Our argument in this book will focus upon a "pneumatic" interpretation of humanhood, personhood and creaturehood in order to help human beings to affirm their daily existence joyfully and accept life thankfully as grace.

In the past, a Reformed model often stressed sinfulness (the no) without affirmation (the yes to creaturehood). This then leads inevitably to a negative dissociation from the world. Such a negative model implies a reduction of human beings to the status of inferiority. On the other hand, the danger in an opportunistic model is that affirmation (yes), without reckoning with the human predicament and impairment (no), could easily lead to an overestimation of human inner potentialities. Such a stance tends to minimize the doctrine of the Fall. It can also lead to an anthropocentrism that relegates humans to nonhuman forms of creatureliness and enhances selfishness/smugness.

The core problem in a human identity and vocation is often the problem of suffering and evil. It seems that a pastoral anthropology should, therefore, always take into consideration the dialectical tension between affirmation (yes to creaturehood), as well as resistance (the no to evil).

• *The human quest for meaning, significance and purposefulness.* It has been mentioned that spiritual direction is closely linked to the existential issues of anxiety (our fear of death, isolation and rejection); despair and doubt (our need for hope), and guilt (our need for freedom and salvation). My basic assumption is that our core human need is *intimacy, i.e.,* to be accepted unconditionally without the fear of rejection. This need is linked to the teleological question, Why? Meaning, therefore, cannot be predicated upon being. It must be disclosed in terms of an understanding of our human identity and vocation, as well as an understanding of God which is closely linked to our human suffering. Hence the need for a *theologica crucis* and the notion of God's compassion and vulnerability.

Being, as such, does not seem to disclose its own *raison d'être,* which should be disclosed. Hence the following question in a pastoral anthropology: In a society in the grips of "future shock," a society conscious of the prospect of nonbeing on a massive, global scale, of violence and criminality, what can Christian faith contribute to the contemplation of the teleological questions, Why? For what reason?

• *The interplay between God-images, spirituality and self-esteem.* If our being human is exposed to the daily threat of death and vulnerability, what contribution can theology make in revising and reframing inappropriate God-images? For example, if God is understood in terms of immutability, what is the influence of such a static understanding on our human need for pathos and compassion?

It is my basic assumption that, in terms of a relational model, God should be interpreted in terms of companionship, partnership and communion. Hence the notion of God as "Soul Friend." To avoid the impression of an intimate, but very private and individualistic "consumption" of God for mere personal matters, the concept of a "Soul Friend" should be supplemented with the notions of a "suffering God" and the "faithfulness of God." The suffering God discloses Him within the reality of our human misery. It safeguards theology from a very romantic understanding of God (the unqualified yes [love] without the no [resistance and judgement]). God's faithfulness fulfils our need for continuity within discontinuity.

Outline

The first chapter is devoted to an outline of the two traditional main streams in pastoral care. It is an attempt to advocate a bipolar model and an eschatological approach in pastoral care. The expectation is that pastoral care should thus overcome the impasse between a theological and psychological reduction. Furthermore, the first chapter deals with an exposition of both the connection between creation and a theological anthropology (persons created in the image of God), as well as the interplay between Christology and anthropology (the impact of salvation on an anthropology of pastoral care). It proposes a realistic approach which moves further than either a pessimistic or an optimistic view of human beings. The assumption is that spirituality should be described in terms of pneumatology (the spiritual person as *pneuma*) in order to understand the theological meaning of a mature faith.

The second chapter is a design for pastoral ministry from the perspective of pneumatology. It describes the character of a mature faith and how it is linked with the more general understanding of adulthood, mental health and human virtues. An attempt is launched to determine the value of a psychology of religion for theological data. Hence the design of a "psychology of grace" which reflects the impact of an integrative approach in spiritual direction.

The last chapter focuses on the distinctiveness of spiritual direction. It explains the link between the assessment of God-images and spiritual direction. It gives an exposition of what is meant by metaphorical theology in pastoral care. It applies the principle of a pastoral hermeneutics to care and counseling and develops a substantial rather than a mere functional diagnostic model. The difference between appropriate and inappropriate God-images is discussed. The final chapter concludes by making a proposal for a God-image which links the naming of God to postmodernity's quest for meaning, humanity and intimacy. Hence the notion of God as our "Soul Friend", our "Partner for Life."

CHAPTER I

THE DOCTRINE OF PERSONS
IN PASTORAL THEOLOGY: ON BEING HUMAN

Pastoral ministry is ministry to *people*.[1] Thus any model and strategy must ultimately be determined by the view of who and what a person is. How pastors deal with people, as well as the therapy they employ, depends not only on the fundamental theological theory, but also on their specific view of a human being (anthropology). Knowledge of God, apart from an understanding of humans, can easily become abstract and speculative. Similarly, a pastoral theology without a clearly outlined theological anthropology, runs the risk of becoming "docetic." As such, it is alien to life and does not allow for the historical context of human beings. Thus, a theological anthropology clearly determines the effectiveness of the pastoral encounter as well as the eventual therapeutic outcome.

Unfortunately, very few works in pastoral theology pay special attention to anthropology. A specific anthropology is often implied, but without giving an explicit description or an exposition on how this anthropology influences counseling and therapy.

The fact that pastoral theologians have paid so little attention to an anthropology in pastoral theology does not mean that they were unaware of the important function of a Christian anthropology. In

---

[1] For pastoral care humanity is a most important issue. P. K. Jewett, [1996], p. 26) answers as follows: "... the 'I' is an 'I' in relation to the 'other,' the divine Thou of the Creator and the human thou of the neighbor. This relationship is one of responsible love."

Grundriss der Praktischen Theologie, Haendler pointed out that
the care of souls is a human concern and this needs a Christian
anthropology.[2]

Within the American context, with its emphasis on psychology,
the danger of a psychological reduction of the human being lurked.
Because of the influence of psychotherapy and the optimistic view
of humans in the individualistic and democratic American society,
the doctrine of persons was in danger of being interpreted solely in
terms of secular personality theories and the empirical research of
the human sciences. Hence the critical reaction in some Christian
models of pastoral care. A good example of this is J. Adams's nouthetic model with, as its focal point, the sinful nature of humans.

In *More than Redemption*, Adams attempts to design a biblical
doctrine of persons. He is convinced that, because of the current
humanistic climate, pastoral theology should pay urgent attention
to an anthropology.

> In considering the human personality, the plight into which it has
> been plunged by sin and what God has done about it in Christ, it is
> truly remarkable that any Christian thinker or writer can begin at
> any other point — or turn to any other primary source — than the
> Bible data that reveals acres of facts about anthropology.[3]

Adams divides his treatment of anthropology in two: Adam
before the fall and Adam after the Fall. Adams uses the perspective of the creation to point out that Adam is both a mortal and a
spiritual being, as well as a moral and a social being. He sees
human beings as intrinsically corrupt and that their sins and guilt
reveal their true wretchedness.

Although Adams's attempt should be appreciated, his discus-
sions concentrate mainly around the human situation before and

---

[2] See O. Haendler, *Grundriss der Praktischen Theologie* (1957), pp. 310-311.
[3] See J. E. Adams, *More than Redemption* (1979), p. 96.

after the Fall. This becomes the central point of departure regarding his understanding of humans. This standpoint enables Adams to address the biblical person mainly in terms of his sinful condition before God. It also explains why Adams concentrates exclusively on our redemption from sin and his dominant soteriological perspective. He pays very little attention to a general anthropology in terms of creation, eschatology and pneumatology.

This deficiency was especially noted by the Dutch theologian, G. Heitink, who realized the need for an extensive anthropology in pastoral theology. Help and care are rendered to people in many forms. Thus, when designing a more extensive anthropology, Heitink finds it necessary to combine knowledge from other human sciences with the biblical view of the human being.[4]

Heitink criticizes reformed theology's traditional doctrine of persons: *simul justus et peccator*. This formula reveals the tension that exists because the person is both evil but also justified. It tends to describe humans in a very negative and pessimistic way.

The real danger of such an approach looms when our humanity and our having been created in the image of God are interpreted mainly in terms of a person as a sinner.[5] Heitink believes that a biblical anthropology comprises more than redemption from sin (soteriology). He therefore argues that the traditional bipolarity, sin/grace, should be broadened by the bipolarity, creation/recreation. Heitink extends this broader bipolarity by means of a Trinitarian approach consisting of: the human being created by God; Jesus Christ the new Person; the Spirit and the person's new

---

[4] By a pastoral-theological anthropology G. Heitink (*Pastoraat als Hulpverlening* [1977], p. 109) understands: "Een theologische anthropologie die bewust aansluiting zoekt bij de resultaten van het onderzoek binnen de mens- en gedragswetenschappen en zich richt op een verstaan van de mens in empirische zin."

[5] *Ibid.*, p. 111.

humanity. He combines this Trinitarian vision of human beings with the growing consensus amongst all helping professions regarding the importance of a holistic and total approach.[6] This results in the following so-called "anthropological consensus":

a) A person is a unity of body, soul and spirit. This rejects a dualistic approach.

b) A person does not *have* relations, but *is* a relation. As human beings, we exist and are relational.

c) Our being is constituted of conscious and unconscious levels.

d) Developmental psychology reveals that a person is a dynamic entity in search of self-realization.

e) Norms and values play an important role in our quest for human and personal identity.

Heitink's attempt should be appreciated, yet it still lacks an extensive theological anthropology. He does not quite succeed in elaborating on the question: what is the theological link between a Christian anthropology and a pneumatology?

J. Rebel's *Pastorate in Pneumatologisch Perspektief* makes a more important contribution in this regard. Rebel pays renewed attention to the relation between Spirit (*pneuma*) and the human being (*humanum*) in pastoral theology. His basic presupposition is that categories which function in psychology and psychotherapy attain their theological meaning within pneumatology. His aim is to prove that in pastoral care psychology influences pastoral ministry through the work of the Spirit.[7] He contends that the current emphasis on psychology, which tends to psychologize pastoral care, results from the neglect of pneumatology with its understanding of the human being within a theological

---

[6] *Ibid.*, p. 108.

[7] See J. J. Rebel, *Pastoraat in Pneumatologisch Perspektief* (1981), p. 257.

anthropology.[8] Rebel is convinced that Van Ruler's pneumatology could contribute towards addressing this neglect, by placing data from psychology within a theological framework. In an article on the meaning of "Clinical Pastoral Education," Rebel points out that this movement has often been criticized because its theological approach is deficient. Yet these critics have not succeeded in designing an anthropology for pastoral care within which pneumatology is justified.[9] The criticism thus remains formal, and pastoral theology still does not seriously consider the pneumatological implications for all human relations and communication. Despite the danger of a psychological reduction, the task of pastoral theology must be to reflect anew on the implication of psychological data for a theological approach in anthropology.

The value of J. Rebel's pneumatological approach is that he pointed out that humanity cannot be bypassed in pastoral care. This theme is important, because pastoral care's challenge is *the application of salvation to the human being in all relations* (my translation).[10] The need to concretize salvation demands that pastoral theology must not allow the church, in its struggle against humanism, pelagianism and synergism, to leave people to psychotherapy while in the process severing the necessary biblical connection between anthropology and pneumatology. People and their inner potential are not detached from theological reflection. Thus, one of the most important tasks of a pastoral theology must

---

[8] "Is de pastoral psychologie niet een denkmogelijkheid bij gebrek aan een goede pneumatologie?" (*Ibid.,* p. 136).

[9] "Ook wordt aandacht gevraagd in de theorievorming en de praxis van het pastoraat voor de pneumatologie. Maar het is hoogst merkwaardig, dat het blijft bij deze al te zuinige constatering, zodat juist in deze publicaties de leer van de Heilige Geest een welhaast vergeten hoofdstuk is" (J. J. Rebel, "Klinische Pastorale Vorming" [1985], pp. 137-138).

[10] See J. J. Rebel, "De pneumatologische Dimensie in het Pastoraat" (1984), p. 107.

be to pay attention to the theme of what it means to be human. It must also ascertain whether provision has been made within a theological anthropology for the viewpoint: the human being as a person is a *living human document*[11] and could, therefore, contribute to an epistemology of pastoral care.

We have no intention of treating a person as an object of research. A doctrine of persons does not assume the exposition of the human being. Our humanity and personhood are dynamic and arise from within a systemic network of relations. We aim to understand and interpret a person from a specific perspective: the human being in a relationship with God. We shall, therefore, investigate whether eschatological and pneumatological perspectives play a decisive role in a pastoral hermeneutics when they are applied to a theological anthropology.

1.1 Pastoral Anthropology from the Perspective of Faith

In pastoral care, we are interested in how the quest for meaning is related to our being human and the context of our Christian faith. *A pastoral anthropology is interested in the issue of spirituality and how our Christian faith can play a role in coping better with life. Pastoral care attempts to relate a theology of comfort to people's struggle with meaning, despair, suffering, anxiety and guilt.* A pastoral anthropology therefore cannot avoid asking how our Christian understanding of the human being influences the process of healing and the way in which we come to terms with

[11] See W. J. de Klerk's attempt (*Pastorale Sensitiwiteit* [1975], pp. 42-43) in this regard. He formulates the pastoral objective in terms of data derived from psychology: self-realization as a process of self-acceptance, self-confrontation, self-integration, self-independence, self-projection, self-servitude and self-transcendence.

fundamental issues. We assume that a close link exists between a doctrine of persons, a pastoral hermeneutics and therapy.

A pastoral anthropology not only deals with problems. Its basic objective is to guide people towards growth and development in faith. Basically, a pastoral anthropology should ask: what is a mature faith, and what is the relationship between a psychological and a theological understanding of maturity? Also: if pastoral care does not focus merely on problems but also on growth, what then are the components of a mature faith which will equip a person to enjoy a constructive life? Pastoral anthropology is about more than just meaning and therapy; it is about the quality of human life as perceived from the perspective of the Christian faith.

Because ethics is a decisive factor when dealing with life issues and meaning, we should reflect on the connection between a perspective of faith and normativity. Our reflection inevitably led to a hermeneutics which tries to understand a person in terms of a relationship with God. We may thus describe our hermeneutical approach as an assessment of Christian faith within different life contexts: an analysis of behavior motivated and generated by faith. Therefore, a design for an anthropology for pastoral care is undergirded by the following hypotheses:

• A pastoral anthropology is not focused primarily on human *self-analysis* in the light of psychological personality theories. Introspection, and an attempt to understand oneself solely from the perspective of an inner self-reflection could easily lead to the danger of narcissism. This, in turn, can lead to isolation and self-obsession (*incurvatus in se ipsum*). Although psychic energy and consciousness play a role in self-understanding, our objective is not in the first place psychoanalysis.

• Pastoral anthropology is not merely about *analyses of behavior*. Human behavior is important in pastoral care, especially when it refers to the notion of responsibility (*respondeo ergo sum*). Yet, when human behavior is viewed from the perspective of faith and sanctification, we cannot be content with only analyses of behavior. In order to understand human behavior, theological anthropology also needs to understand people in terms of a normative dimension (the eschatological perspective). The ethical dimension and the role of the human conscience are, therefore, particularly significant for pastoral anthropology.

• Pastoral anthropology is particularly concerned with *analyses of faith* (understanding people in terms of their relationship with God) and *analyses of ethics* (understanding people in terms of ethos, normativity and virtue).

It has already been pointed out that a pastoral anthropology requires that its doctrine of persons should take account of the interplay between God and the human being (the covenantal encounter). A pastoral anthropology is, therefore, deeply interested in the human quest for meaning, and with the implications which faith in God have for ultimate meaning.

Naturally, other motives are also involved when pastoral theology considers an anthropology. One of the most important is that of human dignity and the significance of humanity. Technology, the rise of genetic engineering in medical science, bio-chemical manipulation of human problems by means of the pharmaceutical industry, human violation of political structures and increasing poverty and social misery have all led to a situation in which people have virtually lost their real identity. Stress, increasingly, causes people to become slaves of work pressure and material achievement. The so-called *achievement ethics* alienates people from their creative dimension.[12] People's isolation within relationships, as well as their struggle for freedom, often results in greater

---

[12] "Aus dem homo faber droht ein homo fabricus zu werden" (H. Thielicke, *Mensch Sein — Mensch Werden* [1978²], p. 313).

enslavement to ideologies. This is why the need for an anthropology is being brought increasingly to the church's attention.

Traditionally the church has viewed a person from different perspectives. Paul's portrayal of a Christian being divided into two
dual polarities is classic. "For in my inner being I delight in God's
law; but I see another law at work in the members of my body,
waging war against the law of my mind and making me a prisoner
of the law of the sin at work within my members" (Rm 7:22-23).
An intense struggle takes place in the very core of our human
existence: the struggle between good and evil.

Although powers greater than the human ego dominate one's
life, yet these are not such that a person is merely a sinner ("What
a wretched man I am! Who will rescue me from this body of
death?"), unable to exalt: "Thanks be to God — through Jesus
Christ our Lord!" (Rm 7:24-25).

Pastoral anthropology is interested in the guilty person who
says: "I," but also rejoices: "Thanks be to God." The question of
how the affliction of the ego is connected to the therapy of thanksgiving is of cardinal importance to pastoral care.

The person who can say "I," not only possesses self-consciousness and a personal destiny. Nor is he or she only a historical
being who is determined by own experience alone. The eschatological perspective sees a person, essentially, as an open, dynamic
and incomplete being, who has a specific task in terms of which
he/she constantly makes responsible choices. The human being
can also say: "*I believe.*" Furthermore, the Christian also knows:
"I must become the person whom *I should be.*"[13] Being human
and the normative dimension of existence thus belong together.

---

[13] "Die Grundbefindlichkeit des Menschen dass er erst 'werden soll, was er
ist,' dass er sich folglich nicht als potentiell fertige Gegebenheit von der Natur
empfängt, nötigt ihn zu der Frage nach seinem Woher und Wohin. Damit stehen
Grund, Ziel und Sinn, seines Daseins zur Diskussion" (*Ibid.,* p. 225).

This ethical stance latches onto the fact that theology operates with the basic assumption: people should be understood primarily from their relationship with God.

Weber is convinced of the connection between a theology and an anthropology.[14] He does not believe that the human being is an incidental theme in theology, while God Himself is the only real main theme. Rather, a person is a theme of theology exactly because God is *the* theme of theology. This implies that a theological understanding of the human being does not see a person as a correlate of God; or a person as emanating from God; or God and human being as identical. Rather, it is a result of the message that God is the Creator and Lord of our existence.[15] God's proclamation of salvation and grace makes the human being the theme for theology. The fact that the Gospel is about a radical transformation of, and new foundation for, human existence, means that the human being appears in theology in terms of a unique perspective: the meaning of our being within the presence of God.[16] People exist because the acts of God are directed to them personally.[17]

Weber's view agrees with the view of Calvin. In his catechism Calvin questions the main purpose of human life (*la principale fin de la vie humaine*), and replies that it is to know God in such a way that He is glorified through human life (*pour estre glorifié en nous*).[18] The question about the human being thus focuses on God's honor and his active involvement in history. An anthropology essentially belongs with theology.

---

[14] See O. Weber, *Grundlagen der Dogmatik I* (1972⁴), p. 583.

[15] *Ibid.*, p. 586.

[16] "Das Thema der theologischer Anthropologie ist der Mensch vor Gott. *Der Mensch!*" (*Ibid.*, p. 587).

[17] *Ibid.*, p. 590.

[18] *Ibid.*, p. 586: For a discussion of Calvin's approach.

We will now examine what consequences such a theological perspective on the human being will have for pastoral theology. How does a theological understanding of a person (namely, as a person before God) influence the development of a pastoral theology? What is the function and place of an anthropology within various models in pastoral care?

1.2 The Two Main Streams in a Pastoral Approach and New Developments

The principle of bipolarity (the mutuality between theology and human sciences) explains why it is impossible to limit pastoral care to either the human and communication skills, or to the Word and salvation. The pastoral encounter makes it impossible to limit human problems to either a psychological reduction, within which therapy focuses mainly on inherent human potential, or to a theological reduction, within which therapy depends on mainly an external source (namely the proclamation of the Word). The interaction between God and humans is too complex and too extensive for unilateralisms. A neutral balance or homeostasis between God and humans can never be considered, particularly if pastoral care wants to retain its theological character. A convergence model, with its focal point in the eschatological perspective, points to the uniqueness of the God-human-encounter. In this encounter the salvation of the Gospel is dominant when determining the quality of faith.

Why are there such profound differences between the two main streams in pastoral theology?

• The difference between the various pastoral models within pastoral theology can be ascribed mainly to the different perceptions and definitions of the essential human characteristics. The purpose

of pastoral ministry, as well as the therapeutic outcome, is determined essentially by a specific anthropology which functions as a
presupposed framework.

• The difference between the two main streams also has a deeper
theological background resulting from the different interpretations of the doctrine of salvation within each model. In other
words, the difference between models could be ascribed to
whether a model encompasses the incarnational motif (Christ's
becoming human) or the soteriological motif (Christ's redeeming
work as Mediator). The choice between an incarnation or a soteriological motif is closely connected to the point of departure
regarding a particular anthropology: namely, either the humanity
of people and their inner potentialities (theologically based on the
principle of incarnation); or the guilt of people and their sin
(theologically based on the principle of justification by faith). We
will examine the influence of an anthropology on various pastoral
models in theology as follows: firstly, the presupposed anthropology and, secondly, its influence on the interpretation of the
doctrine of salvation.

a) The Doctrine of Sin: The Kerygmatic Model

The kerygmatic approach is dominated by the Reformed view
of the human being: *simul justus et peccator*. Guilt before God
and the reality of sin make a person a sinner who is subject to
God's punishment and wrath. A person can be freed from this sinful condition only through Christ's expiatory sacrifice and God's
sovereign mercy. The reality of sinful brokenness and transient
fallibility (death) underlie all human problems. Restoration is
"beyond" the competence of humans and is found only in
redemption. "Therapy" implies proclaiming forgiveness of sins.

The message of salvation in Christ restores human beings to new people and guarantees redemption from sin.

The kerygmatic approach to the human being is determined by the scriptural declaration: "... for all have sinned and fall short of the glory of God, and are justified freely by his grace through the redemption that came by Christ Jesus" (Rom 3:23-24).[19] Human fallibility is central to J. Adams's viewpoint.[20] He views the human being from the perspective of revelation: "The Bible's position is that all counsel that is not revelational (biblical) or based upon God's revelation is satanic." Adams's nouthetic counseling does not ascribe all problems to personal sins: "I have stated clearly that not all problems of counselors are due to their own sins."[21] Nevertheless, the perspective of sin dominates his point of departure to such an extent that a person, being created in the image of God, virtually disappears behind the notion of him/her being a sinner.

The kerygmatic approach has the danger of elevating the Fall, thereby completely distorting the notion of creation in a very negative and pessimistic way. The Fall attains a unique status and autonomy beyond the grace of God. Grace is described as a mere reaction to the Fall,[22] before which grace was not really mentioned

---

[19] Adams's anthropological point of departure (*More than Redemption* [1979], p. 143) should be understood against this background. "Corruption of the whole person, but especially of his inner life, is a dominant and essential theme for every counselor to know to teach and upon which to base all his work."

[20] *Ibid.*, p. 4.

[21] *Ibid.*, p. 140.

[22] Compare Weber's following comment (*Grundlagen der Dogmatik I*, p. 613): "Wo Gottes Gnade nicht allein die Sünde gleichsam umklammert, da wird sie uns zur blossen Re-Aktion, und umgekehrt gewinnt dann die Sünde in der Polarität zur Gnade ein Eigengewicht das ihr nicht zukommt. Eine 'hamartiozentrische Theologie' will in Wahrheit gerade das Schlimme an der Sünde verkennen."

as a factor. Weber speaks of a "hamartiocentric theology" which diminishes our creatureliness.[23]

Weber reminds theology that the retention of people's humanity and creatureliness remains the alpha and omega about human beings. Sin is secondary and not the final word about the human being. The dominance of grace focuses not only on human guilt, but also on a person as having been created with "natural" gifts. Nature and grace are not in the same opposing polar tension as sin and grace. Nature is not identical to sin. Sin is not situated *per se* in matter or in the body. Such a view would bring theology back to Greek philosophy, with its dualism between spirit and matter.

Reformed theology should not view a person only from the perspective of sin. Calvin maintains that, although God transcends our human senses, his glory is perceived in all creation[24] and that an awareness of God lives in the human spirit, and acts as a "natural intuition."[25] A "germ of religion" is present in humans, which results in an ever-present inclination towards religion. Thus, human nature and abilities cannot be obliterated and ignored by a doctrine of sin.

The kerygmatic model wrestles with the following problems: how should the inner potentialities and abilities of humans be rated? To what extent has sin obliterated the image of God? Can the Fall be the hermeneutical key for a theological anthropology?

Nevertheless, the danger still lurks that if a pastoral model abandons its perspective on people as sinners, then the following problem surfaces: do people need grace at all, or have they become so self-sufficient and autonomous that God has become superfluous?

---

[23] *Ibid.*, p. 612.
[24] See Calvijn, *Institutie I, V (s.a.)*, p. 17.
[25] See Calvijn, *Institutie I, III (s.a.)*, p. 8.

b) The Doctrine of the Inner Human Potentialities: The Client-centered Model

The notion of inner human potentialities dominates the more phenomenological and client-centered models. This does not imply that these models ignore the component of sin. Hiltner, for example, comments: "We must regard sin as crucial in many forms of serious impairment."[26] In therapy, healing and change are dealt with as inclusive concepts comprising all forms of healing. The client-centered approach uses Rogers's non-directive, client-centered therapy to introduce the theme of self-actualizing in pastoral care. Hiltner confirms this focal point: "'Client-centered' was intended to show that one begins and proceeds from the best possible grasp of internals — that is, the inner frame of reference of the other person in so far as it can be grasped."[27]

The purpose of this focus on people's inner frame of reference is to help them to become whole. In this therapy, sustaining plays an important role. Sustaining does not imply giving people strength, or offering them an external source of healing, but empathizing with them in such a way that they can start relying on a source of power within their own abilities. The approach in this model is thus more maieutic (supportive) and obstetric, rather than presentative (presenting from outside) and proclamative (prescriptive proclamation).

This framework presupposes a positive view of humankind, which reaches beyond salvation back to creation, and focuses on the psychological potentialities of a person. Sin becomes secondary: inner potential becomes the key to all pastoral therapy.

Clinebell propagates a *holistic liberation growth model of pastoral care*.[28] He formulates the purpose of his holistic growth

---

[26] See S. Hiltner, *Preface to Pastoral Theology* (1958), p. 98.

[27] *Ibid.*, p. 145

[28] See H. J. Clinebell, *Basic Types of Pastoral Care and Counseling* (1984), p. 25.

model as follows: "Pastoral care and counseling involve the utilization by persons in ministry of one-to-one or small-group relationships to enable healing empowerment and growth to take place within individuals and their relationships."[29]

The following six basic anthropological presuppositions, for what Clinebell calls "*a therapy of wholeness*," serve as an example of how human abilities function:

> ... enlivening one's mind; revitalizing one's body; renewing and enriching one's intimate relationships, deepening one's relationship with nature and the biosphere; growth in relation to the significant institutions in one's life; deepening and vitalizing one's relationship with God.[30]

A person grows in an integral way along these six dimensions. For Clinebell, this growth to an integral wholeness is not an egoistic process of self-fulfillment, but a relational process of growth within social dimensions. Therefore, Clinebell declares that the purpose of pastoral care and counseling is "self-other-society-wholeness. Growth occurs in covenants-of-wholeness with others."[31]

Although still within the more phenomenological paradigm, Clinebell's growth model should be assessed as an important additional development. It can be regarded as supplementary to the unilateralisms of both the kerygmatic and client-centered models. It becomes important for a pastoral anthropology to view and assess a human being more in terms of relationships and the dynamics of a caring community, than the individualistic stance of a consulting room. "Wholeness" becomes the new category to describe the objective of a pastoral anthropology and the outcome of therapy.

Currently, the tendency is towards a more hermeneutical approach in which narratives, experiences, contexts, systems and

[29] *Ibid.*, p. 26.
[30] *Ibid.*, p. 31.
[31] *Ibid.*, pp. 31-32.

symbols play an important role in a pastoral attempt to understand human beings and problematic life issues. The implication of these new developments for a theology of pastoral care is that a growth model, a holistic approach and a preventative stance should reflect anew on the implications of different metaphors for God for contextual spirituality.

c) Towards a New Reorientation: Spirituality and a Hermeneutical Analysis of Human Experience

The idea that pastoral care should find its uniqueness within the growth potential which exists in human relations, indicates a progressively dominant tendency in the American model. Where previously the onus was on the pastor to practise counseling in a one-to-one personal relationship, the current tendency is to concentrate on what Gerkin calls: "concern for the corporate process of care in the community of faith and the revolt against modern consciousness, including its psychological paradigm."[32] Gerkin is concerned that the emphasis on psychotherapy will threaten the theological roots of the subject. He pleads for a new re-orientation in pastoral theology. He does not want pastoral care to be limited to psychotherapy, nor does he wish for a return to the unilateralisms of a kerygmatic model. Instead he suggests, as an alternative, a hermeneutical theory of pastoral counseling.[33]

A person's development and life story within the cultural and social field of experience provide the material for a process of pastoral hermeneutics. Hence, Gerkin's description of pastoral counseling:

[32] See C. V. Gerkin, *The Living Human Document* (1984), p. 17.
[33] *Ibid.,* p. 19.

> Pastoral counseling will be here seen as a process of interpretation
> and reinterpretation of human experience within the framework of a
> primary orientation toward the Christian mode of interpretation in
> dialogue with contemporary psychological modes of interpreta-
> tion.[34]

Gerkin suggests a shift away from a practice of psychotherapy
(which is based, methodologically, on decisions and actions in the
light of psychological and psychotherapeutic criteria) to a practice
of hermeneutics (which is methodologically based upon the interpretation of stories of being human in the context of language and
social symbols). The process of a hermeneutics of the human self
is embedded within a narrative milieu. This milieu is determined
by a specific atmosphere or setting, a certain intrigue or "plot," as
well as a unique character and emotional, intellectual framework.
Gerkin's "new basic theory" results in the conclusion:

> I have established the basis for an image of the self as interpreter of
> its own experience and of the life of the soul as that arena in which
> the self's interpretive process must find whatever resolution is pos-
> sible to the force/meaning dynamics of human existence in the con-
> text of its life in God.[35]

This model is thus not about psychological diagnosis, but about
a hermeneutical analysis of human experience, as expressed in the
language of faith and religious symbols. Experience becomes the
source of knowledge for an anthropology. The field of language
and the symbolic frame of reference for human life is viewed as a
narrative event, within which the person asks the question regarding meaning of life: what does all this signify for me? Interpretation and reflection become two important methods in this
approach. This narrative approach employs, as basic material, the
person's choices and their influences on various situations and

---

[34] *Ibid.*, p. 20.
[35] *Ibid.*, p. 116.

relations; their inner and intersubjective conflicts; their desires
and intentions relating to future behavior and moral issues.

Gerkin's hermeneutical theory of the life of the soul envisaged
that change will result when a new structure of meaning is created
for the self, within which the different fragments of the story can
be woven into a narrative unity. This integration develops within
the human eschatological identity before God. Gerkin employs
Clinebell's concept of holism together with this notion of an integral self — a holism within an ecology of relationships.

> This larger view of the ecology of relationships to be integrated
> includes the expectation that the soul is not fully self-dependent in its
> pilgrimage toward wholeness. By means of God's incarnation in the
> world and the activity of the Spirit, God is actively engaged in bring-
> ing about those changes that makes wholeness ultimately possible.[36]

Integration and wholeness are the goals generated by change
within the theological framework of human pilgrimage. Gerkin
focuses on two theological issues in this dynamic process of
change: God's incarnation in Christ and God's suffering on the
cross. Incarnation and suffering become the Christian symbols
from which pastoral hermeneutics allows the process of change to
develop. Gerkin describes this as a process of spiritual direction,
that is, a process within which the integration of self is linked to
the eschatological destiny of human life before God.[37]

Gerkin's viewpoint clearly reveals that the client-centered and
empirical model works from the presupposition that a person does
not only *have* relations, but *is* a relation. This relational dimension
of human existence weaves a network of experiences within
the developing self. It creates a narrative milieu which, through

---

[36] *Ibid.*, p. 146.

[37] Gerkin (*Ibid.*, p. 198) does not want to give up the normative component in
the pastoral process of spiritual guidance. "In the world of psychotherapy, pastoral counseling asserts the normative value of Christian images of what human
life under God was meant to become."

interpretation, brings insight which leads to the re-integration of life. Such a relation-oriented and holistic therapy deals with the following anthropological presupposition regarding epistemology: a person is a source of knowledge within the network of relations. Pastoral ministry thus has therapeutic material at its disposal which could help people to re-integrate their lives (the notion of "inner potentialities" and a person as a "living human document").

The challenge put forth by a hermeneutical approach is how to move further than the kerygmatic and phenomenological models towards a relational approach and a "holistic spirituality," while still trying to maintain the Christian and theological character of a pastoral anthropology. Before moving to a theological interpretation of a hermeneutical stance (Chapter 3) and the pneumatological implications (Chapter 2), we need to reflect more critically on the implications of the afore-mentioned unilateralisms for a pastoral anthropology and the scriptural notion of salvation.

* * *

Within the American context pastoral care developed in very close cooperation with other human sciences. Hence the influence of psychology. Rogers's personality theory contributed to the understanding that congruency between the self and the immediate field of experience is important for any therapeutic approach in counseling. A basic point of departure for effective counseling is the fact that congruency may be increased by means of empathy.

Even greater appreciation should be given to Rogers's emphasis on the basic attitude in counseling. He stresses the crucial need for "deed proclamation" in counseling, where love is expressed concretely in interpersonal relationships.[38]

---

[38] See W. A. Smit, *Pastoraal-Psigologiese Verkenning van die Client-Centered Terapie van Carl Rogers* (1960), p. 151.

Love and acceptance within the pastoral encounter are important issues. Rogers has reminded pastoral care that the primary motive behind a relation-oriented therapy is not the generation of a type of pelagianism or semi-pelagianism, but of effective listening skills. Nevertheless, when acceptance on an empathetic level is elevated to the main criterion for implementing salvation, this can lead to a theological problem. This is especially so when acceptance is regarded as a direct medium of revelation to the detriment of justification. Browning raises this concern in his discussion of contemporary pastoral theology's view of the human being. He believes that Rogerian psychology has played a significant role in shifting anthropology in pastoral care away from the normative component to the more experiential affective component of human life.

> Rogerian psychology held certain propositions about the nature of man which were, for various reasons, attractive to the liberal theological tradition. Rogers taught that human beings are motivated by "one basic tendency and striving — to actualize, maintain and enhance the experiencing organism." This gave rise to a vision of human beings as growing, changing and basically constructive.[39]

The effect of Rogers's influence on counseling led to the romanticizing of emotions[40] and of human organisms, and to the elevation of relationships and the human body as a direct medium of revelation.

The client-centered model has led to the following fundamental theological problems:

• The concepts of self-assertion and self-actualization play a significant role in psychology. The human self-actualizing potential

---

[39] See D. Browning, "Images of Man in Contemporary Models of Pastoral Care," (1979), p. 146.

[40] "There was a tendency to romanticize the body and the so-called 'feelings' of the experiencing organism" (*Ibid.*, p. 148).

is interpreted as a link between God and the human being. In extending this link to include God, the human self-actualizing potential becomes identified with the concept, "image of God." Self-actualizing thus becomes a material principle within a person, and is interpreted as the exposition of the theological meaning of the human being created in the image of God.

The psychology of emotions and self-actualization and the physiology of bodily functions are thus elevated to a theological principle with therapeutic qualities. The empirical level of human emotions, needs and language become the main components of an image of God. The human potential for self-actualization thus becomes a type of remnant and primitive condition (*status integritatis*) which is not affected by sin. The affective psychological component and the human potential for self-actualizing become an autonomous ontic principle. This functions like an untouched "natural remnant," thus serving to implement grace. The danger in this approach arises when the image of God becomes a type of "embryonic principle," which serves as a point of departure for grace and makes grace superfluous. Grace becomes a supplement to the image of God, without the focus of human self-actualization being changed or transformed.

This optimistic overestimation of inner potentialities not only weakens the principle of sin in human life, but it also emphasizes, unilaterally, the human affective, cognitive and conative abilities. In this process, the normative component of life is diminished. A psychology of empathy eventually dominates the ethical dimension and the theological understanding of life in terms of grace and salvation.

• The client-centered model risks interpreting sin in psychological terms and diminishing it to a mere obstruction or pathology. Sin then becomes an obstruction to the human volition for self-assertion, and restricts human ability for self-actualization within relationships. Sin is interpreted as whatever hampers a person, within a holistic view on being human and the potential for human growth. In terms of Rogerian psychology, sin becomes dysfunctional in the personality. Sin results in an incongruency between the self (self-esteem) and the experience of the ego within the phenomenological field of experience and perception. This incongruency does not need an external factor, but can be overcome when inner potential is stimulated through empathetic communication.

An ontology of acceptance forms the underlying principle for this communication model. When a person feels accepted in conversation, then it means that God's acceptance of this person's life has already been relayed. Tillich's concept of *analogia entis* reveals a correlation between a person's being and the Being of God. This correlation results from the association between being (creation) and God as the Ultimate Being. Thus, any factor which disrupts this level of analogy on an ontological level, is described as a form of "sin." This model ultimately relegates sin to mere pathology and neurotic behavior.

• Within the client-centered model's holistic terminology, therapy becomes associated more with holistic "healing," and less with salvation. Therapy is interpreted as a process of healing within psychological and social functions. In this process the external salvific factor becomes incidental and irrelevant. The term "salvation" becomes a kind of general health concept or a condition of psychological well-being (*homeostasis*). Salvation becomes synonymous with wholeness. Those who have received "salvation" are those who have been helped to live congruently — that is to say they have reached an optimal congruency between self-esteem and the ego and have developed self-actualization. Pastoral therapy becomes mainly psychological. Even the nomenclature reflects this shift. The terms congruency, empathy, and self-integration all become concepts which describe and generate a holistic process of healing.

Similarly, the pastoral concept of "salvation" gradually becomes understood as a liberation from all depressing factors in the human psyche and from all that suppresses within the social milieu. But, and this is important: is salvation not more than a psychic event of ventilation? It is impossible to separate anthropology and the doctrine of soteriology within a pastoral model. We will now try to interpret how the doctrine of salvation fits in a pastoral anthropology.

1.3 The Link between a Pastoral Anthropology and the Doctrine of Salvation: Soteriology

A kerygmatic model views humans primarily as sinners and describes them as powerless and miserable. The influence of the kerygmatic model on the doctrine of soteriology is evident in the emphasis that is placed on the forensic character of justification. The significance of Christ's work as Mediator is sought in the salvific event of the cross (expiation).[41]

This model raises an anthropological question. While it is true that a person cannot contribute towards salvation, nevertheless, does soteriology not still have a certain effect on the human psychological and social functions? Reconciliation does not leave the human being untouched, neither does it exclude our human responsibility. The important questions now facing us are: how does it do this? and to what extent?

---

[41] This interpretation of soteriology, in terms of the transfer of guilt on the grounds of Christ's expiatory crucifixion, is known as the synthetic approach to soteriology. The emphasis on the fact that the human being has no share in his/her redemption, is known as the Anselmus tradition. The significance of the synthetic doctrine of conciliation with regard to anthropology, is that people are dependent upon God and his Word for salvation and eventual "healing." Forgiveness then becomes a key issue in a theological understanding of therapy. For the link between Christology and anthropology, see also P. E. Hughes *The True Image* (1989), pp. 211-249.

An "eductive" model[42] (client-centered/phenomenological/empiri-
cal approach) takes human beings and their relational components
as its point of departure. While this model, in its theological
reflection, focuses mainly on God's incarnation and pathos, its
main interest is the *effect* of soteriology (a functional Christology)
rather than its sacrificial character (a forensic Christology).
This model is strongly influenced by Schleiermacher's subjective stance. For Schleiermacher, human religious self-consciousness and a dependence on God became a focal point for a
theological analysis (*slechthinniges Abhängigkeitsgefühl*). The
client-centered model develops the Schleiermacher tradition even
further. It concentrates on the effect and function of soteriology in
human existence. This emphasis is known in theology as the ana-
lytic understanding of soteriology (Abelard tradition). In this
approach, it is not so much Christ's expiatory death that is important, but Christ's death as example (Christ as precursor), and how
it affect our lives. In his *Verzoening als verandering*, Wiersinga
comments that reconciliation is mainly functional and effective. This
approach caused a commotion within the Reformed tradition in the
Netherlands because it meant that soteriology then focused mainly
on transformation: *It is about changing people radically, transforming people, or truly changing relations between people.*[43] Thus, the
emphasis is not so much on Christ and his expiatory sacrifice on the
cross, but on Christ and his identification with suffering.[44]

---

[42] In the eductive model "eductive" implies: "That it 'leads out' something
that may be regarded as either within the person or potentially available to him
(through sources other than ourselves)" (Hiltner, *Preface to Pastoral Theology*
[1958], p. 151).

[43] See H. Wiersinga, *Verzoening als Verandering* (1972), p. 51.

[44] "Men kan wel van 'plaatsbekleding' spreken, maar dan is dat bedoeld in de
zin van solidariteit, van verbondenheid in lot en gehoorzaamheid. Met anderen
woorden: plaatsbekeleding moet inklusief verstaan worden. Het laat ruimte vóór
en wil oproepen tót de eigen aktiviteit van alle leden van de gemeenschap" (*Ibid.*,
p. 51).

Soteriology is significant: in Christ's work of reconciliation there is a transforming power, which enables people to act differently and thus to change surrounding circumstances. This truth should be acknowledged in a pastoral anthropology. Reconciliation is indeed a functional and relational issue affecting our humanity. What is important in a functional model is not *what* Christ accomplished on our behalf, but *how* Christ did it. Of cardinal importance is not the content on the objective level, but the effect on the subjective and social level. This emphasis reveals why this model concentrates more on the subjective and experiential, rather than on the objective and transcendental components. By focusing on the implications of the incarnation, the emphasis falls on humanity and personal identity. Christ's solidarity with the fragments of human life generates an integration factor which, in turn, gives meaning to life. The danger lurking in a functional Christology is that it concentrates so heavily on the life of Christ that his mediatory work of salvation becomes degraded.[45] This separation between person and work has influenced an anthropology within a pastoral model. Less emphasis is placed on the qualitative transformation of being (conversion; *metanoia*) and more on the effective change in psychic functions (well-being/healing). Christ's incarnation becomes the point of departure for a communication model. Counseling skills, the nature of relationships and style of communication are viewed as an embodiment and continuation of Christ's incarnation,[46] thereby attaining their own therapeutic value.

[45] W. D. Jonker (*Christus, die Middelaar* [1977], p. 173) discusses the problems related to a functional Christology in his work, *Christus die Middelaar*. He points out the fact that the problem with a functional Christology is that it not merely attempts to bring about a methodic correction in Christology, but that Christ's function is so strongly emphasized that it puts the question of his Being in the background.

[46] This tendency, for example, is found in H-J. Thilo's pastoral model (*Beratende Seelsorge* [1971], p. 22), when he speaks of the salvatory effect of counseling.

The following diagram has been designed to clarify the connection between the doctrine of persons and soteriology in the two models under discussion. The difference between the two can be seen in the anthropology, method, therapy and effect. Because this diagram oversimplifies a model's basic viewpoints, it does not do justice to the author's overall perspective. Nevertheless, the diagram does not claim to be complete. It merely offers an insight into the dominating thought pattern and anthropological assumptions of each model, and highlights the interplay between an anthropology and a Christology.

A. The Kerygmatic Model: Proclaiming Salvation

Anthropology	Method	Therapy	Effect
a) The bipolarity of sin and grace b) Distress regarding our misery and sinfulness (problem-oriented)	a) Proclamation (Scripture) b) Admonishment Confrontation Directive Advising	Repentance and forgiveness. Function of pastoral care: reconciliation conversion transformation	*Remorse *Confession *Conversion *Redemption

Pastoral care: Liberation from guilt; conversion; proclamation of salvation and forgiveness.
Christology: Redemption through grace on the grounds of Christ's expiatory salvation (soteriology).

B. The Phenomenological (Client-Centered) Model:[47] *Disclosing Inner*
Potentialities (Facilitating)

Anthropology	Method	Therapy	Effect
a) Autonomous and independent self-image	a) Listening skills. Empathy and communication (affective)	Acceptance aid	*Self-insight *Self-help *Self-confidence *Self-integration
b) Inner potentialities (growth-oriented)	b) Relation building/ relation of trust. Non-directive	Function of pastoral care: - healing	*Congruency *Revelation of inner potentialities
c) The human being ture. Objective: self-realization	c) Phenomenological method: - experience, obser- servation and perception	- guiding - sustaining - reconciling - nurturing	

Pastoral care: A holistic approach: self-integration. Client-centered and relational.
Christology: God's acceptance and identification with human need, via Christ's incarnation and suffering on the cross (God's pathos) with a view to salvation on the level of human relations (functional Christology).

The two pastoral models mentioned above raise the following questions for a theological anthropology: is pastoral care about the sinner's redemption, or about freeing a person from blocked potentialities and suppression? Should the relationship between anthropology and the doctrine of salvation concentrate on soteriology (on a person becoming converted) or should it concentrate on humanity (on a person's becoming human within his/her psychic

---

[47] The model could be described as eductive, functional or client-centered. Rogerian psychology influenced pastoral care to a great extent. The reason for calling it a phenomenological model is because phenomenology could be viewed as the undergirding philosophy and method which greatly influences contemporary psychology and pastoral care. The phenomenological method is about description (P. Thevénaz, *What is Phenomenology?* [1962²], p. 91), observation and perception.

and social functions)? Should the justification of the sinner allow for the sanctification of the oppressed and depressed?

These questions clearly reveal that the bipolarity between God and human beings also affects a theological anthropology. If the kerygmatic model's emphasis on sin is chosen, then Christology is easily reduced to soteriology, and anthropology is reduced to harmartology. But if the client-centered model's emphasis on human potential is chosen, then Christology is narrowed down to incarnation (functional Christology) and anthropology is restricted to ethics (the perfection of people through their own actions) and humanity (improving the quality of human life). The solution should probably be sought elsewhere. Hence, the suggestion that a pneumatology could play a role in the development of an anthropology for pastoral theology. But, more of this later. We will now examine the basic components of a theological anthropology. Special attention will be given to the link between our being created by God and our assessment of our self-identity, and the term "image of God."

The notion of sin cannot be avoided in a theological anthropology. Is it possible to develop our identity and humanity without guilt and feelings of guilt? If the perspective of guilt is lost, then this could easily lead to an overestimation of inner potentialities. The doctrine of persons would then operate with the following indirect assumption: an original form of harmony[48] underlies our

[48] "Critical philosophical analyses of the kind of eudaemon and teleological assumptions behind self-actualization theories are now available." In the light of this statement Browning ("Images of Man in Contemporary Models of Pastoral Care," [1979], p. 149) makes the following comment: "All such theories assume that there exists an underlying harmony which unifies and adjusts each person's thrust toward self-actualization. According to this view, primarily Greek in origin, humans do not find community through self-sacrifice and self-transcendence. They find it through specializing in their own self-actualization on the assumption that if every person is true to their own potential — their own complementary capacities will be the result."

humanity. We may return to this harmony through self-actualization. As created beings, humans possess an original and pure integrity (*status integritatus*) which can be revealed as a potential. The achievement ethics of modern culture constantly promotes this optimistic vision of people. Meanwhile, people become more depressed and frequently are exposed to severe stress. This results in what Capps calls "the depleted self: sin in a narcissistic age."[49] By "depletion" is meant an experience of shame and self-failure. Depletion then refers to our nameless shame, our guiltless despair, our sense of mortification for having failed to live lives of significance and meaning. Depletion becomes an indication of a very subtle inner experience of reality. "The words that capture this deeper, inner experience of shame are not humiliation and embarrassment, but words like empty, exhausted, drained, demoralized, depressed, deflated, bereft, needy, starving, apathetic, passive, and weak."[50] Modernity challenges pastoral care to design a more realistic approach to our being human.

1.4 Realism in a Pastoral Anthropology: Humanity and the Interplay between Creation and Recreation

Pastoral theology must grapple with a twofold anthropological question:
• Firstly, the question regarding the character of being human. The traditional church doctrine that humans were created in the image of God, presupposes that people should be interpreted and assessed in terms of their relationship with, and dependence on, God. The question regarding the nature of human beings is

---

[49] See D. Capps, *The Depleted Self* (1993), pp. 97-100.
[50] *Ibid.*, p. 99.

simultaneously also a question about those qualities which determine their human dignity.

• Secondly, the essential qualities which humans possess as creatures of God pose a question about the goal, direction, destination and meaning of our human existence. Or is our being a meaningless struggle which ends in nothingness and hopelessness?

An anthropology is predominantly descriptive in the human sciences. It entails mainly a phenomenological description of human beings through perception and empirical analysis. Knowledge of human behavior, physiology and psychology does determine our humanity and therefore should play an important role in pastoral theology. But a theological anthropology should move further: it should include an understanding of humans as moral and spiritual beings in terms of their awareness of the ultimate, and their relationship with God.

In 1542, in his Catechism's introduction, Calvin asks the classic, universal question of Christian tradition, religion and philosophy: what is the eventual and principle purpose or direction of human existence? (*Quelle est la principale fin de la vie humaine?*) The answer: *summum bonum*.

This question is intensified by the current quest for meaning in a postmodern society which is being determined by pluralism and relativism. If people have no awareness of destiny, then life degenerates into a mere struggle for survival. It becomes impossible to live, in line with Calvin's view, to the honor of God (*c'est de congnoistre Dieu*). Contemporary technocracy, which emphasizes human power, rational knowledge and science, introduces a new crisis in identity: the depletion (nameless shame) of the human ego. Human beings risk falling prey to their own achievements. Human aspirations threaten to dispel the question about who they are and what they should be (ethics). For instance, the role of bio-genetics and genetic engineering increasingly involves the threat of human beings being manipulated by human-made powers.[51] Once again, the question about freedom and meaning arises[52] with the result that normativity and ethics become burning issues. The question facing pastoral anthropology is whether a realistic approach should be designed only in terms of experiential knowledge, or whether a transcendental component (revelation) could shed more light on human destiny.

Theological Anthropology and Experiential Observation — The Empirical and Phenomenological Dimension

Aristotle's philosophical description of the human being as a reasoning/thinking animal (*homo est animal ratione praeditum*) was one of the first in Western literature. He recognized human uniqueness compared to, but also distinct from, animals, and contended that the essence of human beings should be understood and assessed in terms of their rationality and intellect. This approach results in the notion that human beings can be perceived empirically, and that their existence can be recognized by means of a phenomenological perception and rational categories.

We cannot deny that there should be room in a pastoral epistemology for an "empirical approach in human science." In *Fenomenologie en Empirische Menskunde*, Strasser uses the term "empirical" to indicate that the study of human beings should not

---

[51] On the identity crisis Thielicke (*Mensch Sein — Mensch Werden* [1978²], p. 225) comments as follows: "Aus dem homo faber droht ein homo fabricatus zu werden."

[52] "Die Grundbefindlichkeit des Menschen, dass er erst 'werden soll, was er ist,' dass er sich folglich nicht als potentiell fertige Gegebenheit von der Natur empfängt, nötig ihn zu der Frage nach seinem Woher und Wohin. Damit stehen Grund, Ziel und Sinn seines Daseins zur Diskussion" (*Ibid.*, p. 225).

be limited merely to a naturalistic approach. Natural science is about human beings as part of the cosmos. Thus, they cannot be separated from the whole. Although empirical social science encompasses the methods of natural science, it differs from the latter in that social science focuses on the human component.[53] Strasser describes the difference between social science and natural science as follows. Natural science regards human beings as beings produced by nature and as a link in a cosmic process of evolution. They are organisms dependent on a biologically definable milieu, which has resulted from a philogenetic and ontogenetic process of development. *In contrast, in the empirical social science the human being is perceived not as an object, but as the subject, founder and developer of his own Umwelt* (own translation).[54] Because the empirical social science concentrates on the totality of the human being, Strasser dismisses the term "human sciences." Empirical social science does not study the human being as spirit or soul, but the human being as a dynamic being within relationships.

Empirical social science does not verify or observe a person merely as an object.[55] Instead it aims to understand the human being through a process of description. This process yields a form of knowledge of human nature which, in turn, could contribute towards a better interpretation of how human beings live within relationships and concrete situations.

Knowledge of the empirical social science is of inestimable value for a theological anthropology. The value of a phenomenological approach lies in its ability to help a theological anthropology to understand the human being as a person within relationships.

---

[53] See S. Strasser, *Fenomenologie en Empirische Menskunde* (1965), p. 17.

[54] *Ibid.*, p. 18.

[55] That is why Strasser (*Ibid.*, p. 294) rejects empiricism, objectivism and scientism as approaches concerning an understanding of the human being.

Phenomenological knowledge helps theology to concretize its human knowledge and concentrate on human needs. Efficient and accurate phenomenological data about the human being from the fields of medical science, psychology and sociology are indispensable. But can a phenomenological analysis alone suffice for a theological anthropology regarding the quest for meaning and spirituality?

Faith is not abstract: the Christian exists within a concrete field of experience and in a specific historical situation. The Christian faith and the church's concrete ministry could indeed be subjected to a phenomenological analysis, and described in terms of different empirical modes of faith. This analysis could contribute to an effective assessment of the church's ministry and could improve the quality of ministerial practices. Yet, in a theological anthropology a merely empirical analysis of the "Christian" or "believer" is insufficient. Weber concurs when he states that the "Christian experience," as the only source of knowledge and foundation for an understanding of the nature of human beings, cannot satisfy a theological anthropology.

Weber presents the following four reasons for the rejection of a purely phenomenological approach in a theological anthropology:
• What is considered to be "Christian" in a "Christian experience" is not comprehensible in empirical terms. Faith does not depend on human behavior or achievements, but on the faithfulness of God. *It is impossible to express the essence of faith in an empirical analysis.*[56] *God's faithfulness is beyond the human intellect and sensory perception.*

---

[56] On this Weber (*Grundlagen der Dogmatik I*, p. 602) comments as follows: "Ebenso würde auch die umfassendste und eindringendste Analyse der christlichen Erfahrung oder des christlichen Selbstverständnisses nie *das* enthalten, was solche Erfahrung zur *christlichen* macht."

• The Christian experience is full of paradoxes. For instance, within the Christian faith experience there is the phenomenon of temptation. Temptations are often targeted at faith. Luther pointed out the danger that temptations could lead to doubt which could eventually wipe out all faith. In temptation, the voice of the heart and the conviction of reason often bring a person to the nadir of their "own" faith. In the end, people do not believe on the grounds of their experience, but despite their experience. Experience is thus the medium of faith, not the final access to faith.

• We cannot measure the categories "old person" and "new person" by experience. The old person is a qualitative description of a certain human condition: the person alienated and directed away from God. The new creation and the new person are associated with the cross and Christ's resurrection. The new creation is the new order of salvation. This status is impossible for humans to achieve by themselves, but is initiated by Christ and the Spirit.

The new person in Christ is a premise which is essentially determined *extra nos*. This does not mean that human existence is mystically qualified, thereby negating the concreteness of humans as believers. The "in-Christ" formula is given to people on the grounds of their eschatological stance within the new aeon.

• Christian existence has a limited character. In the New Testament, faith is described in terms such as "birth," "death," and "resurrection." Conversion, as a process of birth, death and resurrection, cannot be observed by the relevant person. Nobody can reflect comprehensibly about his own birth or own death.[57]

In summary, the reality of faith cannot be subjected finally to an empirical analysis. The rebirth of a Christian is an act of the Triune God. For a believer, faith is a reality and is perceptible, but the nature and origin of this faith is a gift to the human being, and

---

[57] See *ibid.*, p. 604.

therefore beyond human analysis. This unique character of faith means that the data of an empirical social science cannot suffice for a theological anthropology. Naturally, the experience of sin and guilt in a Christian life is perceptible phenomenologically. But, in a Christian context, awareness of true guilt is impossible without also being conscious of God's presence and of the fact that God made Christ to be sin for us (2 Cor 5:21). Without the perspective of the Gospel (grace), an awareness of sin often becomes reproach and self-castigation about lost chances. It leads to a wounded ego's self-pity and negative self-esteem.

Moltmann points out in *Mensch* that in Scripture the question regarding the nature of human beings is not asked in the context of comparing humans to animals, to the creation, or to other peoples. It is asked within a concrete encounter with God. The real issue is thus not about the impression which God makes on a person, but rather about a calling where God asks a person to do what is virtually impossible. Knowledge of biological anthropology cannot suffice for a theological anthropology.[58] Within cultural anthropology, the character of humanity is considered.[59] In a theological anthropology the focus is on the transcendence of faith. According to Moltmann, the secret of human existence appears in a Christian anthropology which has been enfleshed by the incarnation. The crucified Son of God becomes the criticism of all forms of human deification and absolute autonomy.[60] In the light of God's love via the Crucified, human beings recognize their wretchedness but also rediscover their *humanitas*.

In his anthropology, Barth does not declare the nature of a person on the grounds of phenomenologial observation alone. To

---

[58] See J. Moltmann, *Mensch: Christliche Anthropologie in den Konflikten der Gegenwart* (1971), p. 15.

[59] *Ibid.*, p. 23.

[60] *Ibid.*, p. 152.

him, knowledge about the ultimate meaning of the human being is revelational. Thus, while pure phenomenological knowledge leads to reflection about the "shadow-human being" (*Schatten-menschen*), it does not reveal an understanding of people in terms of the truth of their existence. Shadow knowledge is self-knowledge of the autonomous person, while a theological anthropology deals with people in relation to God. According to Barth, human self-existence should therefore be approached from a theonomous perspective.[61]

A phenomenological approach deals only with fragments and certain perspectives on the human being. Human sciences concentrate on personality and behavior: they cannot offer an integrated understanding of human beings in terms of their God-given destiny. An empirical analysis cannot grasp the theological significance of our being human in the presence of God. Jaspers's existential philosophy proved that the quest for meaning arises in borderline situations such as suffering and death. While existential philosophy can describe this borderline situation, it cannot enlighten us regarding the ultimate. Existential analysis and phenomenological research cannot determine the meaning of our existence: we need *a transcendental factor which reaches beyond phenomenological events.*

In the past Barth's approach has always been criticized as being abstract. However, it should be recognized that he does not deny the value of phenomenological insights. Phenonomenology succeeds in determining human characteristics, skills and potential.[62] Phenomenology also describes human actions as part of the reality

---

[61] K. Barth (*Die Lehre von der Schöpfung*, Kirchliche Dogmatik III/2, p. 148) contends that knowledge of the true human being should be reversed: "... es müsste aus einem autonomen in ein theonomes Selbstverständnis gewandelt werden."

[62] See *ibid.*, p. 335.

of creation (*Technik des Menschseins*).[63] In fact, Barth states unequivocally that exact sciences may not be alien to the Christian understanding of the human being. They only become alien when they absolutize their observations and hypotheses.[64] Thus, while phenomenological knowledge can offer relative knowledge about human behavior, it cannot offer final knowledge about the ultimate meaning of life.[65]

Theological Anthropology and the Perspective of Faith — The Theonomous Approach

Barth's theïstic anthropology describes human beings from the perspective of their relationship with God. God's condescending attention to people makes possible knowledge about their alignment to God. This knowledge is attained by means of the methodology of analogy (*analogia fidei*). Hence, Barth's declaration that humanity becomes a reflection of Divinity.[66]

---

[63] See Barth's following comment (*Ibid.*, p. 238): "Es kann also geben: eine allgemeine und doch echte, weil jenes Zeugnis hörende und verstehende Wissenschaft vom Menschen."

[64] See *ibid.*, p. 26.

[65] Pannenberg (*Anthropologie in Theologischer Perspektive* [1983], p. 16) criticizes Barth on this point and says that dialectic theology has not paid enough interest to the anthropology of human sciences. This is the reason why Pannenberg (p. 20) does not opt for a dogmatic anthropology. He says that such a model is merely interested in the notions of sin and the image of God. He describes his own approach as "fundamentaltheologische Anthropologie." "Diese argumentiert nicht von dogmatischen Gegebenheiten und Voraussetzungen aus, sondern wendet sich den Phänomenen des Menschseins zu, wie sie von der Humanbiologie, der Psychologie, Kulturanthropologie oder Soziologie untersucht werden, um die Aufstellungen dieser Disziplinen auf ihre religiösen und theologisch relevanten Implikationen zu befragen" (p. 21). This is the reason why Pannenberg starts his research with an investigation into the "Humanbiologie" as that discipline which covers a very general range of human dimensions.

[66] The theistic anthropology: "Sie versteht ihn (the human being) von Haus aus nicht autonom, sondern theonom bestimmt, den menschlichen Logos als

A theonomous approach focuses on the following hypothesis: a person's ultimate meaning and the meaning of having been created by God need to be understood in the light of revelation. People can be understood only from an understanding of their relationship with God. Barth's hypothesis should be regarded as a fundamental point of departure for the design of a theological anthropology. A theological anthropology assesses the human being from the perspective of faith.

Heyns views people's relation to God as the fundamental and core relationship constituting their existence.[67] Berkouwer states that the purpose of an anthropology in Scripture is not to create a biblical psychology, but to describe people in relation to God.[68] This statement does not imply that a theological anthropology possesses special knowledge about human beings. Rather, a theological anthropology describes a certain vision and perspective on human beings. Particular attention is paid to people in their spiritual focus through faith in God, as well as to God's involvement with them and their eternal and ultimate destiny. A theonomous approach does not involve an abstraction of human beings, but looks at human beings in the light of revelation concerning their fundamental identity: human beings seen as created by God and their eventual destiny: salvation and resurrection life. Thus the theonomous approach is concerned with the totality of human life in the presence of God (*coram Deo*). A theological anthropology is not about a "systematic doctrine" concerning persons[69] but

---

seiend durch den göttlichen Humanität als Spiegelbild der Divinität" (Barth, *Die Lehre von der Schöpfung*, Kirchliche Dogmatik III/2, p. 240).

[67] See J. A. Heyns, *Teologiese Etiek* (1982), p. 201.

[68] See G. C. Berkouwer, *De Mens het Beeld Gods* (1957), p. 27. On p. 66 he puts it as follows: "Daarom is het te verstaan, dat in de dogmatische 'locus de homine' aandacht gevraagd wordt voor de mens in deze relatie."

[69] On this Berkouwer (*Ibid.*, p. 66) contends: "... dat er nergens sprake is van een ook maar enigzins systematische leer van de mens als beeld Gods."

about an understanding of persons from a certain perspective: the perspective of the Christian faith.

We can now make the following concluding remark: *the design of a theological anthropology for a pastoral theology is not concerned primarily with a fundamental analysis in terms of psychic issues or behavioral modes, but with a fundamental comprehension of human beings in terms of their calling by the grace of God. A pastoral anthropology is not focused on the effort to explain the origin of human beings in terms of a metaphysical model. A pastoral anthropology focuses on those scriptural perspectives which instill meaning in order to help people to discover their true humanity before God and to cope with painful life-issues. A pastoral anthropology opts for that kind of realism which tries to interpret the human quest for meaning in terms of the grace and love of God.*

The goal of a theological anthropology is not a rational exposition of human beings. The goal is merely to understand them hermeneutically: to interpret them in relationship with God. Barth meant this when he said that human reason resides in responsibility and obedience to God. The reality of human potential resides in human freedom and one's calling to be God's partner.[70] *The potential and skill (Fähigkeit) to be God's partner (i.e., faith) is the object of a theonomous approach in anthropology.* A "theo-anthropology" then becomes basically anthropocentric.

It is Barth's conviction that a Christian anthropology should not be abstract. Scripture is not only about a heavenly destination, but also about an earthly being. Human beings are part of the cosmos.[71] But the cosmos alone cannot disclose a human's ultimate

---

[70] "Gottes Partner und nicht nur der einer undefinierten Transzendenz" (Barth, *Die Lehre von der Schöpfung*, Kirchliche Dogmatik III/2, p. 240).

[71] "Anthropologie ist die Lehre vom Menschen im Kosmos" (*Ibid.*, p. 16).

destiny. This can only be understood when a person is viewed from a perspective of faith. Revelation determines the ultimate destiny of humankind. The pivotal question for a theological anthropology thus becomes the meaning of human existence, *coram Deo*. Traditionally, this meaning was always linked to the notion of humans being created in the image of God.

a) Human Beings' Fundamental Structuredness: Created in the Image of God (Creaturehood)

Clearly, it is impossible to build an anthropology upon a single scriptural pronouncement. Genesis 1:26-28 (the creation of the human being in the image of God) and Genesis 2:7 (the creation of a person, endowed with spirit) are traditionally viewed as the *loci classici* for a biblical doctrine of persons.[72] But it is doubtful whether this scriptural information was intended to develop an extensive and systematic doctrine regarding a theological anthropology.

In designing an anthropology for pastoral ministry, we prefer to take the following hypothesis as our point of departure. *Both the terms "image of God" and "a person as a living being"* (nefeš), *refer to the uniqueness of human beings as this is determined by their relationship with the living God. "Image of God" does not refer to a person being perfect, but to a person representing God, while* nefeš *indicates that the source of life is dependent upon God's creative action and faithfulness. This has ethical, moral and*

---

[72] P. K. Jewett ([1996], p. 29) remarks as follows: "This dignity, worth, and responsibility with which the biblical story of creation invests the human creature comes to its sharpest focus, for theologians, in the concept of the image of God (the *imago Dei*)." On the *imago Dei*, see also A-G. Hamman, *L'homme Image de Dieu* (1987), pp. 9-19. "L'image enfin dont parle Genèse n'est pas une qualité surajoutée mais constitutive de l'homme" (*Ibid.*, p. 15).

doxological implications: a person should focus upon God and display God's glory so that the entire creation may become aware of God's presence and grace. People, as living beings (*nefeš*), are distinguished from animals because their entire life, their physical and spiritual uniqueness are determined by God. *Both* nefeš *and image of God thus refer to the spiritual dimension of human existence: human beings have a transcendent dimension to their existence. This dimension is decisive not only for our human ultimate destiny (the "telic" dimension of existence) but also for conduct in general. The spiritual dimension does not exclude the psyche and the body, but views them as vital components of existence before God.*

How our creatureliness is interpreted determines whether these hypotheses are proved to be true. The term "image of God" is not limited to the Old Testament. In the New Testament, people are described as the image (*eikon, imago*) and glory (*doksa*) of God (1 Cor 11:7). Human beings are also renewed in the knowledge of their Creator's image (Col 3:10; Eph 4:24). James 3:9 also refers to a person as being created "in God's likeness." Christ, too, is described as the image of God (2 Cor 4:4; Col 1:15; Heb 1:1-4). In the light of these scriptural passages we cannot ignore the notion of people being created in the image of God.[73]

---

[73] When we come to a description of the meaning of spirituality, it should be borne in mind that the notion of creation is still very important. Without the notion of creation, spirituality becomes foreign to life. M. Fox ("Introduction: Roots and Routes in Western Spiritual Conscience," [1981], pp. 2-3) brings to our attention that Western spirituality was very much influenced by the notion of justification which leads to a sort of ignorance regarding the divine dimension of creation and humanity. "Western spirituality has two basic traditions — that which starts with the experience of sin and develops a fall/redemption spiritual motif; and that which starts with the experience of life as a blessing and develops a creation-centered spirituality. This book's purpose is to put Westerners in touch once again with the more neglected of these traditions, namely that of blessing/creation." Hence, his conclusion: "Christian Spirituality, then is a rootedness of being in the world" (*Ibid.,* p. 12). See also *ibid.,* pp. 7-27.

Berkouwer concludes that both the terms "image" (*tṣelem*) and "likeness" (*demūth*) in Genesis 1:26-27 can be used as alternative terms and are not easily distinguished from each other. In his exposition of the doctrine of humanity in Scripture, Wentsel (1987:593) declares that the terms "image" and "likeness" explain each other according to Hebrew parallelism and are virtually synonymous. The term "image" literally indicates a portrayal or a silhouette.

In *Anthropology of the Old Testament*,[74] Wolff contends that the meaning of this term should be sought in its Canaanite and Semitic origin and background, where the image of God indicates *representation with special authority*.[75] Heyns speaks of an analogy between two heterogeneous supporting points. He seeks the meaning of the image of God in the fact that people were appointed as God's representatives. The phrase "image of God," when applied to Jesus and Son of God, probably describes the *unique relation* between God and the human being and indicates that the *ultimate meaning of life* should not be sought outside this unique relationship.

Unlike Barth, Berkouwer believes that this kinship between God and the human being should not be understood ontologically. Rather, it should be understood in a noetic sense: it imparts knowledge about the character of the relationship between God and the human being and how this relationship is healed in Christ. Berkouwer finds a link between a person being a child of God and being created in the image of God.[76] He declares that the term "image of God" portrays *representation*. In an analogous way, a person, as a creature of God, should represent God's fatherhood, particularly as this is revealed in his compassion and mercy. *In his*

---

[74] See E. Wolff, *Anthropologie des Alten Testaments* (1973).

[75] See also the finding of R. L. Saucy ("Theology of Human Nature" [1993], p. 25), "... being in the image of God means not only that we are God's representative, but that we are representational of God."

[76] See Berkouwer, *De Mens het Beeld Gods* (1957), p. 119.

children, the image of God is reflected in the analogy of their entire lives, corresponding to the life of God.[77] Representing the image of God in this way makes the human focus on God visible. It also reflects the mercy of God in such a way that his compassion is conveyed. A person exists only within this relationship and, as both *nefeš* and *psuché*, focuses attention on God. This God-ward focus manifests itself in love for one another (*analogia amoris*).

Along the same lines as Berkouwer, Wentsel asserts: *The conclusion cannot be other than that the qualification "image" of God typically expresses a person as being totally dependent on God.*[78] The image is not limited to a mere part of human existence, such as the reason, the ethos or psyche. In all our relations and in every fabric of our life, we *are* the image of God. True knowledge about ourselves can be found only within this unique relationship.

The value of the concept "image of God" for a pastoral anthropology can be summarized as follows:

• *Qualitative dissimilarity.* Human existence is unique. This uniqueness is encompassed in the term *nefeš,* which indicates that humans, as living beings, differ qualitatively from other creatures. The image of God is *ontic*. This does not imply that something in a person existed before the creation, but was then lost or affected after the Fall. "The image of God" simply implies that a person *is essentially dependent upon God* and has an eternal destiny.

• *Relationality.* The term "image of God" implies that the destiny of human beings can be understood theologically only when viewed from the perspective of their being dependent on God.

---

[77] *Ibid.*, p. 120.

[78] See B. Wentsel, *God en Mens Verzoend* (1987), p. 596.

[79] See Weber, *Grundlagen der Dogmatik I*, p. 632.

Weber concludes that this term describes human beings in terms of their relationship with God (the noetic dimension).[79] Therefore, the possibility of an *analogia relationis* cannot be excluded in an understanding of the term "image of God." Weber speaks of the *imago Dei* as the continual human destiny to love.[80]

Van de Beek argues along the same lines.[81] Creation does not refer to a perfect creation, but to the relationship between God and cosmos. The doctrine of creation, therefore, should not be used to explain the origin of human beings. Creation is not about the origin of *homo sapiens*. We cannot derive a biology or physiology from the Genesis narrative. Creation refers to the sustaining presence of God and his relationship to the brokenness, misery, pain and suffering of the world.[82] Genesis does not portray a perfect world and paradise, but is a critical narrative. Creation therefore is a critical concept[83] which does not describe the essence of being (the character of creation) but the ought of being (how it should be). Hence the importance of the relationship and of understanding the image of God in terms of who a person should become in relationship with God. Human beings and creation are therefore a symbol of God's presence. People and creation *are* not God as is the case in pantheism where the symbol and the reality *are* the same. Instead, both refer to the caring presence of God.

For Van de Beek the implication of human beings created in the image of God is that every creature should enjoy God and live a life of praise and gratitude.[84] Gratitude, therefore, is the result of, and experience of, the love of God. Creation wants to fortify exactly that kind of experience which honors God in terms of

---

[80] *Ibid.*, p. 633.

[81] See A. van de Beek, *Schepping* (1996), p. 50.

[82] *Ibid.*, p. 47.

[83] *Ibid.*, p. 52.

[84] *Ibid.*, p. 406.

praise and exaltation. In this togetherness with God, humanity has been restored.[85]

• *Purposefulness and the dimension of the ultimate.* The term "image of God" assigns to people the faculties of responsibility and "respondability." Human beings are commissioned to represent and glorify God in all that they are and do. The command to rule, that is, to care for the earth, results from God's direction. Life becomes a vocation and existence becomes meaningful.

Obedience and accountability are definitely part of what it means to be created in the image of God. The fact that the human being, despite the Fall, still remains an image of God, cannot be ascribed to any human quality. The continuity does not lie in our humanity, but in God's faithfulness.

• *Christological dimension.* Jesus, as image of God, is not a prototype for perfect humanity, nor for a new type of person. That Jesus Christ Himself is also described as an image of God, means that a person acquires a new status in Christ.[86] Christians are transformed so that they resemble more closely the image of Christ (2 Cor 3:18), and increasingly reflect the glory (*doksa*) of God. Christ, as an image of God, thus brings human beings back to their original destiny, so that they too represent God. Representation does not imply a single function, but places the entire creation within the new order of God's Kingdom.

---

[85] *Ibid.,* pp. 406-407: "Leven als schepsel is een leven in dankbaarheid. We hebben ons bestaan uit Gods hand gekregen. Hij heeft gewild dat we er zijn. We zijn er niet toevallig, maar we zijn er vanwege de goedheid van God."

[86] The image of God is revealed in the New Testament in terms of Christ's salvific work. See Von L. Scheffczyk ("Die Frage nach der Gotteneben-bildlichkeit in der Modernen Theologie" [1969], p. xxxi): "Diese Einheit mit Christus als Grund der durch ihn vermittelten Gottenebenbildlichkeit ist das grosse Thema der neutestamentlichen Ebenbildlehre. Darin sind die Beherrschen-den Momente der Gnadenhafte Charakter der Christusebenbildlichkeit, die den Sünder dem Ebenbild Christi gleichgestaltet (Röm 8,29) ... ."

This Christological dimension of the term, "image of God," evokes the following question: what is the place and function of Christology in theological anthropology?

b) Salvation: The Function of Christology in Theological Anthropology

Barth's fundamental thesis in his theological anthropology is that people exist *for* God.[87] The fundamental significance of being human lies in living in partnership with God. God has determined human beings' original destiny as existence together with God.[88] Barth developed the notion of togetherness before God, and partnership with God in the thesis: human freedom is receptive. This means that being human implies having accountability and responsibility.[89]

Barth applies these two basic statements concretely to Christ, the Person. Jesus, the Person for God, reveals the significance of being-for-God and togetherness before God. This is Barth's Christological point of departure for his anthropology.[90] But Barth also believes that this statement cannot be reversed: anthropology cannot be synonymous with Christology. A design for an anthropology thus cannot be directly deduced from Christology. What it means to be human, and the Christological dimension of Jesus, the Person, have different points of departure. According to Barth, the

---

[87] See Barth, *Die Lehre von der Schöpfung,* Kirchliche Dogmatik III/2, p. 81.

[88] *Ibid.,* p. 161.

[89] "Mensch sein heisst verantwortlich sein. Mensch sein heisst 'respondieren' gegenüber dem was dem Menschen gesagt ist. Des Menschen Spontaneität besteht also darin, dass er solcher Verantwortung fähig ist" (*Ibid.,* p. 150).

[90] See *ibid.,* p. 51.

difference between an anthropology and a Christology resides in Christ's mediation. Christ is a Mediator. Thus, human nature depends wholly on grace,[91] not vice versa. Despite these differences Barth believes that the importance of Christology for anthropology resides in the fact that a form of analogy exists between Christ's humanity and our being human. This kind of analogy implies faith (analogia *fidei*). This safeguards a theological anthropology against docetism. By founding an anthropology on the human nature of Christ (Christ the human Person), Barth concretizes theological anthropology.

Barth believes that a Christology offers an understanding of the basic trait of human beings: people in their togetherness with, and focus upon, God. This ontological destiny of a person is grounded in the fact that Christ is, a priori, the Fellow-person of all. Each person also is the fellow-person of Christ.

Barth questions whether Christology merely defines the human being by theoretical knowledge at the level of epistemology. Does a Christology merely impart knowledge concerning the condition of the human being, or do Christ and the Word also define people ontologically? God's "Yes" to the human being determines human existence ontologically by a Christology (the humanity of Christ). Therefore human beings cannot but answer "yes" to God's "Yes." People's failure to do this, is the inexplicability of sin. (Sin = structural impossibility.)

In the light of this Christological predisposition, Barth declares that the mystery of humanity resides in the fact that human beings are destined to be God's partners and that they belong to God.[92] A correlation thus exists between human beings as creatures (their humanity), and as God's partners (predestination). In Jesus'

---

[91] *Ibid.,* p. 57.
[92] *Ibid.,* p. 319.

co-humanity, the togetherness in God is revealed from the "inside" to the "outside" in such a way that being human is eventually determined constitutively as togetherness with God and partnership with God. Being created thus implies that the significance of humanity resides in a new understanding of being: "being-in-encounter" which concretely is apparent in the I-you relationship and in the relationship between husband and wife.

Barth does not imply by this link between God and being (creation) that a person is identical to the divine Being. The link is not an analogy in being (*analogia entis*), but an analogy in relation (*analogia relationis*). For Barth, Jesus' being for God and togetherness with God, simultaneously reveals Jesus' co-humanity and becomes the criterion for all forms of togetherness between people.[93] Co-humanity is further developed when people open up towards each other and communicate with one another. Through dialogue, in which people express themselves and address each other, humanity attains the concreteness which enables people to support and sustain each other.[94] Partnership and dialogue constitute a basis for human freedom, and create true humanity. People are attracted to this mutuality in human togetherness and partnership because of the analogy with Jesus: the Being-for-others.

This link between Christology and true humanity (anthropology), gives human existence a symbolic character. Togetherness between people becomes a symbol of the original partnership between God and the human being. This association is truly experienced in human deeds of love. A person becomes a parable (image of God) and an analogy of the relation God-Christ (the Human).

---

[93] "So ist Humanität die Bestimmtheit unseres Seins als ein Sein in der Begegnung mit dem anderen Menschen" (*Ibid.*, p. 296).
[94] *Ibid.*, p. 312.

Barth's attempt to found anthropology on Christology, without allowing Christology to coincide with anthropology, implies the following valuable insights for pastoral care:

- Human beings originate in God and are truly dependent on God for their being.[95]
- On the basis of togetherness and partnership with Jesus, the meaning of human existence resides in predestination: God's yes to people.
- Hearing the Word confirms the reality of human existence.[96] People are addressed by God and attain their humanity by the event of a Word.[97]
- As a result of being addressed, people are called to react to the content of such an event, that is, to respond to grace. Hence, the notion of humanity and vocation.
- The fact of being addressed and being called creates a history through which the transcendental factor (grace) truly transforms our being.
- This transformation within the concreteness of our existence, results in gratitude. To be human means to live with an attitude of thanksgiving. Gratitude becomes the act in which the "hearing of

---

[95] *Ibid.*, p. 167.

[96] *Ibid.*, p. 176.

[97] O. H. Pesch (*Frei Sein aus Gnade* [1983], p. 29) is convinced that a theological anthropology should be based solely on Scripture and not on the human sciences. "Hier [in a theological anthropology] kann der Ansatz aus der Natur der Sache heraus nicht eine humanwissenschaftliche Aussage über den Menschen sein ... sondern nur eine solche Aussage, die sich entscheidend auf die biblische Botschaft als Trägerin der Selbstkundgabe Gottes in seinem Verhältnis zum Menschen stützt. Aussertheologische Aussagen über den Menschen werden von hierher ins Gespräch gezogen, aufgenommen, integriert, beurteilt — aber sie sind nicht der methodische und sachliche, höchstens der didaktische Ausgangspunkt." Having said this, Pesch maintains that every theological theory should essentially address the problem of anthropology without falling prey to the danger of an "anthropocentrism" (*Ibid.*, p. 30).

the Word" is enfleshed and embodied.[98] Barth views thanksgiving as the only form of complementariness between God and people. Gratitude is the essential human "task." People truly exist only insofar as they thank God.[99]

• The spontaneity of human existence is freedom, expressed as responsibility and accountability, by which human beings acknowledge that they have heard and obeyed God's Word. Responsibility is thus characterized by obedience. The notion: "I am" (existence), now changes to: "I want to" and "I ought to" (ethos). People want nothing more than to choose God and to focus on exalting him.

Can this Barthian model of the relation between Christology and anthropology be justified scripturally?

We have already referred to the valuable insights which Barth's Christological approach to anthropology reveal. Yet, one should be aware of a possible danger: a too optimistic view of the human being. In his attempt to found anthropology on Christology, Barth implies that Christ not only shares in human nature via the incarnation, but vice versa: human nature shares in Jesus' nature via the incarnation.[100] The triumph of grace eclipses human nature. Barth thus risks elevating the knowledge about the essence of persons (noetic), in terms of the incarnation, to an ontic event within which they already share in Jesus' humanity (ontic identification). Although Barth wishes to avoid this danger, such an approach can result in the uniqueness of Christ's mediation being undermined and the reality of human misery being underestimated. Hence, the danger of a too hasty anthropology which underestimates human

---

[98] "Danken ist das genaue geschöpfliche Komplement zu Gottes Gnade" (Barth, *Die Lehre von der Schöpfung*, Kirchliche Dogmatik III/2, p. 198).

[99] *Ibid.*, p. 203.

[100] For this problem with Barth, see Berkouwer's criticism (*De Mens het Beeld Gods*, pp. 98-99).

misery and suffering in creation. However, the value of Barth's standpoint resides in his emphasis on the fact that true humanity cannot be understood without Jesus' mediating work.

Anderson, in *On Being Human*, uses this positive contribution in Barth's Christological founding of anthropology, in an attempt to link an anthropology to a Christology. Anderson's basic hypothesis is that the foundation of any theological anthropology lies in the continuity between Jesus of Nazareth as the Crucified and Christ the Lord as the Resurrected One.[101] According to Anderson, the human ontological status, as determined by the Word, enables the transcendence of human existence. When human existence is understood merely in terms of creation, then there is the danger of a naturalistic determinism — human beings remain prisoners of their own natural potentialities and genetic limitations. The danger of perfectionism also arises when people become prisoners of their improved or perfect behavior. In contrast, Anderson contends that the Word of God is the transcendental factor and the determining dimension for the Ultimate. Creation out of nothing thus prevents determinism and perfectionism and makes people depend on God's Word for their new potential: "that which we call human being is differentiated creatureliness, experienced as response to the creative divine Word."[102]

Anderson, working along the same lines as Barth, also finds the meaning of true humanity in the human response to the Word, that is, in human responsibility.[103] To him, the image of God is found in encounter and in relationships, as these are constituted by the Word.[104] The same Word also constitutes people in their need for self-affirmation. Human beings can now say yes to their

---

[101] See R. S. Anderson, *On Being Human* (1982), p. 18.

[102] *Ibid.*, p. 35.

[103] *Ibid.*, p. 37.

[104] *Ibid.*, p. 73.

existence, based on the principle of election: God's predestining grace.[105]

Although election forms the theological foundation for the human need for self-confirmation, Anderson nevertheless regards the covenant as the theological paradigm most able to address the human need for relationships and for belonging. For Anderson, the atonement functions as a paradigm which is able to meet the human need for healing and restoration. Thus, true healing takes place through forgiveness. The *eschaton*, in turn, also functions as a paradigm within which the human quest for meaning can take place.

Anderson applies this information to pastoral care.[106] For him, a Christological approach in pastoral care means that the incarnation provides the basis for all forms of healing. Because of the ontological status of a person in Christ, the incarnation, therefore, also functions as the hermeneutical key to understanding authentic personality. "We go to Christ to learn about Adam."[107] Knowledge about the nature of humans should thus be interpreted via the incarnation.

Is it possible to transfer directly from a Christology to an anthropology? Can one move directly from Christ's incarnation to making conclusions about the true human character? When Christology is linked directly to anthropology via the incarnation, then there is a risk that the uniqueness of Christ's vicarious work will have only anthropological consequences. Christ then becomes only an ideal or model (typology) for perfect humanity. He no longer functions as a Mediator between God and a person, bringing reconciliation between the two. On the other hand, the link between a Christology and anthropology cannot be denied.

---

[105] *Ibid.*, pp. 162-163.
[106] *Ibid.*, p. 199.
[107] *Ibid.*, p. 199.

What then are the implications of a Christology for anthropology? The following implications can be identified:

• *Christology has a relational effect on an anthropology.* The Son, as the image of God (Col 1:15-17, Heb 1:1-4), links our having been created in the image of God, to God Himself. This does not imply that in Genesis 1:26-28 the human being was created according to the image of the incarnate Son of God. The Son, as the image of the Father, links God to the created, through the ontology of creation. This connection means that, because of the way in which humans were created, they are dependent on God. *Christology thus functions as a hermeneutical key to a pastoral epistemology: knowledge regarding our destiny is knowledge about our salvation and a relationship of love with God.*

The term, "Christ as the image of God" (2 Cor 4:4; Col 1:15) could also be said to link human beings with their salvation. Christ as the image of God, refers to Christ's pre-existence as the Son of God, before the creation and the Fall. The image of God indicates Christ's Godliness and implies that God reveals Himself in Christ. The term "image of God" was mentioned regarding the first Adam (Gen 1:27). Paul uses Genesis 1 to explain the unique link between Christ and His "pre-existence" with God. But when Paul applies the term "image" to the second Adam, then a different and opposite meaning arises. A person who is an image of the second Adam is of a different order to that of the first Adam.[108] It is Christ, as the image of God, who enables the reborn person to

---

[108] For the discussion about the unique meaning of the "image of God" within the Christology, see H. Ridderbos, *Paulus* (1966), pp. 66f: "Wij kunnen daarom tot geen andere conclusie komen dan dat Paulus in de bovengenoemde plaatsen de goddelijke heerlijkheid van Christus, zowel in zijn praeëxistentie als in zijn verhoging, heeft aangeduid met een qualificatie, die ook de eerste Adam gold, zij het dan uiteraard in een andere bij de eerste Adam passende, betekenis" (*Ibid.*, p. 72).

share in the new order of peace and reconciliation which has been made possible through salvation.

• *Christology is connected to the notion of soteriology and salvation and, thus, has a transforming effect.* It transforms a person into a new being (2 Cor 5:17), who is gradually being transformed into the image of Christ (2 Cor 3:18). Christology, because of its soteriology (the eradication of sin and guilt) is able to restore human beings to their original ultimate destiny, which is to glorify God. In this sense, Christology has ontic implications for an anthropology. The incarnation does not allow a person to share in Christ's *nature*, but in His *expiatory sacrifice*. By sharing in Christ's redemption, the old person is transformed into a new person.[109]

• *Christology has epistemological implications for an anthropology.* Christology reveals human beings' misery and fundamental guilt. A theology of the cross unmasks people in their existential need: they are lost and unable to save themselves. In Christ, people discover that they are God's children and his possessions. This knowledge leads to a new self-acceptance and to a positive self-esteem: God accepts me; in Christ, God reveals his unconditional *yes* to me.

• *Christology restores people to their ultimate function before God. It supplies a telic dimension in which the search for meaning can take place.* People are healed so that they can mirror the original image of God. Their lives reflect true knowledge, justification and holiness (Eph 4:24, Col 3:10). This redemption is expressed in a transformed life-style, which changes all human relationships and conduct (sanctification of life).

At the same time, salvation also provides people with a new eternal destiny, thus giving them a horizon of meaning. The Adam-Christ parallels in Romans 5:12-21 and 1 Corinthians

---

[109] Hence, the following conviction of Pesch (*Frei Sein aus Gnade*, p. 36): "Ort und Ansatz theologischer Anthropologie liegen in der Lehre von Gnade und Rechtfertigung."

15:44-49, reveals how people now share in the eschatological quality of life, so that their lives attain transcendental, heavenly and ultimate meaning.

• *One of the most important consequences arising from a Christology which describes the structure of our creatureliness, is that it also provides people with a spiritual dimension. It reveals that people are more than mere bodies and souls: a person has a transcendental destiny in life.*

Summary

The essential elements of a biblical doctrine of persons can be summarized as follows:

• A biblical approach assumes that people are dependent on God and should be understood from their relationship with God. *Humanity must be understood in the context of our partnership with God and our co-humanity in Christ.*[110] Humanity necessarily

---

[110] The issue of humanity touches the question of what is meant by a Christian humanism. R. W. Franklin & J. M. Shaw (*The Case for Christian Humanism* [1991], pp. 10-11) describe a Christian humanism in terms of the following chief themes. The first is that in Christ the individual person is rescued from lonely isolation and made a member of a historic community. Christian humanism points to a new reality: a human community that enhances personal selfhood and engages in the struggle for peace and justice. Important is the following: "The corporate fellowship of believing persons is one of God's highest and most humanizing gifts" (p. 11). The second theme of Christian humanism is the discovery that in Christ the world of material reality — the earth, the human body and its senses, the humble objects of daily use — can be a vehicle of the Holy Spirit to bless humanity. Another paradoxical theme of Christian humanism is that full human freedom is realized under the authority of Christ. A third paradox stems from the incarnation: human history is touched by eternity.
The implication of a Christian humanism is that it must clash with a humanism that rejects supernaturalism, that regards human beings as natural objects, that claims to be a religion, or that fosters a doctrine of the "mere" humanity of Christ (p. 9).

presupposes togetherness, which results in fellowship with other human beings. Fellowship is expressed by, and through, mutual love: this restores our humanity. Christian love is unconditional: no explanation or reason is offered for God's love for human beings.

• *Scripture does not approach human beings primarily in terms of their sin and guilt, but in terms of grace and of their new being in Christ.* Scripture thus addresses human beings in terms of their covenantal relationship with God. This relationship is characterized by grace, which heals them to become new beings; the eschatological reality of God's fulfilled promises; victory over sin; and the perspective of the resurrection and glory of God's sovereignty over all destructive powers. *Eschatology makes it impossible to regard sin and human guilt as the primary point of departure for a theological anthropology. The point of departure is salvation. This means that in pastoral care human beings should not be addressed in terms of their negative and destructive components (guilt and death), but in terms of grace: the positive and transforming power of eschatology.*

• The scriptural view of the human being is not primarily pessimistic: it does not bind human beings to their guilt and transience. Neither is Scripture optimistic: it does not ignore sin, nor does it rely solely on human inner potentialities. *The biblical view of the human being is realistic.* It uses the notions of salvation and empowerment to reveal to human beings who they are and can become. Knowledge, which emanates from the relationship with God, creates a *dynamic ambivalence* in a person. A person is a being who can confess: *"I* sinned and *I* trespassed." But a person is also a being who is liberated and can give thanks to God. A person can profess: "I believe." This reality of faith results in thanksgiving and praise (doxology): "I praise God." Biblical realism is a realism of faith. Pastoral care addresses human beings in terms of this realism of faith, and focuses on an eventual doxology.

• The ability to react and to respond to God's loving care and condescension is central to a biblical portrayal of the human. *The fact that people were created in the image of God implies account-ability and respondability.*

The etymology of the concept "responsibility" produces most interesting material which has important implications for a pastoral context. The root of the French *responsabilité* and the English "responsibility" comes from the Latin *spondeo* and the Greek *spendoo*.[111] *Spendoo* is linked to libation. It is defined as confirmation of an agreement on the grounds of blood having been shed; pledging by covenant; making promises and being committed to obligations. It thus appears that the concept "response" is linked to commitments within relationships and to the restoration of bad relationships. Response thus presupposes the juridical context, in which the addressee is accountable and in which the addressee is compelled to answer the addresser. The concept of responsibility presupposes that the addressee can answer and is able to give an account.

According to Brinkerink's research, the concept responsibility suggests a creative tension between "must" (obligation) and "can" (potential), without describing the exact nature of the obligation and potential. Both express the fact that being human implies having freedom, within which reason and volition play an important role. This interpretation of the concept responsibility, enables us to conclude that, because of accountability, people are also moral beings. People are responsible *to* but also responsible *for*. To be human, means to be committed to someone and to live with a vocation to do something for someone.

This meaning of responsibility is important for a theological anthropology. The basic notion in a theological anthropology is:

---

[111] See J. Brinkerink, "Ontstaansgeschiedenis van het Begrip Verantwoorde-lijkheid" (1976), p. 208.

respondeo ergo sum:[112] *I respond (and am responsible) therefore I am. Responsibility presupposes the covenantal context of human existence, within which people are addressed by God's Word and are thus responsible to God. A person is a moral being with ethical obligations.*
• Responsibility and respondability are components of our spiritual dimension. When these are assessed in terms of an eschatological model, then the result is: obedience to God. This leads to the necessity of *faith, which is fundamental for a theological anthropology.* Faith can be viewed as the medium through which pastoral care operates anthropologically. Faith development becomes an important factor for pastoral care.
• Love, gratitude, joy and hope are fundamental to pastoral care. All are components of a living faith which operates within the eschatological tension of the already and the not yet. A theological anthropology therefore remains a dynamic, ever-developing issue. A static anthropology does not comply with an eschatological understanding of the human being. *Love, gratitude, joy, hope and faith are components of Christian spirituality and an indication of a mature functional faith.*

The link between people and creation proves the fact that a scriptural perspective on the human is basically positive. Nevertheless, the scriptural perspective is realistic enough to reckon with a fundamental tension: the tension between unity and brokenness (misery); fellowship with God (faith) and estrangement (sin). A realistic approach cannot ignore the ambivalence which is an ingredient of our being in the presence of God.

Within this ambivalence, Scripture describes the human being in terms of "soul," "spirit" and "body." How do these three different perspectives help us to understand and interpret our *coram Deo* position?

---

[112] See F. Heinemann, *Filosofie op Nieuwe Wegen* (1963), p. 180.

c) Realism: The Ambivalence and Unity of Being Human

A number of questions arise when we try to integrate the various scriptural perspectives on humans. How do body, soul and spirit relate? What does the unity of persons mean, especially in the light of the human ambivalence between good and evil, inner potential and sinfulness? Does a description of human beings in terms of personality and physicality suffice for a pastoral anthropology, or are people spiritual beings with a transcendental destiny? What is meant by "spirituality"?

A Biblical Way of Thinking and Understanding

We will use three specific modes to describe how the relationship between God and humans is portrayed in Scripture. These modes are: stereometric reasoning, synthetic thinking, and perspectivism.
• *Stereometric reasoning.* Concepts like heart, soul and spirit are often used alternately in Hebrew poetry to reveal certain aspects of the human being. Stereometric reasoning allows for the Semitic view of a person as a unit. The Greek dualism of body and soul is foreign to the Semitic approach. Stereometric reasoning is relational and systemic. It does not view a person in terms of different parts, but as a functional unit within a network of relations.
• *Synthetic thinking.* A part of the body, for example the kidneys, is used to describe the human psyche and its position within the whole of our bodily existence. The whole is implied, although only a part is mentioned. A basic organ, for example, the heart, could therefore symbolize various human aspects or potentialities. Since a single concept may have a variety of meaning nuances, a theological anthropology must not emphasize only one concept

when describing the human being. For example, the biblical concept *psuché* should be understood in relation to other important human components, such as emotions, will and bodily needs.

• *Perspectivism.* This approach views human beings in terms of their relationship with God. It presupposes that a person is dependent on God and focused on him. A person is viewed from the perspective of God's condescending love, as this is expressed in a covenant of grace. Covenantal thinking argues in terms of the faithfulness of God and the historic event of a salvific encounter. This perspective reveals the transcendental dimension of human existence. *Transcendence is not used in the sense of a metaphysical dissimilarity, but rather to indicate the theonomous origin and destiny of human beings.* Some have described this transcendental perspective as "the vertical dimension of human life." But, because the contrast between the vertical and horizontal perspectives has caused so much confusion, the term "transcendence" is employed. An attempt is made to detach this term from metaphysical speculation by linking the terms "transcendental" and "spirituality," and by employing the historic characteristics of salvation.

The notion of biblical realism frequently arises. By "realism" is meant the ambivalence between our misery (sinful nature) and our new being (redeemed nature).

Sin, Guilt and Shame

The problem of sin, in a pastoral anthropology, is indeed very complex. The current trend in contemporary pastoral care in a post-modern context is to reinterpret sin in terms of our normal limitations and psychological terminology. The result is that sin is viewed as dysfunctional behavior or an abnormality/disorder, and not necessarily as estrangement from God.

Viewing sin as dysfunctional behavior unhitches it from its ethical implications. For instance, sin is perceived as an impediment in the process of self-actualization, which causes incongruency. Our present culture, which emphasizes achievement (achievement ethics), encourages a more pragmatic and functional interpretation of sin. Thus sin is seen less as unbelief before God, and more as inner alienation or an obstruction of inner potential.

In his book, *The Depleted Self: Sin in a Narcissistic Age*, Capps points out that "wrongfulness" is interpreted more as shame than guilt.[113] "Thus, to speak meaningfully and relevantly about sin, we have to relate sin to the experience of shame — not only, not even primarily, to the experience of guilt."

Augsburger latches onto this concept when he asserts that, with cross-cultural communication in mind, the concept of shame, together with anxiety and guilt, play an important role in the human psyche. "Unquestionably the most common opinion about the emerging psyche is the sequence of the three primary control emotions. Anxiety intimidates, shame suppresses, guilt obligates."[114]

Augsburger points out that Western culture is more guilt-oriented, while Eastern culture (*e.g.* Japan) is more shame-oriented.[115] In a cross-cultural situation, pastoral care should therefore make allowance for both the positive and negative sides of the concept "shame." "Shame is both positive and negative, both the capacity for discretion and, when indiscreet, the consequent disgrace."[116]

[113] See Capps, *The Depleted Self*, p. 3.
[114] See David W. Augsburger, *Pastoral Counseling Across Cultures* (1986), p. 126.
[115] *Ibid.*, p. 119.
[116] *Ibid.*, p. 118.

As a result of cultural shifts,[117] Lasch contends that the narcissist is this century's new type of personality.[118] According to Capps, narcissistic disturbances (usually between neurosis and psychosis) are viewed psychologically as less serious borderline cases.[119] According to Kernberg, the most important characteristics of such a personality are: "Grandiosity, extreme self-centeredness and remarkable absence of interest and empathy for others in spite of the fact that they are so very eager to obtain admiration and approval from other people."[120]

Narcissists are usually dissatisfied and unfulfilled, largely because of an excessive obsession with their self-esteem and physical image. "Seeming to be self-loving and self-satisfied, they instead have a deep sense of personal shame and self-contempt."[121] This disappointment in themselves is nourished by a cultural context which emphasizes work, achievement and consumption. The feeling of shame is also strengthened by an inner experience of exhaustion or, according to Capps, "a sense of inner depletedness and of hunger for admiration and approval, and for positive mirroring of their need to idealize self and others."[122]

Capps uses his empirical research to demonstrate how the eight so-called deadly sins augment the feeling of emptiness, disappointment and inner depletedness. These eight deadly sins offer

[117] The notion of sin has been interpreted differently in different cultures and ages. On the medieval conception of sin and the paradise narrative, see J. Delumeau, *Une Histoire du Paradis* (1992), pp. 81-97.

[118] Cited by Capps in *The Depleted Self,* p. 6. Capps draws the attention to Christopher Lasch's book, *The Culture of Narcissism,* published in 1979. As a cultural theorist, Lasch claims that the narcissist is the dominant personality of our time.

[119] *Ibid.,* p. 12.

[120] Cited in *ibid.,* p. 16.

[121] *Ibid.,* p. 35.

[122] *Ibid.,* p. 39-40.

insight into what contemporary people struggle with in a materialistic age, and are therefore listed below.[123]

Greed: A consuming desire for wealth or affluence, causing
              one to think of little else.
Lust: An abusive and manipulative attitude toward per-
              sons of the opposite sex, treating them as objects or
              pawns.
Lechery: Misusing and manipulating another person as a sex
              object for selfish purposes.
Pride: Self-centeredness, continually expecting or demand-
              ing praise and adulation.
Anger: Ire or resentment, reflected in feelings of intense
              hostility, vengefulness, and inner rage.
Gluttony: Addictive habits, for example, excessive or erratic
              eating or drinking, causing self and others untold
              misery.
Envy: Persistent envy of others who enjoy special advan-
              tages, attention and recognition, coveted for oneself.
Apathy: Apathy or callousness, indifference toward the
              needs and aspirations of others.
Melancholy: Personal bitterness towards life; hatred and disgust
              for associates and for the world.

Capps's research further demonstrates that pastors struggle with
pride, as a result of a self-centered attitude which is continually
dependent upon praise. "Thus the minister is especially vulnerable
to self-depletion."[124]

Capps associates this experience of inner self-exhaustion with
shame. According to him, shame influences people's lives even
more than guilt. "Thus to experience shame is to experience in an

[123] Ibid., pp. 49-50.
[124] Ibid., p. 57.

unusually deep and painful way, a sense of self-estrangement, a wave of self-rejection, even of self-revulsion."[125] This self-estrangement also results in alienation from others. It causes disruption (divided self), various defense strategies (defensive self), and a sense of inner self-failure.

> The words that capture this deeper inner experience of shame are not humiliation and embarrassment, but words like empty, exhausted, drained, demoralized, depressed, deflated, bereft, needy, starving, apathetic, passive, and weak.[126]

The value of Capps's study resides in the way in which it reveals how our sinful condition and the brokenness of our human existence are basic realities which influence conduct and behavior. When human autonomy and freedom degenerate into loveless self-assertion, this affects the very being of a person as well as his/her human dignity. In a sense, sin is, and remains, a transgression of the commandment to love. Hence, it becomes necessary to gain some scriptural knowledge about the true nature of sin.[127]

---

[125] *Ibid.*, p. 76.

[126] *Ibid.*, p. 99.

[127] In a study about the scriptural view of sin, J. H. Ellens ("Sin and Sickness" [1989], pp. 60-61) contends that the concept is complex and has a variety of possible interpretations. The many different faces and aspects of the phenomenon of sin are summarized:

* *hatta't*, failure to achieve exactly what was expected — "a missing"
* *pesa'*, failure to conform to the standard — "a rebellion"
* *pesa'*, failure to do things exactly as they were required — "a transgression "
* *'awon*, distortion or corruption of that for which one was intended — "a perversion"
* *ra'*, nastiness of disposition — "evil"
* *resa'*, insensitivity to what would be appropriate to a child of God, living before the face of God — "impiety."

New Testament words for sin have a similar character and content. They include:

If we accept that responsibility for fellow-persons and acts of justice, as these have been demonstrated by the unconditional love of God, are the essence of a theological approach to ethics, then sin is a transgression of the imperative to love God and fellow human beings. We thereby perpetrate evil when we obey our narcissistic nature and injure our fellow human beings or God's world. Evil results from bad choices. These choices are free in the proximate sense, but are bound in the ultimate sense of conscious and unconscious commitment to unhealthy values. From a psychological point of view, evil stems from ignorance, psychopathology, spiritual pathology, inadequacy and other human limitations and distortions.[128]

The theological understanding of sin indicates the kind of conduct and disposition which is directed against God, and which results in a distortion of our relationship with fellow human beings. Sin, as well as sinful deeds, is the result of a life turned away from God (unbelief). Sin indicates transgression of the law of love and originates from evil inclinations, such as hatred and loveless self-interest. The attitudes of smugness, egoistic self-maintenance, selfishness and self-righteousness all indicate a narcissistic self-centeredness in which there is no place for God and

* *hamartia*, failure to achieve exactly what was expected — "missing the mark"
* *parabasis*, failure to do things exactly as they were required — "a transgression"
* *adikia*, failure to conform to the standard, thus a behavior which is not affirmed or approved — "unrighteousness"
* *asebeia*, insensitivity to what would be appropriate for a child of God, living before the face of God — "impiety"
* *anomia*, failure to adhere to prescriptions — "lawlessness"
* *porneria*, inability to do right and good — "depravity"
* *epithymia*, an urge to act differently from what is appropriate and prescribed — "evil desire."

[128] See Ellens, "Sin and Sickness," p. 67.

fellow human beings. The scriptural understanding of sin is that which occurs when a person does not acknowledge the grace of God and resists the offer of salvation. Such conduct necessarily influences behavior and affects the way in which we express ourselves bodily. The impression could be created that the scriptural view of people as sinful beings is extremely negative. A pastoral anthropology based on this understanding of persons would be essentially pessimistic. On the contrary, this is not the case. *The theme of sin in Scripture does not appear in order to design a negative anthropology. Rather, the notion that people are sinful beings creates a realistic view of them, and has the primary intention of setting them free from sin. Sin should therefore be assessed within the perspective of salvation and grace.* For instance, Löhr points out that in Hebrews the concept "sin" is dealt with in such a way as to indicate that sin is conquerable.[129] Sin should thus not be interpreted within the framework of wickedness, but rather should be understood within the salvific context. Löhr believes that a tragic concept of sin is foreign to the text of Hebrews.[130] Sin is linked to the general fallibility of human beings.

The crucial theological point still remains clear: sin makes sense because sin *per se* is sin against God. It describes the backsliding and disobedience in faith which takes place within the framework of God's merciful revelation. As such, *the basis of a theological anthropology is essentially positive: people are evaluated not in terms of their sin, but in terms of God's grace. Sin should thus be interpreted within a broader framework as freedom from guilt, reconciliation and forgiveness.*

---

[129] See H. Löhr, *Umkehr und Sunde im Hebraerbrief* Löhr (1994), p. 134.
[130] *Ibid.*, p. 134.

Sin should also not be viewed substantially. This approach believes that there is an "inner component" or "material principle" in humans which explains the origin of sin. This is not so. Rather, sin is about irresponsible choices, hypocrisy, false motives and distorted needs of self-interest. Essentially, sin is a problem of distorted relationships.

Throughout the tradition of the Christian church, sin has often been associated with our physicality and embodiment. A close link between sexuality and sinfulness has been presupposed. Hence, the necessity to reflect on the notion of physicality and the role of sexuality within a pastoral anthropology.

Physicality (Body) and Embodiment

"Body" has a comprehensive meaning in Scripture. The body was created by God and is the medium through which human beings exist and express themselves. Therefore the body, as such, is not the principle of sinfulness. Human beings do not merely *have* a body, but as creatures *are* wholly physical. Hence, the notion of embodiment: the I and "soul" are "enfleshed" in a bodily existence.

"Embodiment" indicates the way in which human beings, in their daily living, express their motives and goals through their bodily existence, and thereby reveal themselves within relationships. The fact that people are physical beings means that the body is the carrier and the dynamic expression of human spiritual and ethical impulses. The body represents the vegetative and physiological aspects of existence. At the same time, the body also functions as a whole in a psycho-physical unity, which is determined by the ego, consciousness and a moral awareness (ethics). Body and flesh should thus not be perceived as an external human element, but rather as indicative of the person him-/herself from the perspective of a certain mode of existence: a bodily awareness (embodiment).[131]

The Pauline approach focuses strongly on the difference between *sarx* (flesh) and *sóma* (body). In some instances *sarx* and *soma* are used for the same purpose. *Sarx* can mean natural human beings in their creatureliness (1 Cor 1:29; Rom 1:3; 3:20). *When sarx* is associated with human earthly existence, it implies fragility, weakness and transience. Evil does not reside in the *sarx* as such, because nobody hates his/her own flesh (Eph 5:29). Thus the use of *sarx* does not necessarily have a moral meaning, as so often was the case in Hellenism.[132] Yet Paul does not deny the connection between *sarx* and sin. Paul employs *sarx* in the sense of a person's being and attitude as opposed to God and His Spirit. Therefore, when used in a broader context, *sarx* is often linked to sin. It indicates that human existence is subject to powers which hamper, damage and threaten the principle of the new order (the inner person, 2 Cor 4:16). While the flesh is still the instrument for the Christian's activity (2 Cor 10:5), it is no longer dominant in the new person's activities. The flesh in Scripture also often indicates human desires (Gal 5:16), expressed in sinful practices (Gal 5:19).

In Romans 7, the flesh signifies the human struggle, for instance, between people's tendency to sin and their quest for the good (Rom 7:18). Whether Romans 7 is interpreted as describing the conflict in the non-Christian or that taking place within the new person, as experienced by Paul, this is clear: human beings, controlled by *sarx*, find themselves in a hopeless situation (Rom 7:24) in which they must accept responsibility for their sins.

---

[131] See Ridderbos, *Paulus*, p. 123.
[132] See D. Guthrie, *New Testament Theology* (1981), p. 172.

Both *sarx* and *sóma* belong to the sphere of the temporary and transient, but *sóma* has a more comprehensive meaning in the writings of Paul. The body signifies the concreteness of human existence (Rom 12:1). The body is often used synonymously with the human person (1 Cor 6:15). This comprehensive meaning of the concept "body" can be seen in Philippians 1:20, when Paul expresses the hope that Christ will be magnified in his (Paul's) body, either through his life or his death. Thus, while "flesh" denotes a person in his/her weakness and transience, "body" implies the total person in his/her createdness and corporeal focus upon God. According to 1 Corinthians 15, human beings are resurrected bodily so that their bodies will be clothed with a new quality of imperishability and immortality: a "spiritual body" is resurrected (1 Cor 15:44). The "new body" thus shares in the qualities of the new eschatological reality and may not be degraded as inferior.

The body as means of expression for the human ego thus plays an important role in an anthropology. The indwelling work of the Holy Spirit gives the body a moral and ethical value: it is regarded as God's temple. As an embodied being, a person is the home of the Holy Spirit (1 Cor 6:19). Harmony and unity should exist between the body and the ego. The renewal of the "inner person" means that the body and the ego are not totally coherent: hence, the tension and ambivalence between body and soul. There is an ever-present possibility of an inner discord between the flesh and our new being in Christ. The tension (Rom 7:21-25; 2 Cor 4:16; Eph 3:16) between the "external" and "internal" person (which signifies the difference between the visible, physical existence and the invisible, spiritual dimension of life) should not be viewed dualistically. Rather, it should be viewed as two perspectives on the human. The ambivalence and duality between body and soul form part of the tension, which the eschatological factor intensifies: the "already" and the "not yet" of our salvation.

Embodiment and Human Sexuality

Human sexuality has frequently been identified as the main "culprit" of human sinfulness. Pastoral care should not dismiss sexuality as a problem area, especially when dealing with the notion of embodiment. Nevertheless human sexuality is not primarily attached to the notion of sin. It is impossible to understand embodiment without also understanding humans as *sexual beings* with *erotic desires*. We should view these desires as a dynamic force and constructive component of what it means to be human. Scripture regards sexuality as an important part of a person's creatureliness. In Genesis 1 and 2 it is evident that God created the human as a sexual being. Adam's well-known cry in Genesis 2:23 clearly expresses deep sexual and erotic desires:

> This is now bone of my bones
> and flesh of my flesh;
> she shall be called "woman,"
> for she was taken out of man.

The Bible devotes an entire book to the joy of sexuality. The Song of Songs describes the love between a man and a woman as a delight and includes *eros*. Terrien observes: "The Song was intended as a musical and highly literary piece of *divertissement*. It should then be called, without anachronism, A Musical Masque of Love."[133] The Song is in fact a secular poem of love, without any direct reference to divine love. Nevertheless, a woman's passion for her lover displays a concentration of physiological and psychological observations regarding *eros* which, according to the Songs, is traditionally deemed to be an important component of

[133] See S. Terrien, *Till the Heart Sings* (1985), p. 45.

God's grace. Terrien concurs: "In the Song of Songs the act of love becomes a sacramental gesture that prolongs, enhances, and seals the psychological emotion that precedes it and leads to its consummation. It is a sacramental gesture because it is truly 'a means of grace.'"[134]

It is remarkable that the scriptural assessment of creatureliness does not ignore our embodiment, sexuality and erotic desires. For instance, the notion of *eros* in the ethics of the covenantal love of God is altered profoundly. Its numinous character is transferred from the violence and excesses of the religious orgy to the strictly human vocation of loving care, peace, commitment and devotion. The covenant's objective of peace (*shalom*) becomes the source of harmony. It provides the secret to "corporateness." The poet of the Song of Songs is not embarrassed by the pleasure of two lovers. "There is no shame, no sin of the flesh as such, and carnal love is celebrated in terms of wonderment beyond the limitation of natural phenomena."[135]

Scripture's evaluation and appraisal of human embodiment and sexuality enable us to describe the scriptural view of humans as essentially a God-centered humanism. Scripture does not contend that human beings are self-sufficient beings who exist in a meaningless universe: humans are part of the cosmos. Despite the frightening proportions of all phenomena in the cosmos, creation, and therefore our creatureliness, are still considered part of an ordered and harmonious creation. The presence of God is evident here, despite human misery, suffering and sin. A God-centered humanism thus protects people from idolatry: when they forget their creatureliness, they cause their own self-destruction by their boast of autonomous achievement.

---

[134] *Ibid.,* p. 47.
[135] *Ibid.,* p. 48.

Personality and the Dynamics of "Soul," "Heart" and "Thinking"

The concepts "soul" (*psuché*), "heart" *kardia*) and thinking (*nous*) do not convey what current psychology understands as a personality theory. They describe the totality of our being and accountability in the presence of God. These concepts all emphasize that people are conscious, can make decisions and live responsibly before God.

Paul uses *psuché* and *pneuma* alternately: both indicate human natural life and earthly existence subject to death and transience (Rom 11:3; 2 Cor 2:13). When used together with body, *psuché* and *pneuma* form a unity. They represent life in the fear and consciousness of the presence of God. All three are consequential for realizing new life (1 Thess 5:23). In 1 Corinthians 3:1 a close link exists between *psuché* and *sarx*: both represent human beings as distinct from their Godly dimension.[136]

In the main, the soul indicates human life. But in the Old Testament this is more complicated. The Hebrew equivalent for *psuché* is the concept *nefeš*.[137] Besides indicating human needs, desires and life in general, *nefeš* is also used for the human being as an individual, person and self.[138] The Old Testament context should therefore not be disregarded when explaining the concept *psuché*. When Mark 8:35 speaks of the loss and salvation of the *psuché*, the writer links the Old Testament use of

---

[136] See Ridderbos, *Paulus*, p. 128.

[137] According to P. K. Jewett ([1996], p. 37) "soul" in the Old Testament describes "life" in the physical sense: the breath coming forth from the throat that distinguishes the living from the dead.

[138] For a discussion re the connection between "*nefeš*" and the more personal dimension, see K. Kremer's extensive study, *Seele* (1984), p. 189: "In Verbindung mit dem Personalsuffix übernimmt naefaes haüfig die Funktion eines Personal pronomens."

losing and saving as applied to the *nefeš*. *Nefeš* then indicates a vital power.[139]

The concepts "heart" (*kardia*) and reason (*nous*) are crucial to an understanding of human beings in their uniqueness and personhood. The Old Testament regards the heart as the center of consciousness, emotion and reason. The heart forms the center of a person and is comprehensible and accessible. In psychological terminology, "heart" indicates the dynamics between the I (personal consciousness) and the self (expression of the I, awareness of identity: self-esteem).

For Paul, heart (*kardia*) often signifies the inner dimension of life. He regards the heart as the instrument for exercising faith (Rom 10:10). *Kardia* thus implies the total person's focus upon God. But the heart can also be used in service of sin (Rom 1:24; 2:5). It can cause a person to turn away from God. The heart also is indicative of human emotions (Rom 10:1; 2 Cor 1:4) and is the seat of affection (2 Cor 7:2).[140] Ridderbos concludes that "the heart," as used by Paul and also its use in the whole New Testament, implies in particular the human ego in thoughts, emotions, aspirations and decisions, as well as a person's relation to God.[141] The heart is the center of human existence, through which God illuminates an awareness of the transcendency of life and to which a person responds either positively or negatively (Rom 8:27; 1 Thess 2:4; 1 Cor 4:5).

The term *nous* is closely connected to the term "heart," as the center for human orientation and personal reaction. The human intellect is part of one's physical being and signifies that one can

---

[139] See G. Dautzenberg, "Seele (*Naefaes — Psyche*) im Biblischen Denken sowie das Verhältnis von Unsterbiblichkeit und Auferstehung" (1984), p. 197.

[140] "The terms however, are used mainly to describe emotional and volitional aspects" (Guthrie, *New Testament Theology*, p. 168)

[141] See Ridderbos, *Paulus*, p. 126.

react with understanding to God's revelation. Paul considers it important for the human *nous* to correspond to the mind of God (1 Cor 2:16) and for this *nous* to be so transformed through the work of the Holy Spirit (Rom 12:2) that a person can discern between right and wrong. The *nous* thus represents human thinking, reasoning, volition and decision. The *nous* is not the seat of a natural or inherent knowledge of God, nor is it a godly light in a person, but implies the ability to know God. *Nous* describes human receptivity and the ability to react to God's revelation.[142] The *nous* is the receptive and knowing human organ. But it is also more than merely a knowing organ. It describes the human inner self-directing force: a person's human accountability in religious terms and his/her ability to respond to the ultimate. The *nous* is thus the center of all human actions and decisions. As such, the *nous* should undergo a conversion, which implies a radical transformation of reason and focus (*metanoia*). Ridderbos concludes that, on the one hand, *nous* is the organ which indicates the possibility for human responsible reaction to God's revelation; while, on the other hand, *nous* is a description of what profoundly determines people's being qualities through their thoughts and actions.[143]

This conclusion is extremely important for a pastoral theology. As the organ through which pastoral care wishes to change and transform human beings, the *nous* must enjoy preference in a therapeutic approach. Human beings receive a new identity as a result of the transformation of their hearts and reason. This identity is eschatological, and results from the fact that they are accepted by God's grace, and endowed with a new spiritual direction. Despite the preference given to *nous*, it nevertheless appears that the human *pneuma*, and the description of a person as a spiritual

---

[142] *Ibid.*, p. 125.
[143] *Ibid.*, p. 126.

being, will continously play a fundamental and primary role in a
theological anthropology.

d) Perspectivism: Spirituality and the Transcendental Dimension of Life (Persons as Pneuma)

Pneuma is often used as an alternate term to imply human existence in terms of an inner dimension and an awareness of the ultimate. Paul accentuates the term *pneuma* when he links human
existence to our new salvific condition in Christ and to the reality
of resurrected life. This link between the human *pneuma* and the
work of the Godly *pneuma* is prominent in Romans 8:16. Because
of this connection between the human spirit and the work of the
Holy Spirit (2 Cor 1:22; 5:5; Rom 8:23), the non-believer cannot
possess *pneuma*. Hence, the importance of Guthrie's statement:

> In the Christian doctrine of man the central idea is not psyche but
> *pneuma*. In Paul's exposition of it he modifies the Old Testament
> emphasis on *nèpes* (*LXX* psyche) and switches to *pneuma* because
> he at once considered man from the viewpoint of his experience of
> Christ.[144]

In the light of the previous argument, we can present the following thesis for the founding of a pastoral anthropology: as a
result of the Christological basis of a person's new being and the
pneumatological interaction between God and the human spirit,
the notion of a person as a pneumatic being should play a decisive
role in a theological anthropology. The dimension of *pneuma* in
the new person describes a total submission, transformation and
focus upon God. Such a person is moved and motivated by God in

---

[144] See Guthrie, *New Testament Theology*, p. 165.

a way that transforms the person's volition and thoughts and enables the person to experience new life each day.

According to 1 Corinthians 2:11-12, God transforms the human *pneuma* to such an extent that people realize what God has given them through his grace.[145] 1 Corinthians 2:15 thus speaks of a spiritual person who can judge life from the new spiritual perspective, that is, from the teachings of the Holy Spirit (v.13) These teachings correlate with those represented in Christ's Person and Spirit (v.16). We may thus conclude that the human *pneuma* attains a new dimension through rebirth. It describes a new focus on God, and a new submission to Him. This transformation imparts new meaning to the human spirit. The pneumatic focus makes humans dependent on the transcendental dimension of their Christian life, that is, on the eschatological salvific reality. Their lives in future will be qualitatively determined by this salvific dimension. The Holy Spirit addresses people in their inner being (soul). The new person's *pneuma* can thus be described as a point of connectedness or point of mediation for continuous spiritual growth and the development of Christian faith. As a result of the work of God's Spirit, an association emerges in the *pneuma* of the new person between the believer and Christ (the indwelling presence of God) (Gal 2:20).

This pneumatological point of contact for an encounter between God and the human spirit is significant. It indicates that the continuity between the earthly and the eschatological life is not situated in inner psychic abilities, but only in the faithfulness of God and in his transforming actions through the renewing power of the

---

[145] See W. Russel's remark ("The Apostle Paul's View of the 'Sin Nature'/'New Nature' Struggle" [1993], p. 226): "Rather than a divided self, distraught over an internal battle between flesh and Spirit, Paul pictures a new self, emboldened by the liberating work of the Holy Spirit and a vibrant community, with others of like identity."

Holy Spirit. The Spirit in our hearts acts as the security deposit and guarantee (2 Cor 1:22).

A person whose life is qualified as "spirit" (*pneuma*), lives from the Godly qualification of life, and has been transformed to be totally dependent on God's grace. This new person's dependence on God is emphasized by the pneumatic dimension of human existence. Barth calls the human *pneuma*: God's impact upon his creation; God's movement to people.[146] The human *pneuma* is thus the center of a Christian's understanding or personality. It labels the person as an individual, subject and conscious being, who is totally dependent on God. The *pneuma* constitutes and constructs the *psuché* as a religious and moral being with personal identity. The *pneuma* of the new person endows the *psuché/sarx/soma* with an eschatological identity: one now lives from God's grace and promises. *Pneuma* views the human being from an eschatological perspective, *i.e.,* a person is understood in terms of his/her new being and status in Christ. It defines the human being as *more* than a mere individual. The eschatological perspective views a person in terms of a "corporate personality": the status of all believers in Christ as expressed in mutual fellowship (*koinonia*).

Conclusion

Anthropology in pastoral care should deal with the human being neither from an optimistic point of view, nor from a pessimistic point of view, but in terms of a very dynamic biblical realism. A person is both a sinner who lives within the misery of suffering

---

[146] See Barth, *Die Lehre von der Schöpfung*, Kirchliche Dogmatik III/2, p. 425.

and evil, as well as a creature who has been created in the image of God. Realism means to reckon both with our brokenness and our glory. Our brokenness leads to humility before, and dependence on, God. Our glory leads to praise of God, gratitude for, and enjoyment of, life.

The ambivalence of being human should be viewed neither in terms of a *pessimistic anthropology* (a human being is merely a sinner subjected to evil), nor in terms of an *optimistic anthropology* (a human being is perfect, driven by individual needs and determined by the realization of inner potentialities — self-realization). A *realistic anthropology* reckons with both sin and inner potentialities/need satisfaction in terms of another twofold theological perspective. A human being is both a creature *created* in the image of God (relatedness), as well as a new being *recreated* in the image of Christ (salvation).

Creation refers to an autonomy and freedom which should be exercised within a covenantal relationship with God. Our status as creatures is: deputyship, partnership, vocation and representation. We should represent God in terms of an ethics of love, devotion, service and obedience. Hence, the ethical dimension in a pastoral anthropology.

Recreation refers to a new status in Christ, defined in terms of salvation. As a new being, the conduct of a person is determined by justification (redemption from sin) and sanctification (spiritual growth).

The implication of my argument is that human beings should be viewed and understood in terms of the eschatological perspective. Perspectivism means that who we are in Christ, in the light of the reality of the Kingdom of God, determines our very being (the quality of our status before God). Hence, the implication that both the cross and the resurrection of Christ define our humanity. Humanity and humility are important ingredients of an ongoing process of change and growth. We are never perfect. Because of the eschatological tension (the already and the not yet) perfection should be interpreted as the fruit of the Spirit (virtues) (Gal 5.22-23). Hence the ethical dimension: we should become more and more the new person which we already are in Christ.

A realistic model in an anthropology for pastoral care never estimates persons in purely individualistic categories. Because of the theological notion of the corporate personality, personality is a relational issue. As a Christian, our being human is enmeshed within the dynamics of the body of Christ: the church. The mutuality within the fellowship of believers (*koinonia*) determines our very being.

Being human in a theological approach means two things. Our character and nature are defined by grace, *i.e.*, by unconditional love. Humanity is therefore an effect and result of a relationship with God in which we receive our grandeur and freedom as a human being in terms of God's Yes to humanity: unconditional love as incarnated in Christ. Furthermore, our most basic relationship is determined by a theonomous stance in theology: the relationship of dependence on God, *i.e.*, faith.

To view and to interpret human beings from the perspective of faith, has profound influence on an anthropology for pastoral care. It means that, although the human being is a unity, the spiritual dimension is of the uttermost importance in pastoral care and counseling. To become "whole" in terms of Christian anthropology means: life, peace (reconciliation) with God and salvation as a gift of God's grace. Spirituality as a care for life becomes a key concept for designing a Christian anthropology. If the latter assumption is true, immediately another theological question surfaces: but what is meant by spirituality and what does it imply for spiritual direction in pastoral care? If our theological assumption is true, *i.e.*, that persons as *pneuma* are determined by both Christology and pneumatology, what then is the role of pneumatology in the design of a pastoral anthropology?

In terms of our discussion of a Hebrew understanding of soul (*nefeš*) and the meaning of *pneuma*, we conclude: pastoral care is more than merely "soul care" (*cura animarum*). Pastoral care is care for life (wholeness); life in its fullness as qualified by God and the resurrection of Christ. Pastoral care as faith care aims at an embodiment of life and an enfleshment of the presence of God within all life relationships and structures.

We must now address an important question. If our argument for a theological design for a pastoral anthropology moves towards a paradigm shift (that is, away from the traditional founding of anthropology in the "image of God" to the pneumatic dimension of new life in Christ: spirituality linked to the Spirit of God), what then is the role of a pneumatology in a pastoral anthropology? What is meant by the term "a pneumatic human being"? How does it relate to the term "spirituality" and the scriptural notion of a mature faith?

CHAPTER II

THE ROLE OF PNEUMATOLOGY IN THE DESIGN
OF A PASTORAL ANTHROPOLOGY FOR MINISTRY

If we accept the fact that spirituality, and therefore the *pneuma*-dimension of personality, describes the unique contribution of pastoral care to the anthropology debate, we could assume that human beings clearly have a unique capacity for knowing God. Chamblin distinguishes between two French verbs: *savoir* as a descriptive knowledge about reality, and *connaître* as an intimate knowledge of reality.[1] *Savoir* may state factual truth while *connaître* depicts the experience. Our knowledge of God is fundamentally *connaître* (a knowing of God), although it does not exclude *savoir*: knowledge about God. This knowledge entails exercising the mind (*nous*). But knowing is not purely cognitive; hence, the following undergirding assumption: *Our knowledge of God is a "pneumatic" experience (*connaître*). This makes our "pneuma" the main faculty for understanding faith and "spirituality." Hence, our choice of "pneuma" as fundamental for a pastoral anthropology.*

Scripture does not divide a person into three segments when referring to the triad: spirit (*pneuma*), soul (*psyche*) and body (*soma*). For example, I Thessalonians 5:23 does not dissect a person but speaks of God's sanctification of the human being as a unity, a whole (*holoteleis*). Hence, Paul's plea that our whole (*holokleron*) (spirit, soul and body) be kept blameless at Christ's return.

[1] See J. K. Chamblin, *Paul and the Self* (1993), p. 46.

In justification and sanctification, *pneuma* designates the self's capacity for what Chamblin calls the three kinds of knowledge.

a) Knowledge of self. The Spirit (*Pneuma*) knows what is in a person (1 Cor 2:11).

b) Knowledge of other selves. Through the Spirit (*Pneuma*), Christians are part of the assembly (1 Cor 5:3-4) and know each other through mutual fellowship.

c) Knowledge of God. The *pneuma* is that dimension of the self through which the whole person communes with God. The Spirit (*Pneuma*) testifies with our spirit (*pneuma*) that we are children of God (Rom 8:16).[2]

In pastoral anthropology the "pneumatic person/self" implies the renewed person in Christ. It describes a person as utterly dependent on enlightenment and instruction by the Spirit of God. According to 1 Corinthians 2:13-15, the unspiritual do not receive the gifts of the Spirit of God. Insight into spiritual realities has been given to the spiritual person of 1 Corinthians 2:15 through the tutelage of God's Spirit. God's Spirit imparts a wisdom which makes a person mature (1 Cor 2:6-10) and which is linked to the crucified Christ (the wisdom of God — 1 Cor 1:18-2:8).

The pneumatic person, as the spiritual person in a pastoral anthropology, reveals that a Christian anthropology is about *humility* and the ethos of servanthood (sacrifice). Hatred, discord, jealousy, fits of rage, selfish ambitions, dissensions, factions and envy (Gal 5:20-21) flow from pride, and therefore destroy humanity. Pride places a person in competition with God and with fellow human beings. Humility transforms us into sensitive, loving and empathetic human beings. The incarnation of Christ is about humility (Phil 2:6-7). *When incarnational theology is used in a pastoral anthropology it does not lead to a selfish self-assertion,*

---

[2] *Ibid.*, p. 47.

but to a loving self-renunciation: this is the result of humility.
Humility does not mean that the humble constantly demean and despise themselves, nor do they dwell upon humility; both are subtle forms of egocentricity.[3] *Humility creates caring human beings* and fosters cohumanity (interrelatedness and communion and companionship). The humble are "selfless." This does not mean that the humble are inferior, but they are compassionate and open to the needs of others. In pastoral anthropology, the pneumatic person is caring, and has been made sensitive by the indwelling Spirit of God. Hence, the quest for a pneumatology in pastoral anthropology.

2.1 The Quest for Pneumatology in Pastoral Anthropology

It has already been pointed out that soteriology plays a decisive role in a theological anthropology. Soteriology transforms us, and changes our nature from being sinners (the old Adam) to being reborn. The vicarious work of Christ and his resurrection transforms people. They now live as people whose lives are defined by the eschatology. The function of a pneumatology is thus to concretize this new life in and through daily behavior and conduct. Through a pneumatology, our "being functions" (who we are) materialize the new life. The indicative of the new life sets us free from a life governed by the law (the imperative).[4]

---

[3] *Ibid.*, p. 128.

[4] The important role of the Holy Spirit within the God-human relationship is formulated as follows by Weber (*Grundlagen der Dogmatik I*, p. 598): "Wer die echte Menschlichkeit im Werk des Geistes leugnet, treibt pneumatologischen Doketismus. Wer das Werk des Geistes auf menschliches Sichverstehens aufbaut oder es als dessen Überhöhung oder Überbietung auffasst, der treibt pneumatologischen Subordinatianismus." For the relationship between God, the Spirit, and experiences within postmodernity, see M. Welker, *God the Spirit* (1994), pp. 1-49.

In pastoral theology, the general trend was often to found anthropology on the incarnation of Christ. Although the incarnation has implications for our being human, it should never serve as an example of perfect humanity. The incarnation should not be used to explain the nature of true humanity, but to convey the identification of God with humanity and to serve the mediatory work of salvation. In his humanity and Godliness, Jesus is the Mediator, not the example of perfect humanity. What is at stake is salvation and reconciliation, and not a systematic model for anthropology.

It has already been indicated that a kerygmatic model frequently results in a reduced anthropology: human beings remain mere sinners. A phenomenological and client-centered model frequently results in an over-estimation of the human ability for self-actualization. This model also runs the risk of over-simplification and opportunism, thus creating unrealistic objectives. In a theological anthropology a person's abilities should be viewed with regard to the work of the Spirit. Hence, the role of pneumatology and the importance of an understanding of our human potential from the perspective of faith. Rebel's work on pastoral care from a pneumatological perspective points in this direction.

According to Rebel, Reformed theology enabled psychology (with its emphasis on the *humanum*) to dominate the scene of pastoral theology. This was a result of Reformed theology's underestimation of human beings in the presence of God and the poor attention paid to the relation *pneuma* and *humanum*. Rebel sees it as theology's task to combat pelagianism and a humanistic view of humanity in pastoral care.[5]

Rebel designs his pneumatological anthropology with the aid of Van Ruler's special focus on the place of the *humanum* within

[5] See Rebel, *Pastoraat in Pneumatologisch Perspektief*, pp. 9-13.

salvation, under the primacy of the Holy Spirit. According to Van Ruler, an anthropology cannot be based solely on a Christology. This is because, according to the Gospel, there has never been a "Mister Jesus." In a Christology the human being remains of no significance (a lost sinner), while God is everything (merciful Savior). Whoever attempts to build an anthropology based exclusively on a Christology, risks diminishing the uniqueness of Christ's conciliatory work so that it becomes only a model of perfect humanity. Jesus' mediatory work was not intended primarily for the design of an anthropology. Rather, it reveals an understanding of soteriology. Jesus' intention was to achieve the eschatological salvific reality of the redeemed human being, through which anthropology and cosmology attain a new ethical quality.

A pastoral anthropology, which is based mainly on a Christology, faces a threefold danger:

• Emphasis is placed unilaterally on the incarnation alone. This often results in a functional Christology, which concentrates more on the consequences which our salvation has on our behavior, than on the implication for our condition before God (justification).

• Christ's mediation is reduced to the level of morality. Christ's life becomes an example of perfection. Jesus' conciliatory work becomes a model and example of how a person should live and be. When discipleship becomes more important than faith, it risks becoming merely a set of morals and virtues. Salvation could then degenerate into mere synergism.

As a result, the unique character of Christ's salvific work is lost. People can never be their own Savior before God. A moralistic reduction of soteriology has the danger of perfectionism. The pressure of perfectionism often exposes a person to the cruel reality of failure and limited resources. This in turn can influence a person's faith: the impression is created that the basis of faith is at fault and that the person has not been fully converted. Pressure for a repeated conversion now becomes the new synergistic lever which could liberate the person from his/her depression regarding unsuccessful attempts at faith.

• Christology operates within the dynamics of grace and our sinful nature. Guilt is a reality which cannot be ignored. Nevertheless, when justified by grace, the new person in Christ is *more* than a mere sinner. The Christian now lives from the reality of Christ's victorious resurrection. A Reformed anthropology needs to answer the following question: what is the relationship between humanity and the dimension of the resurrection? The resurrection places humanity within the perspective of eschatology, and implies that humanity should be assessed from the dimension of hope. The fulfilled promises of God (God's faithfulness) have predominance over being a guilty, failing sinner. While sin cannot be ignored within eschatology, nevertheless, humanity should now be understood in terms of salvation and grace. Sin has been conquered. Hence, a hermeneutics of hope in the design of a pastoral anthropology. The significance of Christology is thus that the new person should live from grace and victory, not from guilt and defeat.

Faith in Christ functions as an ontic principle — it transforms a person into the new spiritual being in Christ. Nevertheless, the transformed nature is never equal to the uniqueness of the incarnated Christ. The vicarious work of Christ, the Mediator, prevents a Christology from slipping into a cheap anthropology. The Spirit stands between the two. An anthropology, based on Christology without the Holy Spirit, could develop into an evolutionary model based on a self-actualizing principle. People then develop their redemption out of their own potential, based on the ontic correlation between their own humanity and Christ's humanity. Incarnation then serves as a point of contact between God and our humanity, and no longer as a revelation of God's identification with human need. Only through pneumatology can people find their healed and transformed *humanum*: this *humanum* is a gift of the Spirit.

The human being has a place within theology. Self-actualizing plays a definite role: people are created with the physical, psychic and social potential necessary to materialize their full humanity. But the focus and quality of this potential, however, is qualified both by the Holy Spirit, and by the salvific reality of Christ's conciliatory work. Human potential is thus not autonomous, but charismatic: human autonomy is, and remains, receptive by nature. The Holy Spirit, through faith, enriches, empowers and develops our natural human potentialities. The Spirit does it all; people receive it all (salvation). Van Ruler sees no complementary reciprocity between God and humans, merely a theonomous reciprocity. The Christology-pneumatology link within the context of an anthropology can thus be formulated as follows: within a Christology, salvation is the object and focal point of faith; within a pneumatology, the human I (the totality of a person: body, soul and spirit) is the object and focal point of salvation.[6]

The interaction between Christology and pneumatology is essential to a theological anthropology. In a Christology, Christ becomes human (*incarnatio verbi*). This may not be reduced to a mere principle for a type of incarnation-humanism. The *cur Deus homo* is "mediatory" to an understanding of the human being. Similarly, neither can the humanity of Christ be singled out, thereby overshadowing his Godliness. In a pneumatology, Christ becomes a person's Savior, when Paul's fundamental anthropology applies: "But by the grace of God I am what I am" (1 Cor 15:10).

---

[6] *Ibid.*, p.140, for a discussion of this connection between Christology and pneumatology and the role of Van Ruler's theology.

Christ lives in a person through the Holy Spirit (*inhabitatio Spiritus*). So radical is this in-dwelling presence of Christ, that human sexuality and physicality have a special place in God's revelation: the body becomes a temple of the Holy Spirit (1 Cor 6:19), and the new person is commanded to honor God in his/her body (1 Cor 6:20).

The Spirit's *inhabitatio* enables human beings to be transformed to full humanity. A pneumatology makes the human I, with its potential, extremely important. The human I, or "soul," now becomes the anthropological point of encounter and contact for the Spirit. *God speaks with his truth in our reality. There is no natural theology, but God deals with us by way of dialogue* (my translation).[7] In this dialogue the human I becomes the focal point.

The pneumatological model which I wish to propose for an anthropology of pastoral care leads to what J. McIntyre[8] calls a *dynamic model*. Such a model does not describe the trinitarian relationship, as such. (A trinitarian model with its emperichoretic pattern describes the way in which the Persons of the Trinity interpenetrate one another). In a dynamic model the emphasis is on what the Holy Spirit *does* and how the Spirit is evident in terms of our human conduct and behavior. This is what is meant by the immediacy of the Spirit and the epistemological role which the Spirit plays in bringing men and women to the point of believing in and knowing God.[9] When Christians have to live out their faith and develop a maturity, the Holy Spirit can be recognized as the One who plays a personal empowering role as well as an enabling ethical role. The Spirit penetrates our whole being and effects a process of sanctification. Sanctification, indeed, determines the

---

[7] See W. Rebell, *Psychologisches Grundwissen für Theologen* (1988), p. 385.
[8] See J. McIntyre, *The Shape of Pneumatology*, (1997), p.25.
[9] *Ibid.*, pp. 71-72.

process of maturity because: "The whole person, body, soul and spirit, is the place of dwelling of the Spirit in the believers who have known the redemption of Christ."[10] Sanctification and the Spirit's *inhabitatio* have direct consequences for a pastoral anthropology and its relationship to other human sciences. The encounter between the human I and the Spirit makes dialogue (listening and answering) an important pastoral issue. As a result of this spiritual encounter, human potential and the understanding of the human living document are indispensable as instruments for the development of faith. This pneumatological perspective also makes psychology an important partner for pastoral theology. This link raises a difficult question: what is the difference between a psychotherapeutic interpretation of our human potential and a spiritual and pastoral interpretation of our human potential?

Within a phenomenological (empirical) model, human potential is purely psycho-physical (with the danger of a psychological reduction). Within a pneumatological model, human potential is "charismatic" (with the advantage of spiritual enrichment and empowerment). This means that the Spirit transforms the psycho-physical and social potential within the human level, and gives it a new focus and application. The human potential is now determined by the salvific reality and it functions within the context of the body of Christ. The new person does not merely *have* potential, but *receives* potential (*charisma*). A pneumatological model furthermore implies the interpenetration of being and creation. Creaturehood receives a new point of orientation: integration, healing, wholeness and peace.

In terms of the pneumatology, the new person's potential is called *charisma*. The encounter between the Spirit and the human

[10] *Ibid.*, p. 245.

I focuses personality traits anew. When viewed from an eschato-logical perspective, they now become gifts of the Holy Spirit. This process of transformation implies that the Spirit releases new pos-sibilities in a person. Through His immanent workings, the gifts of the Spirit transform personality traits and physical components by changing their objective and destiny. People are turned away from loveless selfishness towards service and love. The perspective of *diakonia* (service) imparts a new intention and goal to human potential. It diverts it from inherent egoism, to a service-oriented sacrifice which focuses on realizing the salvific gifts. This focus, which is brought about by the Holy Spirit, labels all human poten-tial as charismatic. Human potential, *charisma*, becomes images and symbols of gratitude which are focused on spreading the con-sequences of Christ's mediating work through testifying/witness-ing (*marturia*), joyful gratitude (*leitourgia*) and sacrificial charity (*diakonia*). Psychological potential is employed in a pneumato-logy for a service-oriented missiology: gifts are used in the service of God's coming Kingdom and his justice.

The intention of a pneumatology is to develop our "being qual-ities" in the presence of God: humanity is interpreted as *charisma*. In *The depleted self*, Capps proposes that the courage to continue in the light of failure should be used as therapy for the experience of shame, inner exhaustion and isolation. "For a theology of shame, the challenge is to live with failure."[11] Capps quotes Kohut, who says that narcissists, with their need for positive acknowledgement and appreciation, need "mirroring."[12] Con-structive reflection and mirroring is more than offering empathy. It includes a positive confirmation of our "being functions": this is precisely what a pneumatological confirmation is about. "The

---

[11] See Capps, *The Depleted Self*, p. 98.
[12] *Ibid.*, p. 67.

reliable mirroring that occurs between pastor and parishioners — meeting the needs of both — is, indeed, or rather must be rooted in the mirroring activity of God — the God revealed through Jesus ... ."[13] The question could rightly be asked: what difference does a pneumatology make to a pastoral anthropology? Is the difference not merely in terminology, while the effect remains the same? The difference is as follows:[14]

a) The factor of influence. While psychology is dependent on the counselor's communication skills, in pastoral care something else happens on a deeper level. By means of Scripture (Heb 4:12) the Holy Spirit can judge a person's being (theological diagnosis), create insight (a new vision and future perspective on human life), bring about a radical change (*metanoia* as human transformation) and design a new ultimate meaning (a focus on the eschatological issues in life) for human life. The guarantee for the authenticity of these changes does not depend on human potential, but on the covenantal confirmation of the new person by the Holy Spirit (Eph 1:13-14).

b) The Holy Spirit creates a new dynamic and meaningful objective for human existence. The Spirit transforms the tendency towards internally-focused self-assertion to externally-focused self-denial. Self-denial does not mean self-contempt, but self-acceptance in the light of a new calling in life. Anthropology now attains a new dimension: self-transcendence

---

[13] *Ibid.*, p. 69.

[14] For a further discussion of the connection between pneumatology and an anthropology, re the gifts, see A. van de Beek (*De Adem van God* [1987]), who makes the important statement: "Door de Geest mogen mensen delen in de verzoening en het nieuwe leven in Christus" (*Ibid.*, p. 87). The important role of the Spirit in the edification of the congregation is emphasized by Wentsel (*God en Mens Verzoend*, p. 347): "Hoe kan de Zoon vanuit de hemel zijn gemeente bouwen, bewaren en tot aktie mobiliseren tenzij door de Paracleet door en in Wie Hij zijn levendmakende werk voortzet?"

through love and hope. Eschatology becomes the normative component for the dynamics in pastoral anthropology, that is, the development of faith. Thus, through eschatology[15] pneumatology creates a telic dimension in life: faith is transformed by hope. The content of such a faith is the faithfulness of a living God. Rebel pleads for a "pneumatic pastoral care" which he understands as follows:

> Pastoral care discloses how the Holy Spirit not merely renews, but how, under His guidance, the human being discovers him-/herself *as a person directed, guided and equipped for his/her ultimate goal: being the child and representative of God* (my translation).[16]

c) Within a pneumatology, the development of the human being becomes more than mere growth towards psychological maturity; that is, growth in self-responsibility, stability, self-assertiveness, other-centeredness, and becoming an integrated person. The Holy Spirit applies Christ's salvific work to human life, thereby initiating the development of faith towards mature spirituality; that is, the development in Christian love, hope, gratitude, joy and sacrificial service.

d) The new focus in life (life's telic orientation) implies a radical new pattern of life and change in behavior. "Since we live by the Spirit, let us keep in step with the Spirit" (Gal 5:25). Behavior is now characterized, not by self-centeredness, but by God-centeredness and others-centeredness.

---

[15] The role of the eschatological perspective in connection with the work of the Spirit and the sanctification of human life, is confirmed by the following quotation in a special manner: "De perichorese van rechtvaardiging en heiliging staat — niet ongelijk aan het wederzijds verband tussen christologie en pneumatologie — in dienst van een perspectief, naamlik van de eschatologie, die Calvijn zelf meditatio futurae vitae noemt" (E. J. Beker & J. M. Hasselaar, *Wegen en Kruispunten in Dogmatiek* [1987], p. 67).

[16] See Rebel, "De pneumatologische Dimensie in het Pastoraat," p. 112.

e) By means of the gifts (fruit) of the Holy Spirit, the believer discovers a new morality: service (*diakonia*) within the congregation as body of Christ. This is a radical paradigm shift away from individualistic achievement towards systemic caring. "Each one should use whatever gift he has received to serve others" (1 Pet 4:10). Within *koinonia*, and on the grounds of the principle of loving care for one another (1 Cor 12:25; Gal 6:2), believers become more sensitive to the needs of others and the congregation starts functioning as a caring body of Christ.

f) In pastoral counseling, a relationship is created, an encounter takes place and a communication network is established. This links the components of emotion (affective), reason (cognitive) and will (conative) to the growth of maturity in faith. These components are also linked to the fellowship of believers (*koinonia*). The Holy Spirit creates an encounter between believers, which becomes an exponent of the *communio sanctorum* and an expression of the promise of God's presence.

g) Pastors' identities change. They are, after all, not dependent only on communication skills and counseling techniques. Their basic attitude and disposition is not based on a professional obsession to achieve something through counseling. Their attitude is not completely dependent upon empathy on an emotional level. The sympathy of Christ and God, as interpreted in the crucified Christ, determines the basic pastoral attitude. In the unconditional love of Christ (*agapé*), pastoral ministry attains a priestly character (Heb 4:14-15). The pastor communicates Christ's sympathy to people. In this caring service the believer's action attains an official character. The person now acts in the name of Christ, and becomes an exponent of God's loving care.

h) Therapy is different. Pastoral care is not primarily about psychotherapy, but about a care for life and hope therapy based upon God's promises (promissiotherapy). A person's healing towards becoming a new person, does not reside within him-/herself, but in Christ's salvific work: this renews, transforms, changes and heals at all levels of life. This becomes the main objective of pastoral therapy. Scripture, the sacraments, prayer, *koinonia* and pastoral counseling are the mediums through which this salvation therapy is communicated.

i) Pastors do not direct their work only at individuals, but also at groups and the congregation. The process of reaching maturity in faith is a corporative event, and thus also affects the edification of the congregation, as the body of Christ. The purpose of the gifts of the Spirit is not to overwhelm the personality, nor to rule it out, but to allow the new person to grow in an other-centered love. The edification of the congregation becomes the context within which the gifts of grace (*charismata*) function.

A pneumatology labels pastoral care as an essentially paracletic event. The Holy Spirit becomes the *parakletos* who mediates salvation and determines the nature and character of the pastoral encounter. The pneumatological perspective calls for the following description of the pastoral hermeneutics of care and encounter:

- it is a dynamic and dialogic encounter
- through which the scriptural message of salvation is communicated to, concretized and realized in human beings within their social and cultural context
- so that, on the grounds of Christ's salvific work
- and via the Holy Spirit's mediation
- people are radically transformed to new beings in Christ

- and in association with the congregation (fellowship, *koinonia*)
- accept responsibility for one another
- in order to grow spiritually towards a mature faith
- and to develop a dynamic hope which anticipates the coming

Kingdom of God and Christ's *parousia*.

j) A pneumatology redefines the new person as follows: he/she is a person endowed with gifts of grace (*charisma*) which serve as a core potential for the development of faith skills.

2.2 Personality in terms of Pneumatology: the "Charismatic Person"

The term *charisma* clearly plays an important role in a pneumatologically oriented anthropology. But what is meant by gifts of grace? A theological anthropology makes the following distinction between these gifts.

Common Gifts

The common *charismata* describes the condition of the new person's life before God. A person's share in the corporative dimension of Christ's salvific work is a basic gift of grace, which liberates (Rom 5:15-16) and gives eternal life (Rom 6:23).

Particular (Individual) Gifts

The Holy Spirit entrusts certain gifts (also called *pneumatika*) to specific believers, each according to the person's need, so as to equip them better for the ministry and for their comforting function. These gifts are focused on charitable work, and are summarized in Romans 12:7-8, as serving, teaching, encouraging, generosity, leading and showing mercy. The gifts focus on service and intensify the dimensions of spirituality, piety, dedication and devotion.

Gifts for Life and Creaturehood

These gifts are known as the fruit of the Holy Spirit (Gal 5:22). The fruit signifies the totality of Christ's redeeming work and God's fulfilled promises, as these are concretely focused upon and realized within faith behavior. These gifts are love, joy, peace, patience, friendliness, kindheartedness, faithfulness, humility and self-control. A person with these gifts is described in Scripture as wise and sensible (Jas 3:17): this person's life is always focused on a wise and right relationship with God. The purpose of these gifts of grace is that people should use them to make peace (Jas 3:18) and to design a new pattern of behavior (Gal 5:25). These gifts constitute the imperative to which the new person is subject. They are also a necessary result of the indicative which a pastoral anthropology employs. The purpose of these gifts is not to create super Christians, but to empower them to edify the church and to live differently in the world. They should be utilized in terms of priesthood, servanthood and stewardship. They endow Christians with a new vocation in life, *i.e.,* to foster hope and promote humanity as cohumanity. Christians become peacemakers (Jas 3:18).

1 Corinthians 12-14 describes the basic criteria for practising these gifts (*fides quaerens actum*) as:

• *Confession*: In a theological anthropology, in order to distinguish between gifts of grace and mere personality traits, one must ask whether the gifts express *agapé* love and whether they correspond to a confession based on the "resurrection formula": "Jesus Christ is the Lord" (1 Cor 12:3; Acts 2:36).

• *Service in the body of Christ*: The gifts were not meant to be dramatic or sensational personal characteristics, but symbols of service in the Kingdom of God. The gifts operate with "concern for each other" (1 Cor 12:25). The gifts are meant to empower Christians and to prevent a negative self-underestimation (1 Cor 12:15-17). At the same time, the gifts are also meant to correct all self-overestimation and narcissistic self-satisfaction.

• *Love*: 1 Corinthians 13 describes *agapé* love as a basic characteristic of the true Spirit-inspired *charisma*. Love, as a gift of grace, is both the new person's joy and pain. Love enriches the new person, but also demands painful self-denial, service and patience.

• *Edification of a congregation*: 1 Corinthians 14:5 regards the *oikodomé* motif as being central to a more profound motivation to apply the gifts of grace: "so that the congregation may be edified." *Koinonia* acts as a regulative principle in applying the gifts of grace. It prevents an inward focus and improves the congregation's witness in the world.

• *Other-centeredness*: *Charisma* correlates with a certain disposition: "Each of you should look not only to your own interests, but also to the interests of others" (Phil 2:4). The gifts are not intended for self-enrichment, self-praise or self-satisfaction. According to 1 Corinthians 14:6, the gifts should be useful (*sumteró* and *ófeleó*): they should put other believers' benefit before one's own interest.

• *Peace*: 1 Corinthians 14:33 describes presenting and establishing God's new order as the purpose of the gifts. This should bring mutual peace and serve to edify the congregation. The gifts are focused on the establishment of justice within the coming of the Kingdom.

Sanctification and the Characteristics of the Christian Faith

Paul uses the categories "old" and "new" to describe human transformation which results from the work of the Holy Spirit. Death and resurrection in Christ are described as a transformation from the "old self" to the "new self," as taking off the old self and putting on the new self (Col 3:10).

This transformation is a "transcendental" process of change, and precipitates a new qualitative condition of life. It is an effect of the renewing work of the Spirit, and is linked to baptism (Col 2:11-12).

The new life originates and derives its meaning from the fact that in baptism the believer is "clothed with Christ" (Gal 3:27). According to Ridderbos "the washing of rebirth" (Tit 3:5) signifies the renewal as a reality brought about by the Holy Spirit, which is bestowed on the believer through baptism.[17] The Spirit thus brings about a revolution in the human heart: the person is now under the reign of grace. This revolution of the heart, as a qualitative change of life, means that the individual, together with all humankind, shares in the new reality. Human accountability and susceptibility for revelation now become the point of encounter for God's Spirit.[18]

The believer's new being in Christ should not be conceived of individually. Although the renewal does have implications for the individual, the new being should nevertheless be understood corporatively. The new being is the mature person (*'aner teleios*). This implies the entire congregation. As the believer is corporatively included in Christ's vicarious work, so all believers together, within the context of the congregation, are the "new

---

[17] See Ridderbos, *Paulus*, p. 248.
[18] *Ibid.*, p. 250.

person." The new person's being-in-the-Spirit is not primarily a personal, but a "body" category.[19] 1 Corinthians 12:27 describes this corporative comprehension of the new mankind as the body of Christ. The Spirit does not first bring about salvation to the individual believer, and then take possession of all to form a new "corporative personality." The sequence is reversed: by virtue of the corporative bond with Christ, all now are the new, pneumatic person in the Spirit (Rom 8:9). The new person's being is continually subject to a twofold tension. Firstly, there is the tension caused by the eschatological reserve: the already and the not yet. While, on the one hand, the new person already shares completely in the fullness of salvation, on the other, the person lives in hope. Paul describes the tension experienced by the new person in Ephesians 4:7-15. In verse 15 Paul speaks of all who are perfect; but in verse 12 he says that he does not yet possess the resurrection from death, and is not yet perfect. This eschatological tension means that the new person, as a concrete believer, is that same person who previously *was* the old person (in terms of a sinful condition under God's wrath), but now *is* a new person (in terms of the new condition under God's grace). A person is new, insofar as he/she already *is* that new person in Christ, but should *become* that more and more.[20]

Secondly, there is the tension between the indicative and imperative. This means that, on the one hand, the new life should be proclaimed as fruit of God's salvific work in Christ through the Holy Spirit (the indicative of justification). But, on the other, salvation is proclaimed as an imperative to which a person should react responsibly. According to Colossians, the old person has already died (indicative), and thus should eliminate the remains of

---

[19] *Ibid.*, p. 241.
[20] See Barth Kirchliche Dogmatik IV/1 (1953), p. 606.

the old life. The tension indicative-imperative means that, while a person does not share in the *cause* of salvation, he/she nevertheless has a responsibility regarding the *application* of salvation. The imperative is founded in the indicative. Both indicative and imperative are not totally extraneous and separate from the human being. A person appropriates salvation and applies it to his/her life through the medium of faith. *Both indicative and imperative are subjects of faith, on the one hand in its receptivity, on the other in its activity* (my translation).[21]

The eschatological perspective has value for a theological anthropology because it provides a distinction between person and works. No longer is the new person the victim and slave of his/her work, nor does the person have to achieve in order to be a person. In contrast to the present success morality, which emphasizes achievement, production and efficiency, the Gospel assesses human beings in terms of their new condition in Christ. People's *being* qualities are more fundamental than their *knowing* and *doing* functions. A distinction exists between people's personal being (identity) and works (behavior): this has a liberating effect on their identity and self-esteem. People are more than the sum total of their works or behavioral actions. They *have* identity and *receive* identity because of salvation; their new existence is a gift of God. Jüngel regards the new person as the receiving person, who gratefully receives his/her existence as a gift and, in accepting, also receives his/her humanity and identity as a gift.[22] *The*

[21] See Ridderbos, *Paulus*, p. 282.

[22] In this connection Jüngel (Der Menschliche Mensch [1987], p. 25) comments: "Dass Gott widersprechende Mensch ist der undankbare Mensch, der sich nichts geben lassen, der nichts nehmen will. Er will sich selbst verwirklichen. Deshalb lebt er unter der Diktatur von Imperativen ... . Doch ihm fehlt die Oase des Indikatives, in der er nichts weiter ist als er selbst — eine menschliche Person aber eben so eine Gott entsprechende Person."

result of this receiving is that people are not dependent on themselves for their real identity. Thus, instead of self-realization, we may speak of pneuma or faith realization. True identity is discovered when the new person is turned away from pride to humility: this process involves the death of the old person. Pneuma realization implies that human beings receive their humanitas *at the instant of* humilitas. *The* humilitas *of pneumatic people is their real greatness — a greatness that enables them to praise God in everything. Humility is the anthropological consequence of predestination and justification.[23] New people are humble people, and therefore also sensitive and caring.*

The eschatological reserve and the polarities of indicative-imperative bring to the fore another dimension of the new person: the process of sanctification.

Sanctification is the process through which the Holy Spirit applies the implications of this new reality of salvation to our daily behavior. Because the person is sanctified in Christ and God Himself is holy, he/she should become holy in all conduct (1 Pet 1:15-16). Sanctification now reaches the moral life of the person and of the whole congregation (Col 1:22; Eph 5:26-27). In a special sense, the human body and sexuality also become part of this process of sanctification. Sexuality is regarded as a gift of God. It is not excluded from this new life: the new person remains a person with a body and sexual needs. According to Scripture, humans are sexual beings. People should thus glorify God in their bodies and in their souls: both belong to God (1 Cor 6:20).

Sanctification labels people as moral beings. This morality should not be viewed only in terms of moralism. Rather, sanctification

---

[23] Graafland (*Van Calvijn tot Barth* [1987], p. 30-31) describes humility as the efficiency of the predestination for human beings. Sanctification remains the purpose of justification only by means of *humilitas.*

labels a person as a moral being, who is thus called to respond to
salvation (vocation in life).

> The concept sanctification is indeed about morality, but in one spe-
> cific sense and from one very special point of view, that is, from the
> moral answer and our respondability due to the fact that we belong
> to God, our Lord. It is the moral renewal *sub specie electionis* and
> *sub specie ecclesiae* (my translation).[24]

Because the new person — the pneumatic person — is a
believer, the following categories can be used to describe the person's faith: already and not yet, indicative and imperative, justification and sanctification. In other words: faith is the new person's
way of living and faith precipitates a process of growth towards
maturity and spirituality.

The nature of this faith could be summarized as follows:

a) *Faith as receptivity and responsibility: obedience.* In the
   Gospel, the righteousness of God is revealed by faith (Rom
   1:17) and is received through obedience arising from faith
   (Rom 1:5). Thus faith, as obedience, means that faith attains
   an instrumental and receptive character. Two issues are high-
   lighted when faith is called an instrument. Firstly, it implies
   human receptivity. *This means speaking about the emptiness
   of faith, its voidness and purely passive nature* (my translation).[25] We embrace grace through faith: *fides quae creditur.*
   Secondly, faith is also an instrument of salvation. As such,
   faith is not a lifeless, "bloodless" process, which leaves
   untouched the concrete human being and his/her existence.
   The subjective effect of faith in human life (*fides qua creditur*)
   implies activity: responsibility, accountability, decision-making and a changed life-style. These are all human reactions

---

[24] See Ridderbos, *Paulus,* p. 291.
[25] See Berkouwer, *Geloof en Rechtvaardiging* (1975²), p. 187.

to God's salvific actions. The Holy Spirit imparts faith to believers. Grace, in turn, creates in believers an attitude which confirms grace within their concrete existence. Thus, grace incorporates people.[26] Faith should be "enfleshed" and "embodied" in a new life-style.

b) *The confessional character of faith.* According to Romans 10:10 consent and content of faith belong together. A confession, or *homologia*, implies the consent which enables a person to repeat the content of faith with conviction and to testify together with other believers. 1 Timothy 6:12 speaks of the good confession before many witnesses. This confession goes hand in hand with the struggle of faith. The Gospel can be cited and repeated by believers with a power of conviction which convinces others of its authenticity.

c) *Faith as Person-centered.* Faith is not determined by an issue, but by a Person: the resurrected Christ. In Romans 3:22 faith in Jesus Christ is linked to the historical reality of Jesus and the fulfillment of God's promises in Christ, the Messiah. Faith, therefore, implies a personal relationship and communion with God.

d) *Faith is linked to the tradition of the congregation and the church.* In 1 Corinthians 15:1-3, Paul links the Gospel to the doctrine of Christ's crucifixion and resurrection. This means that faith cannot be isolated from the traditional doctrine of the church. The congregation itself is the carrier and protector of the truth of the Gospel. The congregation is called "the pillar and foundation of the truth" (1 Tim 3:15), and should be protected from heresies. The most basic heresy is the view that Christ did not come in the flesh (the cursing of the historical Jesus). This heresy affects the content of the Christian confession in its very core (1 Cor 12:3; 1 Jn 2:22).

[26] See Berkouwer, *De Mens het Beeld Gods*, p. 186.

e) *Faith as wisdom.* Faith presupposes a knowledge which is based on the triumph of Christ's resurrection. In 2 Corinthians 2:14, Paul speaks of the knowledge of Christ which allows a person to share in the triumph of the Gospel. The content of faith is: "God ... who raised Jesus our Lord from the dead" (Rom 4:24). Christ's resurrection is the exegesis of the cross: our salvation is an act of God which has finally conquered sin and death (see also 2 Cor 4:14). Christ, crucified, has therefore been called "the wisdom of God" (1 Cor 23-25), but this "wisdom" is considered by worldly standards as "the foolishness of God."

f) *Faith as trust in the faithfulness of God.* Faith accepts the content of the Gospel as God's truth. The absolute truth of the Gospel resides in God's faithfulness to his covenantal promises. Trust in the faithfulness of God thus forms a characteristic of faith. For example, Romans 4:21 says that Abraham believed that God has the power to fulfill his promises.

g) *Faith as sharing in the power of resurrection.* Faith allows a person to share in God's power. Ephesians 1:19-20 describes this power which God exercises in believers as the power to resurrect (see also Col 3:12). In Philippians 3:10, Paul expresses the desire to know Christ and to experience the power of His resurrection.

h) *Faith as a mode of hope.* A close link exists between faith and hope. Hope focuses faith on the invisible dimension of eschatology. Romans 8:24-25 says that we have been saved in hope: we therefore wait with expectation for the invisible. Hebrews 11:1 defines faith as: "... being sure of what we hope for and certain of what we do not see."

Faith's victorious character does not exclude agony, tension, intense struggling and suffering. Rather, the process of sanctification involves an ongoing process of development, in which the believer grows towards a mature faith. Paul uses this pastoral formula to summarize the purpose of his ministry regarding Christ as hope for glory: "We proclaim him, admonishing and teaching everyone with all wisdom, so that we may present everyone perfect in Christ" (Col 1:28). James 1:4 links the perseverance of faith to the following goal: "... so that you may be mature and complete, not lacking anything." 1 Corinthians 14:20 urges people to become mature in their thoughts. Ephesians 4:13 provides the classic text for spiritual or faith maturity: knowledge of faith is linked to the unity of the church so that all can be "mature, attaining to the whole measure of the fullness of Christ."

2.3 The Objective and Goal of Pastoral Care and Counseling: Maturity in Faith and the Embodiment/Enfleshment of Life (the Telic Dimension)

Theological discussion of our Christian faith reveals that Christian maturity is *sui generis*. Because of its corporate dimension and its association with justification and salvation, it cannot be coupled with theories from other human sciences. What is necessary, therefore, is a growth model that is not alien to the notion of faith in Scripture. Hence, the suggestion that faith is best depicted as a process of development which influences a more general concept of maturity.

In his article on Christian adulthood, Bouwsma argues that Christian life is conceived as indefinite growth.[27] It is the product of an engagement with temporal experience which involves the entire personality. Growth takes place within the realities of struggle and pain. Hence, the concept of life expressed in the figure of

---

[27] See Bouwsma, "Christian Adulthood" (1978), p. 87.

the Christian as wayfarer (viator) or pilgrim. Christian adulthood depicts a voyage into the unknown.

The essential condition for Christian adulthood is our capacity for growth. Bouwsma's interpretation does not regard the worst state of a person as being sinful (sins can be forgiven), but rather the cessation of growth, arrested development, or remaining static at any point in life. The refusal to grow can be regarded as a clear indication of the Christian understanding of immaturity. "A further symptom of his immaturity may be seen in man's perennial tendency, implicit in his claim to divinity, to absolutize his understanding of the universe in a frantic effort to hold his anxiety in check."[28]

The source of this immaturity is a person's alienation from God, and thus also from his/her true self. In terms of salvation, the first step in the direction of spiritual growth is a person's acknowledgement of helplessness. This acknowledgement is the point of departure for a faith which admits its own "faithlessness" (a person has no resources for saving him-/herself) and realizes that the only available resource is the grace of a loving God.

Christian adulthood, or a mature faith, starts with *confession* and *conversion*. Through faith, a person is dramatically relieved of his/her false maturity and claims to a self-defined "manhood." Christian adulthood is a result of salvation. The Gospel frees a person for "adulthood." "But this is an adulthood that involves, always, the whole man. Thus its goal is symbolized not by the immortality of the soul but by the resurrection of the body as representing the total self that must be made whole."[29]

In Scripture wholeness and maturity are *organic* and *corporate* concepts, and not purely individualistic. "The Pauline description

---

[28] *Ibid.*, p. 88.
[29] *Ibid.*, p. 90.

of growing up in Christ, though it has obvious implications for the individual, is primarily concerned with the growth of the Christian community; it is finally the church as one body, and perhaps ultimately all mankind, that should reach 'mature manhood.'"[30] Maturity, in terms of ultimate growth, presents the question of "maturity in faith" as the goal and objective of the pastoral encounter.

In Scripture *teleion* gives a description of maturity and growth as it is linked to the presence of God and the quality of our Christian being. *Teleion* is also connected to the conduct of life and the ultimate goal of Christian faith. This link means that *teleion* has moral and ethical implications. For example, love is linked to perfection (Col 3:14; Eph 4:16). But perfection does not imply ethical perfection or moralism: it is an ongoing process towards completeness and meaningful relationships. This growth is not individualistic, but is a corporate process, which is linked to the dynamics of the body of Christ (the church); it aims at life (fullness and wholeness).

A mature faith is thus "perfect" because of God's faithfulness and the completeness of our salvation. It is victorious because of Christ's resurrection. When *teleion* is used to describe maturity, its close link with eschatology should be appreciated hermeneutically.

Teleion can be viewed as a variant term for sanctification. It operates through the Spirit's victorious power. Hence, Ridderbos's important conclusion regarding spirituality and maturity: *The latter is the full effect and unfolding of the gift of salvation regarding the preliminary and temporary (1 Cor 14:20; Eph 4:13) as well as the ultimate and the eternal (1 Cor 13:10; Phil 3:15)* (my translation).[31]

---

[30] *Ibid.*, p. 94.
[31] H. Ridderbos, *Paulus* (1966), p. 299.

In his book on New Testament theology, Goppelt links *teleion* with Christology and soteriology.[32] For example, in the book of Hebrews, maturity is linked to an ongoing sanctifying process, which includes severe suffering (Heb 2:10-11). Goppelt argues that maturity in faith is closely linked to the mediation of Christ and our redemption from sin (Heb 10:14). Goppelt's explanation gives *teleion* a pastoral meaning: *it is the attempt to prepare people to encounter God, to live in his presence so that they can correspond to the will of God, to his ultimate goal for us* (my translation).[33]

The following important questions arise: what is meant by a mature faith? Does this concept not introduce a fixed goal in pastoral care which could hamper the dynamics of pastoral counseling? What is the connection between a mature faith and the development of spirituality?

The mature Christian is a spiritual being in Christ. The terms "Christian spirituality" and "a mature faith" share a similar meaning and can be understood as variant terms, although spirituality is used in a slightly different context. Both should be distinguished from the Greek dualism which existed between spirit and body. Both mature faith and spirituality describe the reality of Christian conduct. Both are connected to the eschatological characteristics of salvation. Spirituality and maturity also have existential implications for our daily life-style.

We have chosen the term "a mature faith," or "maturity in faith," to describe how Christian spirituality is understood in terms of the content of faith and Christian theology. "A mature faith" describes the goal of pastoral care and counseling. This goal results from our findings about the characteristics of a pastoral anthropology: the Christian as a spiritual, pneumatic person, who

---

[32] See L. Goppelt, *Theologie des Neuen Testaments* (1980³), p. 582.
[33] *Ibid.,* p. 582.

is endowed with charisma by the Spirit. The term also explains the unique contribution which pastoral care can make to counseling and therapy, which distinguishes it from psychology. The psychological concept of maturity is not necessarily similar to what is understood by maturity in the pastoral context. This is because maturity in faith, and therefore our Christian identity and integrity, is always closely associated with the *communio sanctorum*, the fellowship of believers. Moreover, the term, "a mature faith" also indicates the telic dimension of a pastoral anthropology.

Scripture uses the Greek word *teleion* (and its related forms) to describe the process of growth in the fullness of salvation and the development of faith towards perfection and maturity.

The noun *telos* originally derived from a root word, meaning "to turn." The turning point functions as a hinge in which one phase is closed and the next begins. When this term is applied in a religious context, it attains the meaning of a specific goal: that is, to bring people closer to God. *Teleios* can function as a noun, referring to the one who founds all. As a verb it means to begin, fulfill or complete something. In Hebrews 12:2, *teleion* refers to Jesus' work in connection with the accomplishment of faith. Jesus is portrayed as the One who helps people to attain and fulfill the goal of faith — Jesus is the Pioneer and Perfecter of our faith. Thus mature faith depicts a process fulfilled by Christ Himself.

In the Old Testament, *kâlâh* is often used synonymously with *teléo* and means to fulfill and complete. It also frequently functions synonymously with *sálém*, thereby indicating the process of healing and the integration and perfection which are conditions of peace, integration and perfection. "The stress lies on being whole, perfect, intact."[34]

Teleios is often used to describe the process whereby the human heart turns towards God, binding itself in total surrender to God.

---

[34] See R. Schippers, "Telos" (1978), p. 60.

"It is used of the heart which is wholly turned towards God" (1 Kings 8:61; 11:4) and of the person who has bound himself wholly to God (Gen 6:9; see Deut 18:13).[35] In Proverbs 11:3, *teleiotes* (from the stem *tám*) signifies perfection, and indicates the person's integrity. In Exodus 29:22,26, *teleiosis* is used in a cultic sense and implies human devotion to God. Within the apocalyptic literature, *synteleia (qés)* is used. It functions within the eschatological context to express end or completion. There is also a close link between *telos* and the concept *eschatos*.

The *LXX* uses *eschatos* in a temporal sense, as a translation of the stem *'ahar*, meaning end, finality, outcome, the last. The prophetic language has a future-oriented formula for the end of the days, which indicates Israel's expectation of a new direction linked to God's redeeming actions. In the Synoptic Gospels, the term *eschatos* signifies a total change of the prevailing order, in which the last will be first (Mk 10:31). Within the Adam-Christ typology (Rom 5:12-21; 1 Cor 15:21), the Second Adam signifies a reversal of the total order in life and represents Christ's work of salvation and the new mankind which is created in his image. The resurrected Christ becomes the eschatological prototype of God's new humanity.[36] The term *eschatos* not only indicates the new era (*kairos*) which dawned with Jesus' birth, but also describes the process of fulfilling and revealing in which God completes his final purpose or plan for this world. For example, in the future chronology death as the last enemy should be destroyed (1 Cor 15:26), in order to reach the great *telos* of history: God will be all for all (1 Cor 15:28).

In the New Testament, the link between *telos* and *eschatos* cannot be ignored. Both concepts function within the context of the

---

[35] *Ibid.,* p. 60.
[36] See H-G. Link, "Eschatos" (1976), p. 59.

Kingdom of God and the dawn of the new order of reconciliation. Christ Himself is the end and fulfillment of an old order, which was determined by law (Rom 10:4; 1 Tim 1:5). Within this context, *teleios* may be applied to the new person's being. The maturity of 1 Corinthians 2:6 is linked to God's wisdom, which is revealed to the pneumatic person. It has already been argued that faith is a corporative category. So too is *teleion*. According to Colossians 1:28, all people should be brought to spiritual maturity. In Hebrews, *teleioó* indicates the process of dedication and sanctification of life which allows people to stand before God like the Old Testament priests. This is made possible by Christ's sacrifice which liberates completely from sin (Heb 10:14).

We may conclude that a mature faith involves a process of integration, devotion and sanctification which enables a person to meet God. Within this encounter, God desires to bring the implications of Christ's salvific work to completion. A mature faith is thus part of a process of fulfillment. It reveals the ultimate purpose of history: the sovereignty and glorification of God, together with the final destruction of the power of death.

The Theological Nature of a Mature Faith

It has become clear that one should regard maturity as a comprehensive concept, which includes both psychological and spiritual components. Yet, the concepts of maturity and spirituality are more fundamental for the Christian faith than for psychology. Although the two are closely related and influence each other reciprocally, mature faith nevertheless has a unique character, which must not be confused with what is understood by psychological maturity.

While it is inevitable that a mature faith will incorporate and reflect traits of a general psychological understanding of maturity, the two are not analogous. A psychological understanding of maturity ought to influence and stimulate the development of faith. In turn, a mature faith should heighten the quality of a psychological understanding of maturity.[37] Nevertheless, we have chosen the concept "maturity in faith" or a "mature faith" because, in theology, maturity cannot be assessed and understood apart from its eschatological context. "Maturity in faith" describes salvation in terms of a pastoral anthropology which operates with both Christology and pneumatology.

The following four theological functions define qualitatively what is meant by the concept "maturity in faith."

• *The soteriological function: maturity and the redemption of the new person.* Maturity in faith describes the Christian predisposition as a result of redemption in Jesus Christ. The Holy Spirit is the point of contact between faith and salvation. A mature faith thus indicates a process through which human beings are changed radically by the Holy Spirit. They turn from the old life (away from God) to the new life (towards God). Henceforth, they do not live under the judgement of the law, but through their freedom in Christ. The mature person in Christ is one who shares in the justification of Christ's vicarious death. And, it is because of the indicative character of justification, that our being human can be affirmed in a positive manner. It leads to the affirmation of being

[37] J. Overduin (*Worden als een Man* [1967], p. 489) points out the fact that "spiritual" maturity has a unique quality and that it is the vertical dimension of maturity which makes it radically different. "Wij komen tot de conclusie, dat psychische en geestelijke volwassenheid ieder naar eigen aard zijn, en dat de ene volwassenheid niet te herleiden is tot de andere, en dat ze wel in elkaar ingrijpen en in elkaar functioneren, en dat ze elkaars stimulans zijn, en dat ze niet altijd behoeven samen te vallen."

and creaturehood. A mature faith can, therefore, never be detached from a thankful embracement of creation. Redemption necessarily implies also *re*-creation.

Maturity in faith implies the knowledge that all guilt has been abrogated though reconciliation with God. As a result of forgiveness, the Christian is a transformed person, and therefore also a "healed" person. The breach between the I and the self has been healed (as a result of the new order of peace and justification in Christ). Thus, in terms of theology, congruency means: peace with God and peace with oneself. This peace creates a dimension of integration within the human being.

• *The pneumatological and moral function: maturity and surrender (sanctification).* In Hebrews, maturity is associated with human surrender and devotion to Christ. Maturity describes our Christian service, and is directly linked to our calling to witness in the world (vocation). By testifying, believers prove that they are prepared to follow Christ and to vouch for the truth of the Gospel in the midst of persecution.

True human devotion to God occurs as a result of Christ's high-priestly work (Heb 10:14). In Christ the believer has been sanctified for a specific purpose: to witness to the Gospel. People are equipped for this task by Christ: "Because by one sacrifice He has made perfect forever those who are being made holy" (Heb 10:15).

By "maturity," the Bible implies a process of growth, daily surrender, conversion, and a continuous focus on Christ and on the coming Kingdom of God (sanctification). People grow in sanctification as a result of gratitude for their redemption in Christ. In this process the old person dies and the new begins to live. Spiritual people develop a sensitive power of discernment between right and wrong. A practical, applied knowledge of faith develops which creates a new moral awareness and conscience. Humility develops instead of selfishness and jealousy. A change in disposition takes place, which is expressed in deeds and a new life-style. Mature people in Christ reveal new characteristics because their volition and their hearts' attitudes have changed. This influences their temperament and character and deepens the psychic aspects of their lives. Henceforth, the human I no longer orients itself to its own interest, but to Christ's interest and to the Kingdom of God. This new orientation signifies a practical life of bearing fruit through the Holy Spirit. "But the fruit of the Spirit is love, joy, peace, patience, kindness, goodness, faithfulness, gentleness and self-control" (Gal 5:22-23). It is the Spirit who now determines the new person's behavior.

Life of such devotion and surrender culminates in love (1 Cor 13), and presupposes a continuous process of growth. Thus, maturity in faith describes a life lived out of what we have in Christ (already), and what we should increasingly become (not yet) (1 Jn 3:2). Maturity then becomes a metaphor for the embodiment and enfleshment of the purposefulness and significance of life in its totality (wholeness).

Ethically, *teleion* does not mean an eventual terminal point of perfection, but a qualitative new way of living which leads to an integrated, stable personality and abundant joy.

> When applied to man and ethics therefore, *teleios* denotes not the qualitative end-point of human endeavour but the anticipation in time of eschatological wholeness in actual present day living. Christian life in the N.T. is not projected idealistically as a struggle for perfection, but eschatologically as the wholeness which a person is given and promised.[38]

• *The eschatological function: maturity and purposefulness (hope)*. "Maturity in faith" depicts an incomplete process of pur-

---

[38] See Schippers, "Telos," p. 65.

poseful development. It therefore presupposes a continuous process of anticipation in hope.

In Christ, and through the Holy Spirit, God guides the entire creation to an ultimate goal: when all creation glorifies God. This goal includes sovereignty as a total victory over the powers of sin, evil and death. Although these powers have already been destroyed in principle, the complete materialization only takes place with Christ's coming (parousia).

Inter alia, teleion is linked to the end as the fulfillment of the complete salvific history, when God will be all in all people. God's glory, or doksa, as the ultimate eschatological purpose of creation, reveals the victorious future on which people's hope is focused: God's victory is the final confirmation of the Kingdom's sovereignty. Noordmans formulates the Christian's victorious position as follows: in Christ we have the is (the already) of our resurrection. We have been resurrected in Him. But the how and when Christ keeps to Himself.[39] The coming of Christ (parousia) therefore is a process already taking place and will ultimately culminate in a joyful, praising hallelujah (doxology).

• The corporate function: maturity, the edification of the body of Christ and the missionary outreach to the world. "Maturity in faith" no longer applies only to the Christian as an individual, but is also used to describe the individual as part of a greater whole: the body of Christ. Paul regards the entire congregation of Ephesus as mature people in Christ. Although maturity does not exclude individual believers, nevertheless a believer cannot become mature in isolation. Maturity, as a process, presupposes the fellowship of believers (koinonia). As a corporate category, it presupposes the other (cohumanity). Mature people are formed through mutual edification of one another and by acceptance of

---

[39] See O. Noordmans, Versamelde Werken (1979), p. 93.

responsibility for one another. Growth in faith is thus growth of the body (congregation) for its own edification in love (Eph 4:16) and unity.[40] The eventual purpose of edification becomes witness and mission into the world. A mature faith is, therefore, never "inner-directed," but always "world-directed" — the missionary outreach to the world.

2.4 The Dimension of Spirituality in a Mature Faith

The connection between maturity in faith and dedication and sanctification is of great importance to pastoral care. How a mature faith is linked to the dimensions of piety and spirituality has been discussed frequently in pastoral literature. Various attempts have been made to describe the relevance of faith for everyday practice by using the term "spirituality."[41] Wainwright describes spirituality as:

... the combination of praying and living. It is this embodiment of prayer in life that the New Testament writers describe in such phrases as "a living sacrifice," "spiritual worship" (Rom 12:1).[42]

Spirituality has also been defined as:

• Spirituality is not merely inner feelings; it is about the human integration and coherence of an experiencing and acting person.[43]

---

[40] About unity, see Ridderbos, *Paulus*, p. 489.

[41] It is noteworthy to take cognizance of the fact that affections, indeed, play an important role in spirituality. For example, in the thirteenth century Carthusian spirituality linked rationality with love and affection. "Even the scholastic modes involve affectivity in every stage ..." (D. D. Martin, & J. van Engen, *Carthusian Spirituality* [1997], p. 27).

[42] Wainwright, cited by E. Yarnold, "The Theology of Christian Spirituality," *The Study of Spirituality*, eds. C. Jones & G. Wainwright (1986), p.9.

[43] See N. S. T. Thayer, *Spirituality and Pastoral Care* (1985), p. 13. E. H. Cousins ("What is Christian Spirituality?" [1990]) refers to the difficult task of defining Christian spirituality. A comparison of different traditions shows that reflection and experience are components of spirituality. Both are connected

- Biblical spirituality is social spirituality. It is spirituality of the kingdom of God, of a pilgrim people. Spirituality is progress towards maturity. The emphasis is not on inner peace and adjustment, but rather on movement and pilgrimage. In the spiritual progress of which the New Testament speaks, the centrality of love is emphasized in contrast to knowledge or mutual enlightenment.[44]

- *Spirituality is an indication of hope ... . It enfleshes our faith within our daily existence* (my translation).[45]

These definitions of spirituality[46] indicate a movement away from the Reformed approach, which linked spirituality to the transcendental dimension of salvation only. Attempts are being made at present to apply God's grace to the everyday field of experience and to current social problems. Spirituality is thus described as an awareness of transcendence in the midst of existential and social

to an awareness of the presence of God. "... spirituality is concerned with the experiential, with the inner — but not apart from the outer — with the real, the transcendent, the divine" (p. 43). When one comes to defining Christian spirituality, love has the primacy. Linked with doctrinal themes, Christian spirituality "... proceeds through the community of the church" (p. 43). "Thus the Christian path consists of the awakening of the personal center of the human being, by God's personal grace and Christ's compassionate, redemptive, personal love within the Christian community, in a journey that leads to personal union with the tri-personal God" (p. 44).

Spirituality could also be interpreted merely from a sociological point of view. J. M. van der Lans ("Voorwoord" [1984], p.8), in an introduction on the social dimension of spirituality, defines it as the way in which people mold their way of thinking and philosophy of life, especially when they deal with borderline experiences.

   [44] See K. Leech, *Spirituality and Pastoral Care* (1986), pp. 9-10.

   [45] See M. Seitz, cited by G. Ruhbach, *Theologie und Spiritualität* (1987), p. 122.

   [46] D. Tieleman (*Geloofscrisis als Gezichtsbedrog* [1995²], pp. 109-110) is convinced that between gnosis and agnosticism there is room for that spirituality which focuses on humanity and postmodernity's quest for meaning.

conflicts. This awareness of God results in two actions. Firstly, it results in prayer. This is communion with God, and the focus is on growth in faith. Secondly, it results in charitable deeds of love within society. The focus here is on renewing and changing the structure of the political environment. The piety of pious inwardness makes space for the piety of pious outwardness: the sanctification of social practice within human relationships.[47] Transcendence is interpreted increasingly in terms of God's condescendence.

The renewed interest in spirituality reflects our yearning for the transcendent dimensions in our lives. This transcendence should not only impart meaning to our lives, but it should also be "practical." Thus spirituality is directly linked to experiencing God's presence in the world and practising the Christian faith.[48]

For Benner Christian spirituality implies involvement with life. "Christian spirituality relates to and affects all of life."[49] It also influences psychological functions. Benner regrets the separation between religion and psychotherapy which has taken place in the twentieth century. As a result of this separation, a radical shift has thus taken place in pastoral care. There has been a movement away from "soul" care to healing of the mind. As "… psychotherapy came to displace soul care … the focus of care moved from the soul to the mind."[50] Benner describes spirituality as "the response to a deep and mysterious human yearning for self-transcendence and surrender."[51] He believes that people should be liberated from being self-encapsulated. Psychotherapy could play an

---

[47] See D. J. Louw, "Spiritualiteit as Bybelse Vroomheid in die Teologie en die Gemeentelike Bediening" (1988), p. 12.

[48] See W.E. Oates, *The Presence of God in Pastoral Counseling* (1986).

[49] See D. G. Benner (ed.), *Psychotherapy and the Spiritual Quest* (1988), p. 103.

[50] *Ibid.*, p. 25.

[51] *Ibid.*, p. 104.

important role in this process: "psychospiritual maturity is characterized by integration of personality, which occurs within a context
of significant interpersonal relationships and surrender to God."[52]
Our discussion thus far points towards a more integrative model
which tries to link both a spiritual and psychological stance. It
seems that a pastoral approach is inevitably confronted with the
demands of psychotherapy. Hence, the important question: how
does such a holistic venture influence and challenge a Reformed
model with its theocentric focal point?

Reformed Spirituality[53]

"Spirituality" is an ambiguous term. It may mean the human
need for a transcendental factor which can impart meaning to
daily life. Or it may be used to describe a certain faith tradition's
understanding of God and of liturgy, and how these are reflected
in the person's devotion to God. What exactly is meant by the
term "Reformed spirituality"?

It is extremely difficult to achieve a conclusive definition of the
term "Reformed" because historical, cultural and denominational
factors all play a role in the interpretation.[54] Nevertheless, despite

---

[52] *Ibid.*, p. 133.
[53] For a description of Reformed spirituality see D. J. Smit, "Wat is Gereformeerde Spiritualiteit?" (1988), pp. 182-193. W. D. Jonker ("Die Eie-aard van
die Gereformeerde Spiritualiteit" [1989], p. 2) says: "Gereformeerde vroomheid
bestaan uit 'n lewe uit die genade van God omdat dit opkom uit die volkome
gerigtheid op die objektiewe heilsgawe van God in Christus wat deur die Heilige
Gees in ons eksistensie verwerklik word." For further literature about the issue of
spirituality within pastoral care, see G. L. Borchert & A. D. Lester (eds.), *Spiritual Dimensions of Pastoral Care* (1985), and M. Cox, *Handbook of Christian
Spirituality* (1985[2]).
For the influence of our Christian confession on spirituality and how it structures our
awareness of our self, see A. Zegveld, *Tot Vrijheid Bestemd* (1994), pp. 1-11, 223-228.

the variety of viewpoints evident in the history of the Reformation and despite the different uses of the term, two central focal points appear to exist: God's dominion/authority, and the central position of Scripture. "The uniqueness of the Reformed churches, of the Reformed confession and consequently of Reformed theology is simply their allegiance to the Scriptural principle."[55]

Reformed theology, based on *sola Scriptura* and *tota Scriptura*, as well as the sovereignty of God, employs the following dynamic components:
• The theocentric focal point, based on the theological presupposition of *predestination*. This implies a life before God (*coram Deo*): a person lives by the grace of God, and grace is perceived as a relational concept.[56]
• The truth as revealed through Scripture is the point of departure. This has the practical implication of the demand for continual reformation: *semper reformanda*. Reformed piety focuses on a life founded on Scripture. *One may even speak of a* corpus doctrinae, *in the sense of the sum total of the Christian doctrine* (my translation).[57] *Sola Scriptura* and *tota Scriptura* belong together. Since everything happens around and through Scripture, the combination Word and Spirit is decisive for an understanding of God's influence in the world.
• A continuous interaction between knowledge of God and an understanding of ourselves. This is based on the presupposition that human knowledge acquires a receptive character. Self-knowledge is regarded as a response to revelation. A person is essentially a responding being and therefore also a responsible being.
• Reformed theology's aim is to structure a person's life around

[54] See F. H. Klooster, "The Uniqueness of Reformed Theology" (1979), p. 33.
[55] *Ibid.,* p. 39.
[56] See W. van 't Spijker, "Tussenbalans" (1993), p. 326.
[57] *Ibid.,* p. 325.

the functions of the local church. There is close interaction between the concepts "office and congregation," and "office and *charisma.*" The ideal of the unity of the church and the priesthood of believers is continuously applied in a Reformed ecclesiology.

• Reformed theology regards the believer's calling within society seriously. The *pietas* should figure in the *praxis*. Hence, the principle of a *die praxis pietatis*.[58] This *pietas* is nurtured daily by the *unio cum Christo*.

A "typical Reformed spirituality," attempts to offer a pure formulation of scriptural truth. It thus possesses a strong confessional element. The congregation and the institutional church with its offices form the point of orientation in a person's life. *The Reformed believers always experience their Christianity closely linked to their church membership* (my translation).[59] The intense interest in the field of society means that the relationship between church and state is of great importance. Similarly, another typical characteristic of Reformed spirituality is the assumption that the Gospel should penetrate all walks of life, like yeast.

A Reformed spirituality thus has the following theological implications:[60]

a) The believer's entire life focuses on the honor of God: the principle of God's sovereignty.

b) A believer is dependent on God's revelation (his Word) in order to attain knowledge of faith.

c) The sinner is radically lost and is solely dependent on God's mercy for his/her salvation.

d) A believer shares in salvation and in God's gifts of grace through the work of the Holy Spirit. Faith implies a continuous process of forgiving and renewing, trust and service.

---

[58] See W. H. Velema, *Nieuw Zicht op Gereformeerde Spiritualiteit* (1990), p. 55.

[59] See J. Veenhof, "Spiritualiteit in de Gereformeerde Kerken" (1992), p. 159.

[60] See Velema, *Nieuw Zicht op Gereformeerde Spiritualiteit*, pp. 82-83.

Sanctification is thus viewed as the necessary consequence of justification. The process of developing faith includes the tension between *fides quae* (content) and *fides qua* (action and experience).

e) The tension in the development of believers' growth in faith is determined by the eschatological tension: the already and the not yet of human salvation. The expectations of Christian hope and the awareness of the transience of human achievement emerge from this eschatological tension.

The Reformed model is valuable because it takes a theocentric attitude to life and the world seriously. The problems in this model arise from Reformed theology's underestimation of the role of creation in its doctrine of persons (creaturehood) and what place should be given to the empirical dimension of experience in an epistemology. The modern emphasis on relativity and relationality has challenged the Reformed model to shift from a more substantial and metaphysical ontological paradigm to a more hermeneutical paradigm, in which historical and cultural contexts are taken into consideration. The demand for an "integral spirituality" means that the term *praxis pietatis* must make room for the aspect of human experience within specific contexts. The notion of an integral spirituality thus becomes an important issue for practical theology.

Integral Spirituality

Increasing attempts are made to link spirituality to the quality of being human. Spirituality thus becomes a term which links, as well as constructively integrates, a psychological understanding of maturity. Of paramount importance to this link is the notion that spirituality should be understood in terms of human relationships.

In *A Practical Theology of Spirituality*, Richards uses the definition: "True Christian spirituality is living a human life in union with God."[61] Spirituality is experienced within human relationships. He discusses seven human issues in Scripture and links them to the individual and corporate aspects of Christian faith.[62]

Human issue	Individual aspect	Corporate aspect
Identity	Responsibility	Accountability
Intimacy	Prayer	Worship
Sinfulness	Confession	Forgiveness
Lordship	Choice	Freedom
Mortality	Suffering	Compassion
Holiness	Morality	Justice
Commitment	Discipleship	Servanthood

Spirituality is actualized when Christian faith is integrally linked to our being human. The general conclusion of an inter-disciplinary study on spirituality points in the same direction: "Christian belief discloses a further human reality, and so it also offers a further explanation of the human."[63]

Spirituality should lead to an integration of the various aspects of being human.[64] An integral spirituality should improve the quality of human dignity. The presence of God in a person's life should contribute to life's meaning and humanity. It should link

---

[61] See L. A. Richards, *A Practical Theology of Spirituality* (1987), p. 244.

[62] *Ibid.*, p. 245.

[63] See D. A. Helminiak, *Spiritual Development* (1987), p. 165.

[64] See D. Dorr, *Integral Spirituality* (1990²).

the inner and the private dimensions to the external dimensions of life: our social context and public character. Integral spirituality thus means a vocation within creation: wholeness and peace.

Spirituality deals with our experience of faith in the midst of reality. Spirituality thus contributes to the formation of a biblical piety, which promotes the development of a mature faith which is always other-directed and world-directed.

Biblical Piety: Devotion (Eusebeia)

In the New Testament, spirituality is best defined by the concept *eusebeia*, by which is meant devotion, piety and godliness. Paul often uses *eusebeia* in the same way as he uses faith and sanctification.[65] Hence, *eusebia* should be viewed as a vital component of the process of faith development.

The roots of the concept *eusebeia* precede the New Testament. The wisdom literature in the Old Testament provides the background for an understanding of devotion and godliness. In the Old Testament, piety indicates wisdom and an active obedience to God, in contrast to all hypocrisy and superficiality. *Eusebeia* involves the fear of God and practising the Torah in the midst of daily life experiences. For example, the book of Proverbs may be seen as a kind of life-focused *eusebeia*: faith in action.

In the Greek-speaking world *eusebeia* has a strong moral meaning.[66] *Eusebeia* indicates the kind of attitude or disposition one has towards the gods when one is indebted to them. The concept soon obtains the meaning of a human virtue: "*Eusebeia* is

[65] See G. Friedrich, "'Eusebes'" (1971), p. 182.

[66] "Like 'hosios' (holy) which frequently stands alongside 'dikaios' (righteousness), 'eusebes' and 'eusebeia' denote a moral attitude in the Gk-speaking world" (W. Günther, "Godliness, Piety [*Eusebeia*]" [1976], p. 93).

one of the virtues of man who is righteous and acceptable to the gods."[67]

The use of the term in the New Testament has a unique character. *Eusebeia* is perceived neither as a cultic rite, nor as a prescriptive legalistic code. *Eusebia* is not a moral issue residing primarily in human virtues, nor is it a psychological quality, dependent upon personality traits. In the New Testament, *eusebeia* signifies the believer's total attitude towards life as based upon faith in Christ. This new life-style is exercised in the awareness of God's presence. It also has ethical implications. Piety desires not only to care for faith, but also for God's entire creation. Paul's argument in 1 Timothy 4:2-4 reveals this concern. When Paul reprimands the ascetic heretics because they despise and negate the creation and human needs, he is probably addressing a sectarian group which was displaying early gnostic traits as a result of the influence of certain Hellenistic-Jewish groups. *Eusebeia* was emphasized specifically to combat the dualistic separation of the spiritual and physical.

Paul's letters to Timothy emphasize the notion that piety, as an expression of the awareness of God's presence, reflects a certain life-style and behavior and is expressed concretely in the congregation. Piety is not an inwardly directed quality which concerns only psychic processes, but a corporative issue of the entire congregation. 1 Timothy 3:16 associates *eusebeia* with the revealed truth of faith: the mystery of godliness. The congregation is the pillar and the foundation of this truth (v.15). 1 Timothy 3:9 also describes this truth as "the deep truths of the faith." The *eusebeia* in verse 16 is also linked to the hymn about Christ in the rest of verse 16. *Eusebeia* is thus associated with Christ's incarnation, with the confirmation of this salvific reality by the Spirit and with

[67] See *ibid.,* p. 92.

the eventual glory and doxology. Christ's appearance in a body (incarnation) was preached among the nations. The Spirit's vindication of Christ is confirmed by the angels and the focus is on Christ's ultimate glory. The doxology of both cosmology and congregation intercept one another in this hymn. *Eusebeia* thus focuses on the hallelujah, as expressed by the congregation within the creative tension that exists between the cosmic order and the coming Kingdom of God. Doxology should thus be viewed as the essence of *eusebia*.

We can contend that when 1 Timothy 3:16 is read with 1 Timothy 4:7-8 ("train yourself to be godly"), *eusebeia* means: faith in action; operational faith; faith as sanctification and transformation of life. This devotion has an eschatological dimension: "... godliness has value for all things, holding promise for both the present life and the life to come." When spirituality is understood as *eusebeia*, it involves devotion and the exercise of faith by means of the revealed truth. A mature spirituality therefore denotes faith in action, and focuses on a person's life being devoted to God.

Eusebeia helps us to draw the following conclusions about the connection between maturity in faith and spirituality:

• Spirituality, as godliness, denotes an existential knowledge of God. This knowledge is based on obedience to God. Faith is thus not an abstraction from life, but rather a matter of conduct (embodiment).

• Spirituality has an eschatological dimension. It functions within the tension between salvific truth and daily life. This tension generates a struggle, which in turn reflects the character of the development of our faith.

• Spirituality denotes a changed life-style (new ethos). It is linked to the ethical dimension of the Christian faith, and has implications for our daily lives and creaturehood.

• Spirituality, as piety, is not merely a psychic event of inner, emotional experiences, but of faith experiences regarding the presence and will of God for our life. Spirituality involves subjectivity and indeed has implications for the existential and human dimension of Christian faith. Nevertheless, spirituality should basically be interpreted as an exponent of a living faith. It is fulfilled *coram Deo*, experienced in the fellowship of believers and exercised within the world.

Summary

Although a mature faith and spirituality denote more or less the same subject matter (that is, grace and salvation), spirituality should nevertheless be viewed as the experiential and operational dimension of faith (the living dimension of faith). Spirituality is linked to the notion of wisdom in Scripture. It functions in close association with justice and therefore has a social dimension. Spirituality reflects the quality of a *personal stance* before God as well as an embodiment/enfleshment of the presence of God. It reveals a condition and a conduct which indicates the uniqueness of the Christian understanding of God. It therefore determines the identity of the human I. Hence, the importance of a psycho-pastoral model which takes seriously the interplay between a pastoral anthropology and a psychological understanding of maturity.

2.5 The Interplay between Faith and Personality: A Psycho-Pastoral Model[68]

Each person has a certain structure which is connected to his/her personal composition. I can be myself only in a certain

---

[68] Pesch (*Frei Sein aus Gnade*, p. 42) calls such a model "pastoral" and "polemic." "Kurzum, man kann theologische Anthropologie 'pastoral' und 'polemisch' treiben. Man kan das menschliche Fragen stellen, ja zur Rechenschaft vor dem Anspruch des Glaubens auffordern."

body and only in a specific phase of life. My character, aptitude and psychosomatic composition are part of my constitution. That which I am (ontic), is determined by the fact that I am, biologically and physiologically, male or female. The human constitution is co-determined by heredity and gender.[69] The extent to which people can identify with certain characteristics is important in the process of maturity. Insight into the specific nature of the human total aptitude and into the basic "raw" material or potentialities provided in their psychosomatic make-up will determine the quality of the process of identification. The human psyche, with its important dimensions of consciousness and unconsciousness, thus plays an important role in the development of maturity. Our physique and psyche are the most basic components through which faith is experienced and made visible. Faith is enfleshed daily by personality and behavior. Hence, the need for a pastoral model which takes the psyche into consideration.[70]

The Human I: Conscious and Unconscious

There is disagreement in psychology on how to draw the difference between the I (ego) and the self. Jung, for example, differentiates

[69] H. R. Wijngaarden (*Hoofdproblemen der Volwassenheid* [1952], p. 69) concludes: "dat men bij de beschouwing van de individuele mens rekening dient te houden met de mogelijkheid van tal van constitutioneel bepaalde, als erfgoed in de karakterstructuur meegekregen eigenschappen, also een tendens tot geldingsdrang, heerzucht egocentriciteit, passiviteit, gulheid, enz."

[70] According to K. Müller (*Wenn Ich "Ich" Sage* [1994], pp. 18-19) there is a conflict in Roman Catholic theology over the position of the human subject in theology. "Skepsis und Mahnung zur Vorsicht gegenüber einem Subjektivismus überwiegen." According to Pesch (*Frei Sein aus Gnade*, 24) the subject as focal point of theological reflection should be viewed as the challenge put by modernity to theology. He calls it: "Wende zum Subjekt." The danger in any theological

between "I" as the center of being and the "self" as center of the total personality. To him, the self is not only the center of the personality, but also its extent: the circle of self includes consciousness and unconsciousness.[71] However, how one differentiates between the I, which is surrounded by the limits of a deeper, uncharted field (that is, the human spirit and thus impossible to understand fully), and the self (which transcends the I and cannot be fully understood), the reality still remains: the psychological dynamism of our humanity takes place between I and self and is an inexhaustible source of energy which transcends and evades our deepest analyses.

There are general dimensions to a person's being. Self-consciousness is linked to the unconscious, and part of the dynamism of the human being is the relationship between the two. You are aware of the things that you know you do not completely control.[72] Zijlstra believes that the unconscious consists of the following aspects:[73]

• *The relational aspect.* There is always the awareness in the unconscious that the I is different from other people and other things. Others are a mirror in which I see myself as being different. Others also cause my resistance because they are different. The relational aspect of the unconscious allows one to play certain roles intuitively which one is not directly aware of, but of which one can become aware.

• *The preservation aspect.* The unconscious acts like an archive of experiences. This lies just below the level of consciousness and penetrates the human consciousness as memory.

anthropology is that theology becomes a function of anthropology. "Die *Theologie degeneriere zur Funktion menschlichen Selbstverständnisses*" (*Ibid.*, 27).

[71] See W. Zijlstra, *Op Zoek naar een Nieuwe Horizon* (1989), p. 36.

[72] *Ibid.*, p. 35.

[73] *Ibid.*, pp. 36-44.

• *The potential aspect.* The human being has dormant abilities, images, and insights into structures and associations with reality. The potential of unconsciousness acts like a collective primitive form of experience, which is waiting to be actualized (Jung).
• *The warning aspect.* The unconscious alarms us when our knowing function becomes unilateral and rigid. If a person ignores this warning, the unconscious rebels by means of neurotic symptoms such as anxiety.
• *The chaotic-creative aspect.* A person can use disorderly and undifferentiated experiences to become creative. Hence, the importance of psychological symbols.
• *The autonomous, dynamic aspect.* The unconscious contains our passions as well as a hidden source of knowledge which is linked to the entire cosmic reality. Hence, the important role of dreams.
• *The religious aspect.* The unconscious is the world in which the human self transcends itself and makes contact with the transcendental factor of our being. The dynamism of good and evil is within this transcendence and constantly plays a role in human behavior. A person can rise to the level of the "godly" or descend to the depth of the "demonic."

Our self-awareness and self-image are not determined by the unconscious alone, but are also directly linked to human conscious abilities: Jung calls these conscious abilities thought, emotion, perceptions (sensual) and intuition (hidden possibilities which appear in the conscious as images ["*Gestalt*"]).

To conclude, one can say that the relationship between I and self,[74] as well as between conscious and unconscious, is thus part of the dynamics of our personality. Material arising from the

---

[74] "Het ik staat niet tegenover het zelf, en het zelf is geen beperking van het ik, maar het zelf is de mogelijkheid van het ik om zich uit te drukken; het ik wordt dus door het zelf alleen gelimiteerd tot zichzelf" (Wijngaarden, *Hoofdproblemen der Volwassenheid*, p. 31).

unconscious is not meant to cause disintegration in human beings, but to instill creativity and a realistic self-insight: this is made possible by the acceptance of the I. Consciousness of material from the unconscious also creates a dynamic openness through which I should grow to new levels of responsible behavior. Hence, the importance of the relationship between I and self for a pastoral anthropology.

The holistic and systems approach of biblical anthropology enable us to contend that the dynamics between the I and the self play a decisive role in the manner in which our development of faith is expressed. The psyche thus plays an important role in the process of becoming an integrated person and a mature Christian. The ego, or inner self-consciousness, acts as an organizing and creating principle, not only in one's personality, but also in one's spirit.

For more clarity, we could distinguish between ego and self as follows: the ego is each person's directing principle; it is the personality's dynamic organizing and creative principle as it is expressed in thought, will, emotion and bodily action. The human moral consciousness and our sense of accountability and responsibility are components of the ego. Because of the ego, human beings can choose and act in freedom. In this creative process, one becomes conscious of oneself. The self is the aspect of awareness which constitutes the more knowable part of oneself. This self-consciousness in which the ego becomes the object (the self), is determined by needs, urges, habits, character, traits, hereditary inclinations and sexuality. It also plays a decisive role in our self-esteem.

The human psyche implies the totality of the human being, as determined by intellect, will, feelings, emotions and physicality. Physicality must not be viewed as inferior to the psyche. A person is a psychosomatic unity: the reality of the psyche is expressed in physicality.

The psychic dimension of our existence is not limited to the subjective self-conscious. The ego, as the organizing and creative principle, has the capacity to exceed itself. When it does so, the ego is called the human spirit:[75] it represents the transcending dimension of the human spiritual capacity. The psychic and physical aspects of the human spirit are also focused on external norms and values. By linking this with preceding information about the pneumatic person, we may assume that the human spirit is a receptive and sensitive organ: it is receptive for the eternal dimension and to the grace of God.

Human identity involves the integrated functioning of the body, soul and spirit. This means that identity is linked to a given constitution and to the understanding of self. People should know how they are constituted and what the given structure of their being is. People have an aptitude and a certain "autobiography"[76] for which they should accept full responsibility and which should be creatively unveiled and discovered through a process of growth and self-development. Emotions and thoughts play a decisive role in this process.

---

[75] We have already referred to the concept "pneuma" in the theological exposition. Within the general meaning of the concept "spirit" in literature, there is significant correspondence between the scriptural use of "pneuma" and its meaning in philosophical literature. C. A. van Peursen (*Lichaam-Ziel-Geest* [1961²], p. 143) views the spirit as an integral part of the human entire existence: "Deze totaliteit is de geest als de gerichtheid van de mens. Het is een gerichtheid die vanuit de mens als ik ontplooit en waaraan dat ik zich eerst manifesteert." To Van Peursen (*Ibid.*, p. 153) the human spirit is the principle of exceeding and transcending in the act of focusing.

[76] G. W. Allport (cited by A. T. Möller, *Inleiding tot die Persoonlikheidsielkunde* [1980], p. 123) speaks of the raw material which is present from birth. He distinguishes between three aspects of personality which are part of this raw material: the constitution (the total physical composition), intelligence (the capacity of the central nervous system) and temperament (typical reactions of the autonomous nervous system and the endocrine glands).

Emotions/Feelings (the Affective Dimension)

Human beings should understand their psyche as a dynamic totality, which is composed of: emotions, thought, volition, conscience and body. This unity is indicated by the fact that a person not only *has* a body, but *is* a body. Human physicality thus involves an embodied soul and inspired body. Emotions and thought form part of this inspiration and physicality: both play a decisive role in communication. In order to fully understand the dynamics of communication and counseling, attention should be paid to both the person's affective and cognitive dimensions.

Feelings and human emotions play a vital role in personality. People are their true selves in and through their emotions. Emotions and feelings also provide a better understanding of the dynamics between the I and self, and promote the understanding of others. Emotions can be described as the porthole which gives insight into the inner experience of the human I or soul. They indicate the person's immediate reaction to a specific situation. Emotions are part of the reality of a personality. In order to understand other human beings, we must take cognizance of their emotions and feelings. For this, we need empathy.

In *Handbuch der Psychologie für die Seelsorge*, Sieland contends that the dialogue between the church and psychology is hampered due to the fact that a polemic has developed regarding the role of emotions. The impression has been created that emotions are bad and thus do not have a place in a theological anthropology. Emotions are linked to lust, while asceticism is held to be the Christian ideal. Even Christ is portrayed without humor or joy.[77]

Yet, God reveals his glory at a merry, rural wedding in Palestine (Jn 11). In fact, the wedding is so merry that Jesus is criticized

---

[77] See B. Sieland, "Emotion" (1992), p. 111.

as a glutton and a drunkard. The Gospel is not a message that lacks emotions and human experiences. On the contrary, the Bible is full of emotions. God often experiences regret and remorse. The Bible reflects deep "psychological insight" when it describes people's depressed state of mind when they are experiencing emotional distress (Ps 42:12).

The word "emotion" is derived from the Latin *emovere*, and means "surging up."[78] Emotions indicate vitality, movement and turmoil. They are an aspect of the human ego. Laux and Weber describe emotions as complex organized conditions consisting of cognitive assessment, acting impulses and physical reactions.[79] Emotions are expressed by sensual experiences, inner processes and physical reactions, such as grief, as well as cognitive processes, such as assessing, imagining, remembering and expecting.

Emotions are not readily noticed. They are hidden conditions which are expressed in feelings or dispositions, and which indicate an attitude toward life. Emotions thus reflect values and convey messages about the unconscious within the level of the conscious. According to Sieland, emotions have a dual purpose: pleasant = aimed towards the positive, and unpleasant = aimed away from the positive.

Emotions play an important role in pastoral care, especially when assessing the personal value of abstract concepts. For instance, because the term "father" is emotionally laden with associations, its value and meaning are determined greatly by an emotional context. Emotional associations may also play an important role in images of God and in the pastoral assessment of their role in faith. For this reason, we will return to these links and associations between emotions and rational concepts

---

[78] *Ibid.*, p. 112.
[79] Cited in Sieland, "Emotion," p. 112.

in Chapter 3, when we deal with the problem of a pastoral diagnosis.

Thinking (the Cognitive Dimension)

Emotions and thinking clearly influence each other. The mind itself should be viewed as an integral part of human and psychological processes. The mind represents the cognitive dimension of a person. It plays such an important role in personality that the philosopher Reneé Descartes views reason as the most constitutive part of the human ego: I think therefore I am (*cogito ergo sum*).

We shall now turn our attention to the dynamics of the human mind, as expressed in operative functions and content-bound reasoning skills.

Processes of thinking are mainly determined by content and specific operations. Both content and operation are perceived as modalities of the mind and, according to Todt and Heils, consist of the following seven components.[80]

Operative Components

a) Coping skills: understanding and concentrating.
b) Memory and thought: recalling, recognizing and reproducing verbal and numerical material and images.
c) Creativity and fantasizing: ideas, control of different information, imagining, envisaging and noticing various perspectives.
d) Competence: this includes judging information, analyzing, solving problems and reasoning.

[80] See E. Todt & S. Heils "Denken" (1992), p. 178.

Content-bound Components

e) Verbal skills (speech).

f) Mathematical or numerical thought.

g) Figurative thought (image forming).

Beside these components, thought can be divided into: problem-solving, productive thought (insight), and systematic thought (in a network of relationships and contexts).

Pastoral care's focus is on a better understanding of the function of thinking and understanding problem-solving behavior. It is therefore important to keep two forms of problem-solving thought patterns in mind: inductive thought and deductive thought.[81]

Inductive thought means making conclusions by means of sensual perception, simplified by classification and comprehension. Inductive thought also employs analogues: structuring known and trusted data (existing traits) in order to identify the characteristics of a new field of reality.

Deductive thought means making conclusions from an existing premise. A well-known example of deductive thought is the so-called syllogism. For example:

All men are mortal.
Socrates is a man.
Therefore Socrates is mortal.

The difference between left and right brain thought has received much prominence lately.[82] According to this theory, the left lobe of the brain controls the verbal components: logical, analytical, rational, critical, digital and time-focused skills are linked to this lobe. The right lobe of the brain is more visually, spatially and

[81] *Ibid.,* pp. 179-195.
[82] *Ibid.,* pp. 193-194.

non-verbally adjusted: synthetical, intuitive, analogical and spatial skills are linked to this lobe.

One of the goals in counseling is to induce people to take responsible decisions for purposeful behavior. Thus cognizance should be given to the structure of planning thought (productive thought): collecting information → model designing → prognosis of future possible conditions and consequences → planning and executing action programmes → monitoring and reviewing operational strategies for putting formulated goals into action.[83]

The dynamics of thinking clearly proves the creativity and capacities of the human mind. These not only bring about logic and insight, but also produce comprehension, which links imagination to reason. The human mind thus plays a decisive role in how a person views him-/herself and the world. Perceptions are determined by the content of rational concepts.

2.6 The Nature of Mental Health and a Psychological Understanding of Maturity (Adulthood)

Maturity, mental health and adulthood are interpreted differently in psychology according to the specific base theory undergirding each model. For this reason, Bee, in *The Journey of Adulthood* (1992[2]), tries to describe different theories which shed light on different patterns of change occurring during adulthood. In addition to biologically-influenced changes or changes produced by shared experiences within a cultural or social context, processes of internal change are of the utmost importance.

> The basic idea is that each of us must face and cope with a set of tasks or dilemmas in our adult life. In the process of coping, we

---

[83] *Ibid.*, p. 193.

undergo a series of inner adjustments. We may become more "integrated," we may learn to express a wider range of emotions, we may become more "mature." Movement through the family life cycle or other shared experiences may be part of what triggers this set of inner changes, but the internal transformations may go beyond this.[84]

Bee defines adulthood as the period from the age of 18 to death.[85] During adulthood, a person is influenced by ageing (decline) and maturation (processes of change with age, governed by underlying physiological processes, largely determined by genetic code). It is very difficult to identify those elements which are common during adult trajectories. Bee therefore describes the wide variety of existing theories according to their relative emphases on development versus change, as well as describing the presence or absence of stages in each theory.[86]

The process of maturity includes the components of both *development* and *change*. We cannot ignore the notion of stages. It is possible to identify fixed sequences of experiences of events over time. Both the notions of development and change are important in a pastoral model. A developmental model therefore assumes a goal toward which the believer can move progressively. Thus the following concluding remark: *In a pastoral model, it is important that the goal does not necessarily imply "improvement," in the sense of perfection, but rather "transformation," in the sense of qualitative change towards meaningfulness and purposefulness. The goal should never be interpreted as a fixed "end goal" which must be "achieved." The goal, that is, our new status in Christ which is founded by the principle of salvation, is a qualitative stance in life, which determines the quality of our responsibility*

---

[84] See H. L. Bee, *The Journey of Adulthood* (1992²), p. 10.
[85] *Ibid.*, p. 15.
[86] *Ibid.*, p. 64-65.

and respondability. The goal functions as a motivating component; it functions like the axis of a spiral movement. We interpret "development" in the same way as Lemme.[87] He understands development as systematic changes in behavior over time, resulting from interaction between the individual and the internal and external environment. Normative influences play a role in this process of adult development. The term "normative" implies that development is very similar among individuals and across cultures.[88] In addition to the possibility of similarities, to my mind "normative" also refers to a set of norms or values which can be either external or internal. Lemme regards "non-normative influences" as unique experiences which contribute to uniqueness in our development. Nevertheless, it is very important that we understand that human development and mental health is an ongoing process: the so-called life-span developmental perspective.[89]

Mental health is very complex in both psychology and psychiatry. Often, more attention is paid to the correlates of abnormality than to those of normality. Mental health practitioners are frequently more preoccupied with efforts to relieve a person's distress and to resolve conflict, than with identifying the criteria of mental health. This approach implies the definition of health as the absence of illness or problems.

Our discussion in this chapter leads to the conclusion that the mental health profession should once again identify maturity and the optimal development of the individual across the life-span as a legitimate goal in counseling. It is therefore of the utmost importance

---

[87] See B. H. Lemme, *Development in Adulthood* (1995), p. 8.

[88] *Ibid.,* p. 9.

[89] *Ibid.,* p. 11: "A life-span developmental perspective views human development as an ongoing process, beginning at the moment of conception and continuing until the moment of death."

that we identify the criteria associated with psychological health and well-being. These criteria will inevitably reflect the philosophical life stance, cultural values and anthropology which undergird psychology.

Hubbard's popular book, *Dianetics*, reflects the life values of our functionalistic culture, and provides a good example of this reflection. Hubbard views human nature as constructive and good. "Man is good. Take away his basic aberrations and with them go the evil of which the scholastic and the moralist were so fond."[90]

"Dianetics" means an adventure and exploration into *terra incognita*, the human mind.[91] Hubbard concludes that dianetics is a science of the mind which discloses hitherto unknown laws about thought.[92] In order to exercise dianetics, a person needs to understand that survival is the goal of all human beings. Hubbard calls survival the dynamic principle of existence.[93] The driving force behind this principle of survival is the urge towards pleasure,[94] which implies avoiding and minimizing pain. The basic presupposition of such a simplistic and opportunistic model is that a human being is a self-determined organism.[95] The goal of mental health, as identified by this model, is therefore the pursuit of happiness and the overcoming of every obstacle which would block the achievement of this goal.

A much more realistic approach to mental health is acceptance of maturity (responsibility and respondability) as a basic issue for psychological health. For example, Rayner views both responsibility and reflectiveness about issues as valid expressions of maturity.[96]

---

[90] See L. R. Hubbard, *Dianetics* (1986), p. 26.
[91] *Ibid.*, p. 26.
[92] *Ibid.*, p. 531.
[93] *Ibid.*, p. 29.
[94] *Ibid.*, p. 33.
[95] *Ibid.*, p. 42.
[96] See E. Rayner, *Human Development* (1978²), p. 162.

Gerdes argues along the same lines. Several characteristics of maturation are described.[97] The combination of a realistic assessment of life, the ability to make important choices, self-acceptance, the existence of an integrative and meaningful view of life, and the acceptance of responsibility, all play a constructive role in the development of a mature person.[98]

Heath's study reveals that a growing consensus exists amongst philosophers, psychologists and various religions that maturation is an important goal in life.[99] Heath makes use of a developmental model which describes the different dimensions of maturation. He assumes that four principal facets determine the effectiveness of the whole person: cognitive skills; interpersonal skills; values (purposeful long-term goals), including metavalues such as honesty, truth, fairness, compassion, integrity, commitment, courage and freedom; and self-insight, self-understanding and an identity which includes the positive stance of self-confidence.[100]

This model is undergirded by five developmental principles, which organize the growth of minds and character.[101] These principles encourage a person to become:

- more reflectively aware: symbolization;
- more other-centered, empathetic and caring;
- better integrated within relationships and contexts;
- more stable, mobile, enduring and selective;
- more autonomous.

Goldberg's framework for psychological health has three essential characteristics: self-awareness, relationship and action.[102] In order to attain mental health, individuals should not only engage

---

[97] See C. Gerdes, "Rypheid" (1981), p. 92.

[98] *Ibid.*, p. 93.

[99] See D. H. Heath, *Fulfilling Lives* (1991), p. 33.

[100] *Ibid.*, pp. 34-35.

[101] *Ibid.*, p. 38.

[102] See A. D. Goldberg, "Hillel's Maxim" (1992), p. 108.

in self-exploration, but should also love and respect themselves. Achieving a sense of identity requires recognition by others, not merely of normative and socially recognized accomplishments, but, more importantly, recognition of the ideographic and unique aspects of one's being.[103] Self-identity also entails a sense of personal responsibility and the belief that one has personal control over one's life. Control is not achieved without conflict: conflict is essential to growth and health. The discomfort, that comes with the search for a meaningful existence is thus not a sign of illness, but a manifestation of the human condition.[104]

Currently there is a growing awareness that mental health is determined by social factors. Ruble *et al.* draw our attention to the influence of social support and group dynamics on self-esteem.[105] Group identity and social roles obviously affect self-esteem. For example, labeling and stigmatizing could play an important role in the development of a negative self-esteem. Social structures, such as school and family, affect feelings of self-confidence and personal control. Closeness, trust and warmth help to foster positive mental health.[106]

Scholars in the human sciences accentuate increasingly the impact of spiritual issues and religion on mental health and health care.[107] Brown pioneers this approach.[108] An increasing consensus is currently developing that religion is more likely to help solve the problems of the mentally ill than to cause their illness or

---

[103] *Ibid.,* p. 108.

[104] *Ibid.,* p. 108.

[105] See D. N. Ruble *et al., The Social Psychology of Mental Health* (1992), p. 12.

[106] *Ibid.,* p. 13.

[107] See M. Dombeck & J. Karl, "Spiritual Issues in Mental Health Care" (1987), p. 183.

[108] See L. B. Brown (ed.), *Religion, Personality and Mental Health* (1994), p. 195.

distress. Brown discusses the relationship between religion and personality and concludes:

> Expecting those who are "mature" to have no need of God as an explanatory hypothesis is, however, more moralistic than data-based, since it introduces other constructions of the meaning of religious doctrines and practices for individuals.[109]

Bergin's empirical research confirmed this finding.[110] "Overall there was no correlation between religion and mental illness." Studies by Bishop view the church as a healing community.[111] "The special qualities of the *koinonia* provide for an intensity of healing experience that may extend beyond that of the secular healing community."[112]

The process of psychological development and spiritual growth clearly do not exclude each other. In both, our responsibility, our important life issues, and our values play a decisive role. Mental health is often defined in the light of socially desirable features. Because the point of departure in psychology is personality, criteria for mental health therefore include: positive attitudes towards the self through an ability to "self-actualize," a sense of autonomy, and social or environmental control. For example, Jourard and Landsman's comparative analysis concluded that mental health included such characteristics as positive self-regard; realistic self-perceptions; creativity; an ability to care about others and the natural world; to do productive work; to have an openness for new ideas and people; and to love.[113] Yet it is difficult to manifest all these characteristics without possessing positive values.

---

[109] *Ibid.*, p. 5.

[110] See A. E. Bergin, "Values and Issues in Psychotherapy and Mental Health" (1991), p. 399.

[111] See L. C. Bishop, "Healing in the Koinonia" (1985), p. 15.

[112] *Ibid.*, p. 20.

[113] See S. M. Jourard & T. Landsman, *Health Personality* (1980⁴), p. 131.

Psychology, religion and spirituality should therefore be viewed as complementary to each other in the process of developing mental or spiritual health.

Gareis believes that personal or psychological maturity, or mental health, is coherent with the meaningfulness and purposefulness of human life. Mental health is thus associated with a person's response to a sense of destiny.[114] An integral component of this response is formed by having a positive attitude:[115]

* towards yourself;
* towards your fellow-person;
* towards the transcendental (God);
* as well as a self-conscious disposition towards life.

According to Gareis, life should be enjoyed as a gift and a challenge. In order to live in this way, love and fulfillment of love, security and trust, life skills and creativity, and experience of success, acknowledgement and appreciation are all necessary. To him, the main purpose of the process of personal development is joyful living.

Roux draws attention to the uncertainty and to the differences in opinion that exist about what exactly should be understood by "psychological maturity."[116] His description of the five characteristics of psychological maturity can be summarized as follows.[117]

* A coherent view of life (an integrated and committed conviction). This includes values; flexibility; autonomous behavior (the ability to act with interdependence; to accept responsibility; to plan and to act independently, and to deal with problems; a normal need for acceptance and acknowledgement); and purposefulness.

---

[114] See B. Gareis, "Entwicklung und Lebenslauf" (1992), pp. 264-265.

[115] *Ibid.,* p. 265.

[116] See G. S. Roux, *'n Psigo-opleidingsmodel om Teologiestudente tot Psigiese Volwassenheid te Begelei (s.a.),* p. 5.

[117] *Ibid.,* p. 6.

- Spontaneity. Contact with emotions; an openness to immediate events and demonstration of emotions (constructive emotional expression).
- A positive self-esteem comprising two important poles: self-knowledge and self-acceptance.
- The ability for intimate personal relationships. Acceptance of others, and effective communication.
- Altruism, including altruistic concern for others; external problem-centeredness; genuine interest and compassion expressed in involvement with others (social orientation).

This summarized description of psychological mental health and a psychological understanding of maturity (adulthood) indicates clearly that the core factors on which all these characteristics hinge are love, integrity, freedom (autonomy) and responsibility. Only when people have accepted responsibility for their own lives, can the process and development of maturity be directed meaningfully.

2.7 Identity and Growth

The quality of the human answer to the question which life poses about the significance of identity, is decisive for the direction and purposefulness of life.[118] The answer to the question, "Who am I?", depends on the quality of the human reaction, and on the degree and quality of human responsibility (*respondeo ergo sum*).[119] The human quest for identity also raises questions about the nature of our freedom.

---

[118] H. Berkhof (*Christelijk Geloof* [1973], p. 91) is wary of describing the human as a responsible being. Responsibility could place a person too much in the cadre of command and duty. Therefore he speaks of the person as an "antwoordelijk wezen" (responding human being).

[119] In this regard Heinemann (*Filosofie op Nieuwe Wegen*, p. 180) comments: "Deze grote speelruimte van het antwoorden heb ik op het oog, wanneer ik het eerste principe als *respondeo, ergo sum* formuleer. Ik antwoord, daarom ben ik."

In a theological anthropology, "identity" means that people discover that God calls them to respond to their destiny: to love God and their fellow human beings. People display the quality of their responsibility and the genuineness and sincerity of their obedience to God in the way that they love. But identity is also about people being called: the principle of vocation. Although people are called, they have the freedom to choose how they will respond. Nevertheless, responsibility implies that human freedom is not unlimited. "Freedom" means the awareness that our choices are not unlimited, but are determined by the ethical principle of unconditional love. This love includes an acceptance of ourselves, founded on grace: God's yes to human beings in and through Christ. Such freedom, when based upon God's grace, gives rise to true self-acceptance. True self-acceptance means that people will never underestimate themselves (the danger of self-underestimation and inferiority complexes), nor will they overestimate themselves (the danger of self-overestimation and haughtiness). In a Christian ethics of love, our neighbor functions as a watch-dog, thereby preventing us from sliding into the abyss of selfishness.

The principle of responsibility, which leads in turn to self-acceptance, presupposes awareness. People within a specific stage of development need to be aware that they should display real insight in the specific claim made on their personal functions during this stage. Their development and growth is determined by the extent to which they accept responsibility for the development of their potentialities in life. A developmental model in a pastoral anthropology should always deal with the ethical principle of love, because it is an important director in the process of disclosing and discovering inner potentialities.

Erikson's growth model supplements and elaborates on the concept of development and growth.[120] Erikson contends that people

---

[120] Erikson's growth model applies the epigenetic principle meaning that in all development an inherent scheme or groundplan is present. The different

develop according to an inherent scheme. Each of the eight stages of human development have a pair of concepts in a polar tension towards each other, which indicate the nature of the personal crisis in that stage. People grow through crises to a specific identity, depending on whether or not the positive pole gets the upper hand. Erikson's growth model is linked to development in psychoanalysis and ego psychology. He follows Marie Jahoda's definition of a healthy personality: "a healthy personality actively masters his environment, shows a certain unity of personality, and is able to perceive the world and himself correctly."[121] He develops his model from a developmental stance: how does a healthy personality grow or accrue from the successive stages of increasing capacity to master life's outer and inner dangers?

Erikson answers this question, as well as that of human identity, by introducing the "epigenetic principle"[122]: "Somewhat generalized, this principle states that anything that grows has a *ground plan*, and that out of this ground plan the *parts* arise, each part having its time of special ascendancy, until all parts have arisen to form a *functioning whole.*" [123] Erikson views his diagram as a sequence of stages and a gradual development of components. In other words, the diagram formalizes a progression through time of a differentiation of parts. The implication of such a developmental model of identity is that each item of the healthy personality is systematically related to all others.[124] Erikson views each successive step as a potential crisis because it requires a radical change in perspective. He views crisis in a developmental sense. "Crisis"

components of the development scheme ultimately grow to a functional whole. For an exposition of Erikson's model see R. Riess, *Seelsorge* (1973) p. 84, also M. Klessmann, *Identität und Glaube* (1980) p. 50f.

[121] See E. H. Erikson, *Identity and the Life Cycle* (1959), p. 51.

[122] *Ibid.,* p. 52.

[123] See also E. H. Erikson, *Identity. Youth and Crisis* (1974²), p. 92.

[124] *Ibid.,* p. 93.

does not connote the threat of catastrophe, but is seen as a turning point: a crucial period of increased vulnerability and heightened potential.[125]

Despite the deterministic undertone in Erikson's epigenetic model, the value of his approach lies in its insight into the dynamics of personal identity. Against the background of existing ambiguities he describes the development of a healthy personality in terms of a life-cycle compiled of different stages.[126]

Stage 1: Infancy and the mutuality of recognition. Basic trust (confidence) versus basic mistrust.

Stage 2: Early childhood and the will to be oneself. Autonomy versus shame and doubt.

Stage 3: Childhood and the anticipation of roles (play age). Initiative versus guilt.

Stage 4: School age and task identification. Industry versus inferiority.

Stage 5: Adolescence. Identity versus identity diffusion.

Stage 6: Beyond identity (young adult). Intimacy and dissociation versus self-absorption.

Stage 7: Adulthood. Generativity versus stagnation.

Stage 8: Adulthood (mature age). Integrity versus despair and disgust.

Erikson describes stage 5 as the most crucial in the process of development and maturation. It is a decisive turning point in which the following seven dynamic bipolarities all play a part:[127] identity versus identity confusion; temporal perspective versus time confusion; self-certainty versus self-consciousness; role experimentation versus role fixation; apprenticeship versus work

---

[125] *Ibid.,* p. 96.

[126] See Erikson, *Identity and the Life Cycle*, pp. 55-100; *Identity. Youth and Crisis*, 95-141.

[127] See Erikson, *Identity. Youth and Crisis*, p. 94.

paralysis; sexual polarization versus bisexual confusion; leader- and followership versus authority confusion; and ideological commitment versus confusion of values. Within the dynamics of identity, the polarities are: task identification versus sense of futility; anticipation of roles versus role inhibition; will to be oneself versus self-doubt; and mutual recognition versus autistic isolation.

Erikson's exposition of the crisis of identity sheds light on the fact that identity should be viewed as a process, the outcome of which includes: identification; anticipation and role-definition; self-assertion and autonomy; self-acceptance within the mutuality of appreciation. In terms of psychology and a developmental model, we conclude that maturity presupposes a process of matu- ration in which identity plays a decisive role. Whether identity takes place and diffusion is overcome will determine the quality of adulthood: intimacy, generativity and integrity. Fidelity is the cor- nerstone of identity, in terms of Erikson's understanding of the life cycle. "Fidelity is the ability to sustain loyalties freely pledged in spite of the inevitable contradictions and confusions of value sys- tems."[128]

Of utmost importance for our discussion is the fact that Erikson links to each stage a set of "virtues," which can be viewed as qualities of the human ego. These qualities are part of the dynamic interplay between conscious and unconscious forces. Erikson mentions: hope, will, purpose, competence, fidelity, love, care and wisdom.[129] The latter three indicate adulthood.

Another interesting result of Erikson's research on the human life cycle is that the basic human strength is hope:

---

[128] See E. H. Erikson, "Reflections on Dr. Borg's Life Cycle," p. 28; see also E. H. Erikson, *Youth: Change and Challenge* (1963), p. 19; for the problem of identity confusion see *ibid.*, p. 11.

[129] See Erikson, "Reflections on Dr. Borg's Life Cycle," p. 25.

Hope is the enduring belief in the attainability of primal wishes, in spite of the dark urges and rages which mark the beginnings of existence and leave a lasting residue of threatening Estrangement.[130]

The ultimate strength is described as wisdom:

Wisdom is the detached and yet active concern with life itself in the face of death itself, and that it maintains and conveys the integrity of experience in spite of the Disdain over human failings and the Dread of ultimate non-being.[131]

Human development takes place between these two strengths or virtues. Another important finding is Erikson's admission that maturation is neither without value nor completely non-directive. Purposefulness plays a very important role:

Purposefulness is the courage playfully to imagine and energetically to pursue valued goals, uninhibited by the defeat of infantile fantasies, by the guilt they aroused, and by the punishment they elicited.[132]

In conclusion, identity and maturity should never be regarded as already having been reached and attained.[133] *Maturity is a qualitative term linked to the question of the purpose and significance of human existence. Both maturity and identity are relative terms, dependent on the particular stage in life. In a developmental model, it is important to distinguish between maturity as a chronological issue (age and physiological and biological development); an emotional and perceptional issue (self-esteem and self-acceptance) and a spiritual issue (understanding the meaning of the presence and will of God).*

---

[130] *Ibid.,* p. 26.

[131] *Ibid.,* p. 26.

[132] *Ibid.,* pp. 29-30.

[133] This is the reason why maturity cannot be taught and J. Firet (*Het Agogisch Moment in het Pastoraal Optreden* [1977³], pp. 232f) rejects maturity as a pedagogic ideal to be reached during the normal process of growth.

"Identity" is derived from the Latin *idem* meaning same, and conveys the idea of continuity. Identity presumes a continuity between the human I and behavior; hence, the importance of congruency. Congruency happens when self is a true reflection and portrayal of the conduct and experiences of the human I.[134] Congruency is about remaining faithful to oneself, communicating authenticity and truth.[135]

Identity is a dynamic process. The development of identity, therefore, is not linear, but a zigzag movement between experiences of the human I and the response of the environment. The movement acts like a spiral in which experiences of life during each stage of human development play a decisive role.

The direction and objectives of each person's life also play an important role. Human development takes place according to choices made, which reflect a person's norms and values.

This means that identity is inextricably linked to a process through which the ego can transcend itself towards becoming that which it should be or towards reaching its chosen goal in life. Identity comprises transcendence; the quest towards one's destiny involves a movement away from oneself. Identity signifies orientation to a value system, as well as the integration of a goal in life for all daily relationships. One can only arrive at a constructive self-evaluation in terms of an awareness that life is significant and is being directed by purposeful values. Living a meaningful life means viewing one's responsibility as a vocation.

It is impossible to integrate all the theoretical models in psychology into one theory. The different models should be considered according to the different perspectives they give to the complexity of personhood, identity, maturity and adulthood. The

---

[134] See Möller, *Inleiding tot die Persoonlikheidsielkunde*, p. 94.
[135] See Heitink, *Pastoraat als Hulpverlening*, p. 69 on this issue.

different aspects such as type, temperament, trait, mental health, maturity, adulthood, personal development and maturation all have this in common: the understanding that the significance and meaningfulness of personal existence is dependent on one's stance in life and quality of being. Whether mental health or maturity is viewed in terms of integration, the internalization of values, positive self-esteem, altruism, openness, self-assertion, self-acceptance, autonomy or other-centeredness, they all lead back to the most basic question in life: whether one lives an egocentric and selfish life of destructive self-maintenance, or an other-centered life of unconditional love. The discussion thus leads inevitably to the question of the interplay between values and virtues, and their influence on maturity.

2.8 Maturity and the Interplay of Values and Virtues

The connection between values and identity and their influence on meaning, play an important role in the design of an anthropological model for pastoral care. The relation between values and faith has a decisive influence on the development of spirituality. The role played by ethics in Scripture's understanding of a mature faith has already been pointed out. Similarly, when considering communication and the methods of a pastoral therapy, a pastoral anthropology must make particular allowance for the value component of human life.

Values play an important role, not only in a theological anthropology but also in psychology, where values are being acknowledged increasingly as an essential component of personal identity. According to Meissner,[136] values form an integral part of personality:

---

[136] See W. W. Meissner, *Life and Faith* (1987), p. 123.

"The value system represents an organized system that serves an integrative and directive function within the mental apparatus, thus indicating a high level of psychic activity."

An anthropological model in pastoral care must make allowance for the guiding and motivating role which values play in human behavior. Amongst others, Allport described the role of values as the motivating factor in personality. "Allport sees values as beliefs upon which the individual acts by preference. Thus, values serve the functions of directing cognition and motivating behavior."[137]

Values focus in two directions: on the content of a person's faith, which ultimately determines the person's priorities in life; and on preferences and disapprovals based on basic needs. "Yet values have their roots in the basic driving forces of human nature, namely, narcissism, aggression, libido, and the basic instincts that provide the motive power of life."[138]

Augsburger perceives values as the core factor in motivating people: "Humans are evaluating beings. To exist is to choose."[139] This statement links up with a theological anthropology which accepts *respondeo ergo sum* as its core presupposition.

Three aspects are generally included in an understanding of values: values are steering principles for directing human behavior meaningfully; values imply cultural customs and habits; and thirdly, values imply internalized norms (awareness of "the ought").

Augsburger distinguishes between different types of values.

These values are moral (what is just), ideal (what is admirable), aesthetic (what is beautiful), political (what is socially possible), affective

---

[137] See *ibid.*, p. 220.
[138] *Ibid.*, p. 213.
[139] See Augsburger, *Pastoral Counseling Across Cultures*, p. 145.

(what is held dear) and so on. These values provide patterns for living, criteria for decision making, and units of measurement for evaluating oneself and others.[140]

According to Meissner the association between values and needs means that values form a basic element of the desirable. "The desirable is what is felt or thought proper to want."[141]

In addition to the link between values and needs, an interplay also exists between norms and values. Norms have an imperative character and inevitably lead to obligations. For example, as has been pointed out already, Christian ethics is based upon the principle of love. Love therefore obtains a normative character. When a person internalizes love, it becomes a value. Values could be defined as internalized norms, expressed in directed behavior and conduct.

The cultural context of values plays a crucial role in the development of a mature person. In a certain sense, the social system regulates behavior as a result of those values which are inherent to that cultural situation. Social values reflect the symbols of a cultural tradition. Cultural values are thus part of a system of symbols. Consequently, values provide a link between an individual and the tradition of a certain cultural group.

A religious group's tradition, in turn, influences the value system of a cultural group. The symbols of a social group frequently emanate from a process of interaction between cultural context and religious content. Consequently, religious convictions can be a dominant factor in the creation of cultural and personal values.

Meissner summarizes the most important aspects of values and explains the important role of values in the establishment of identity and the development of maturity:[142]

---

[140] *Ibid.,* p. 148.
[141] See Meissner, *Life and Faith*, p. 19.
[142] *Ibid.,* p. 222.

• Values are intrapsychic and often part of the non-observable part of a person's existential orientation within a certain social milieu. They may be introspected and experienced.
• Values provide certainty, security, durability and permanence to human behavior. Values are durable, and form a more or less permanent aspect of a person's psychic composition.
• Values are intentional structures. Values guide one and can be formulated as concepts which promote purposeful behavior. Furthermore, values are concepts and ideas and can, therefore, be verbalized and rationalized.
• Values are explicit or implicit. Sometimes they are partly conscious, but they could also be altogether unconscious. Often values operate on a more pre-conscious level.
• Values are action-oriented. Values often play a role in decision making and offer a framework within which actions take place.
• Values are goal-oriented. "This telic dimension of the value-system has a channeling effect insofar as it organizes or tends to organize the various drive-derivative aspects of personality and directs them toward specific goals."[143]
• Values are linked to the biological needs of an organism. Needs concerning sexuality and love play a huge role in the honing of values. Although the interplay between values and biological needs is tricky, values are nevertheless derived biologically.
• Values are motivational. They channel psychic energy and direct behavior.
• Values are selective and decisional. They are subject to preference behavior. This selective nature of values means that personal decision plays an important role in the formation of values.
• Values are normative. When values attain an obligatory character, thus having ethical implications, they attain a normative character

[143] *Ibid.*, p. 224.

which appeals to a person's sense of responsibility and moral sensitivity.

The following questions must be answered: what implications do values have for human beings? Is there a link between values and moral development? These questions bring us to the issue of character and human virtues.

Discussion of values should be viewed against the background of the role played in human identity by the four classic human virtues: justice, courage, temperance and wisdom/prudence.[144] The debate about the interplay of values and virtues focuses on the moral dimension of personal development. The concept "virtue" can also extend beyond its moral meaning. "'The virtues' to us are the moral virtues, whereas *arete* and virtues refer also to arts and even to excellences of the speculative intellect whose domain is theory rather than practice."[145]

There is a current revival in reflection on the role of virtue in human behavior. From a philosophical perspective, Galston comments: "The past two decades have witnessed a multi-disciplinary revival of scholarly interest in the virtues."[146]

The current debate regarding values cannot be separated from post-modernist thinking. The latter is deeply rooted in the Western concept of democracy, and especially in American thinking. Values

---

[144] For an exposition of the meaning of the four cardinal virtues, see J. Pieper, *The Four Cardinal Virtues* (1966), p. 6. According to Pieper, classical theology viewed prudence (the ability to make right decisions) as the cause of the other virtues: justice, fortitude and temperance. D. Capps (*Deadly Sins and Saving Virtues* [1987], p. 19) contrasts Erikson's list of virtues (hope, will, purpose, competence, fidelity, love, care and wisdom) with the traditional list of seven deadly sins: pride, envy, anger, sloth, greed, gluttony and lust (*Ibid.*, p. 11).

[145] See P. Foot, *Virtues and Vices and Other Essays in Moral Philosophy* (1978), p. 2.

[146] See W. A. Galston, "Introduction" (1992), p.1. See also G. Trianosky, "What is Virtue Ethics all About?" (1990), p. 335.

and virtues are most important for both a principle and dispositional ethics. At its heart burns the question of freedom and the
implications of freedom for our understanding of humanity.

Billington provides an exposition of the debate on values and
virtues against the background of the prevailing quest for freedom.[147] The most common threat posed by a post-modernist
understanding of values and virtues is the basic schism between
freedom and responsibility. The decoupling of this link is mainly
due to the influence of materialism. "This materialistic perversion
of the ideal of liberty, this freeing of freedom from responsibility,
may represent the most immediate present peril to our civic health
and perhaps even to our survival."[148] Moral criteria are gradually
being replaced by aesthetic criteria in the name of entertainment.
This is not done as a result of true reformist conviction, but more
often as a result of the elite's spiritual boredom in an affluent
society. Television is the main culprit.

Billington warns against the real danger of creating a new generation of "vidiots":

> Television corrodes involvement let alone commitment in the civic
> arena, fostering a passivity and spectatorism that destroys resolu-
> tion. In this sense it threatens basic civic decencies and shared social
> goals among a pluralistic people.[149]

Pastoral care must seriously consider the challenges posed by
the way in which Western life-style and communities shape character. Pastoral care cannot ignore the influence of post-modernist
thinking on the continuities and the habits of behavior that make
us who we are. It is the task of pastoral care to offer an "ethic of

---

[147] See J. H. Billington, "Education and Culture Beyond 'Lifestyles'" (1986),
pp. 1-6.
[148] *Ibid.*, p. 2.
[149] See *ibid.*, p. 3.

discernment" in which the final discernment is an "inspired intuition" and piety for God's presence in this world. In a Christian context, virtues are part of the challenge to "enflesh" the Gospel. A discussion on the historical context of virtues reveals the difficulty in synchronizing the different perspectives. For example, Aristotle's and Homer's understanding of *arete* differs from that of the New Testament. The New Testament not only promotes virtues such as faith, hope and love, but views humility (the moral for slaves) as one of the corner-stones in the formation of a Christian character.[150]

MacIntyre's conclusion is of importance to the debate on the interplay of values and virtues.[151] In both the New Testament's and Aristotle's comprehension, despite differences, virtue has this in common: it empowers a person to attain that characteristic essential for exercising human *telos*.[152]

Contemporary Protestant ethics incorporates two important concepts: *vision* and *character*. How we see the world influences our disposition. Related to vision is what Hauerwas calls character: the moral determination of the self.[153] Possessing character is even more basic than possessing individual virtues. Character describes the way in which beliefs, intentions and actions enable a person to acquire a moral history which befits his/her nature as a self-determining being.

In a Christian context, virtues and character can never be traits "possessed" by someone. Basically, they are gifts which a person

---

[150] See A. MacIntyre, *Der Verlust der Tugend* (1984²), p. 245.

[151] *Ibid.,* p. 249.

[152] "... eine Tugend ist eine Eigenschaft, die den einzelnen in die Lage versetz, sich auf das Erreichen des spezifisch menschlichen Telos zuzubewegen, gleichgültig ob es natürlich oder übernatürlich ist (Aristoteles, Neues Testament und Thomas von Aquin)" (*Ibid.,* p. 249).

[153] See S. Hauerwas in J. W. Crossin, *What are They Saying about Virtue?* (1985), p. 42.

receives. Meilaender's suggestion that virtue is needed for prudence, and that one cannot achieve moral knowledge and *do* the
right *deed* without *being* virtuous to some extent, is not totally
irrelevant for our discussion.[154] This interplay can help a Protestant approach to exchange its stance on the constructive role of
experience and emotions, for a more existential understanding and
interpretation of grace.[155] Protestant theology frequently regards the matter of virtues with
skepticism.[156] This is largely a result of the fear that virtue might
be viewed as a mere habit and not as responsible behavior; that
the whole idea of virtues would promote perfectionism leading to
selfish behavior; and that virtues would lead to autonomous
behavior, thereby endangering human dependence on God.

The fact that the meaning of the term *arete* (virtue) in the New
Testament differs from that in Greek philosophy also strengthens
the Protestant's negative judgement of values. In the New Testament *arete* does not describe the human attitude, but obedient
behavior in the light of a Godly command.[157] Protestant skepticism

---

[154] See G. C. Meilaender, *The Theory and Practice of Virtue* (1984), p. 24.

[155] "In ihrer Antropologie herrscht das Moment der Subjektivität im Sinne
des Selbstbewusstseins oder der Reflexion vor. Das Fühlen und Empfinden aber
und damit die Erscheinungen des affektiven Lebens ziehen keine theoretische
Aufmerksamkeit auf sich" (K. Stock, *Grundlegung der Protestantischen
Tugendlehre* [1995], p. 15). The role of virtues for a Protestant understanding of
the human is that it conveys faith as a reality with implications for everyday life.
"Eine Tugendlehre die dem Wirklichkeitsverständnisses des Glaubens in refor-
matorischer Sicht entspricht, hat nun für die Kommunikation in der kirchlichen
Öffenlichkeit aber auch für den Beitrag des Christentums zum öffentlichen
Diskurs der Gesamtgesellschaft grösstes Gewicht und weitreichende praktische
Relevanz" (*Ibid.*, p. 17). See *ibid.*, pp. 15-21.

[156] See E. Herms, "Virtue" (1982) p. 481. For a further discussion of recent
literature about virtues within philosophy, see G. E. Pence, "Recent Works on
Virtues" (1984).

[157] See Herms, "Virtue," p. 487.

also increased when, as a result of Thomas Aquinas's view, virtues became confused with Aristotle's more philosophical approach, thereby opening the way for a natural theology.

Yet Scripture does not exclude individual responsibility, self-consciousness, responsibility for personal growth and the quality of human conduct.

> Ethics, which implies the concept of action as responsible behavior, necessarily also implies the idea of an author of action whose lasting constitution makes it possible to distinguish between his single acts and his potencies or capacity for free and self-conscious action ... [158]

In *Back to Virtue*, Kreeft[159] goes beyond the existential paradigm and significance of virtues. He argues that without virtues, civilization is at risk.

> I want to prove three principles, which are related logically in a syllogism:
> 1. Without virtue, civilization dies.
> 2. Without religion, virtue dies.
> 3. Therefore without religion, civilization dies.

Kreeft implies that virtue is necessary for the survival of civilization, while religion is necessary for the survival of virtue. Without moral excellence, right living, goodness, purity, chastity and effectiveness, our civilization is on the road to decline. Civilization needs justice, wisdom, courage and temperance.

A pastoral anthropology cannot ignore the fact that being human includes knowledge and abilities which are part of our personal make-up. This assumption is reflected in the fact that wisdom in Scripture is not purely a spiritual issue. Wisdom has an edifying function in the development of the human ethos. It

---

[158] *Ibid.,* p. 492.
[159] See P. Kreeft, *Back to Virtue* (1986), p. 192.

incorporates an existential knowledge, which reflects discernment and insight concerning general moral issues. Values and virtues should therefore not be seen as separate entities. Both possess a normative and directive function and play a decisive role in determining the character and quality of our personality. *The important contribution which virtues make to maturity lies in the fact that virtues describe the qualitative value of our "being functions" and the characteristics of our basic stance in life.*

For one central issue behind the "Being vs Doing" debate is the virtue theorist's contention that the moral value of Being is not reducible to or dependent on Doing; that the measure of an agent's character is not exhausted by or even dependent on the values of the actions which he may perform. On this view the most important moral traits are what may be called "spiritual" rather than "actional."[160]

Virtues thus promote spirituality, a genuinely integrated lifestyle, human dignity and constructive behavior. "Let us say then … that virtues are in general beneficial characteristics, and ones that a human being needs to have, for his own sake and that of his fellows."[161]

Another important role of virtues is that they aim to influence the human will and to determine human intentions and motives. Human moral disposition is determined by the quality and nature of one's intentions, which cannot be separated from real contexts. Virtues therefore promote the quality not only of individual lives, but also that of society.[162]

Values and virtues provide a driving force in human behavior. They form an integral part of the human will and give rise to

---

[160] See R. B. Louden, "On Some Vices Of Virtue Ethics" (1984), p. 232.

[161] See Foot, *Virtues and Vices and Other Essays in Moral Philosophy*, p. 3.

[162] For the role of liberal values in a pluralistic society, see S. Macedo, *Liberal Virtues* (1991), p. 257.

purposeful and motivated behavior. Positive values contribute towards growth into a virtuous and responsible person. They therefore promote the development of identity and give rise to an integrated life-style and congruent behavior.

2.9 Towards a Psychological Interpretation of Scriptural Texts

Thus far we have discussed the way in which the human I is determined by consciousness and unconsciousness; the role of emotions and thinking in the dynamics between the ego and the self, the characteristics of human personality; the nature of mental health and adulthood; identity and growth; maturity; and the interplay of values and virtues. These issues all present a new challenge to a pastoral anthropology to rethink its stance on a psychological interpretation of scriptural texts. Our exposition of psychological data and the value of personality theories for all pastoral anthropology enables us to pose the following question: is it acceptable for a pastoral exegesis of biblical data and a pastoral hermeneutics to make use of a psychological interpretation of anthropological information to assess what the church has traditionally regarded as revelational material?

In the literature dealing with anthropology in Scripture little attention is given to the hidden or unconscious dimension of our being. Lurking in the human "heart," in our I-awareness or ego-identity, is a dimension unknown to oneself, but known to God and his Spirit. This hidden dimension is known as the *krupta kardias*, the hidden things (secrets) of the human heart. This dimension is deeply involved with human emotions and the motives from which actions unwittingly arise. For example, Paul refers to "what is hidden in darkness" (the unknown) which God will bring to light. He links this to the intentions (*boulás*) of the heart which the Lord will also reveal. In Romans 2:16, Paul says that God will judge the human hidden things (*krupta tón 'anthrópón*) on judgement day. In the previous verse, Paul refers to the Gentiles. By nature (*phusei*), the Gentiles do things according to the law because the works of the law (God's intentions with people) are written in their hearts (Rom 2:15), and the human conscience (*suneidésis*) testifies to this. This connection between God's law and human psychology (heart and conscience) is of special significance to a pastoral anthropology. This depth dimension of the human being is also described in 1 Corinthians 14:25: the non-believer enters the congregation, hears the prophesy, and becomes convinced that the hidden and secret things of his/her heart are revealed.

In the Old Testament, Deuteronomy 29:29 tells of the hidden things that belong to God's special domain. Psalm 19:12 also mentions faults hidden from the author, but known by the Lord, and for which he should be absolved by the Lord.

In Scripture, there is thus a definite link between the hidden unconscious dimension of our being and God's knowledge of it. The context of 1 Corinthians 2:6-16 is the dimension of the hidden wisdom of God, which is revealed by God through his Spirit to people (v.10). Once again, this revelation, is associated with the human spirit's knowledge (*pneuma*). The following important question arises: to what extent may we determine this scriptural information existentially and psychologically so that a "psychological exegesis" in theology may be created?

Theissen asks this question in *Psychologische Aspekte Paulinische Theologie*. According to him, the general conclusion amongst exegetes is that any psychological interpretation of scriptural matter is a poor form of exegesis.[163] Theissen's basic hypothesis

---

[163] See G. Theissen, *Psychologische Aspekte Paulinischer Theologie* (1983), p. 11.

nevertheless is that some or other form of "psychological" interpretation of the text can be accommodated.[164] By "psychological
exegesis" he implies the attempt to view the text as expression
and fulfillment of human experience and relations.[165] Theissen's
intention is not to distort the text anthropologically from a certain
psychological perspective.

He does not wish to read information
about the human between the lines of the text and thus to force a
psychological interpretation onto the text which is not inherently
there. Similarly, he believes that a psychological exegesis does not
work back to the psychic motives of the biblical author, thereby
attaining a better understanding of the author. Its purpose is not
psychoanalysis.

A psychological interpretation of Scripture risks reducing the
Christian faith to a psychic phenomenon, which makes no
allowance for the unique character of faith and its salvific content.
Theissen's attempt towards a "hermeneutic psychology" is nevertheless important because he alerted us to scriptural matter which
sheds light on human psychic processes. Theissen points out that
the believer's relationship with Christ strengthens an "inner dialogue" in which there is a clear association between conscience,
the hidden things of the human heart and God's knowledge
thereof.

Theissen concludes that the "unconscious" is not an unknown
theme in Scripture. It was not Jung, but Paul who first mentioned
human unconscious impulses.[166] The *krupta kardias* (hidden things
of the heart) should thus be understood as those intra-psychic
processes of self-accusation, self-blame, inner conflict and the
quest for true liberation. According to Theissen, God's omniscience,

[164] Weder ("Exegese und Psychologie" [1988], pp. 57f) explains this attempt
of Theissen in his discussion of the latter's exegetical methodology.

[165] See Theissen, *Psychologische Aspekte Paulinischer Theologie*, p. 11.

[166] *Ibid.*, p. 66.

as a type of transsubjective power, is able to reveal the unconscious human dimensions and to sharpen the human conscience. A "psychological exegesis" is based on the following theological presuppositions:

• God's omniscience sees through inner human motives: "God's cardiognosis."[167]

• Human insight (psychic capacity) is not able to judge one's own being. A person's own insight is too limited to do this and thus needs the insight of God's Spirit. There is an essential reciprocal connection between a cardiognosis of God and a pneumatology.

• The deep level of memories, motives and impulses creates an inner reality which operates in combination with the human conscience. Human emotions, memories and conscience are part of our creatureliness and are the media through which revelation takes place. A pastoral anthropology must allow for this dimension.

The issue of a psychological interpretation and reading of different scriptural texts was raised in a very challenging way by Drewermann. He attempts to ascertain whether depth psychology could contribute to the interpretation of scriptural texts.[168] He argues that historical events should be evaluated in terms of conflicts and problems in a person's unique psyche. A psychological approach must make use of what he calls the "rule of inner experience" (Innerlichkeitsregel). The meaning of discourse is disclosed when things, persons and issues, (e.g. the parables) are understood as images of an inner, psychic reality. Religious meaning emerges when hermeneutics allows us to experience, through words, the emotion and conduct of anxiety and imprisonment.[169] The reader of scriptural texts should ask: what is the meaning of

---

[167] Ibid., p. 66.
[168] See E. Drewermann, Tiefenpsychologie und Exegesen (1992³), p. 753.
[169] Ibid., p. 754.

the Word for my own existential experience and being? Without this, exegesis loses its immediate impact.

Drewermann uses the principle of personal simultaneousness: this reveals the existential characteristic of his model. Being, and the question "Who am I?," are more fundamental to this model than the question "What should I do?" Inner truth and knowledge have priority over behavior and external actions.[170] The task of hermeneutics is to bring the deeper levels of existential anxiety to consciousness. If it fails to do this, hermeneutics faces the danger of becoming merely a process of moralizing. Faith is more basic than ethics. Faith develops when the ego is confronted with its own existential anxiety, and is restored to the being it should be, and increasingly can become.

The function of depth psychology is to uncover the paradox of anxiety and belief, neurosis and self-discovery, suppression and truth. Existential anxiety provides the context within which the contrast and distinctiveness between God and humans is interpreted. Depth psychology therefore prevents being from becoming merely action (the danger of a moralistic interpretation). It also prevents theology from understanding the contrast between God and human beings in terms of a metaphysical abstraction — the Protestant notion of the *extra-nos* character of grace.[171] Understanding God's Word should create a basic experience of trust which liberates being from anxiety. Drewermann's argument implies that the tension between historical fact and the content of faith is bridged within the inner experience of the psyche.

Drewermann's viewpoint, when applied to the field of pastoral care, means that therapy's task is to reveal the symbols in the psyche which create a feeling of basic trust. The therapist should

---

[170] *Ibid.,* p. 755.
[171] *Ibid.,* p. 757.

not "preach" and proclaim the images of trust. (This approach would make the person feel forced.) The therapist should rather step back and create an environment of trust. Healing and salvific symbols should not be taught, but should be experienced through basic trust.[172]

It could be argued that Drewermann's model endangers the factual and historical character of biblical tradition. The danger of a psychological reduction is evident. Is the indwelling presence of the Spirit of God not more than a "psycho-drama"? Nevertheless, the value of Drewermann's approach lies in the way it arouses us anew to the existential implications of biblical truth. A hermeneutical interpretation becomes sterile when it does not touch the deeper level of our emotions and existential experience.

Drewermann describes the task of religion as bringing peace to our existential anxiety.[173] He assumes that religion cannot change a person. Religion's task is rather to free our reason (*Vernunft*) from anxiety-based delusions. Religion can initiate a "dream of trust" (*Traum des Vertrauens*), for instance, the ritual of the Eucharist, with its dimension of forgiveness and spirituality. Such a dream is more than a "principle of hope." It actualizes an alternative for our personhood, it reveals what we suppress in the unconscious and it creates a new identity. Drewermann calls it the "self-healing of the psyche in the light of a diagnosis made within the unconsciousness."[174] Symbols in religion, such as the Eucharist, function as a psychological event which bring about a "psycho-drama" of healing. The intention of such a psycho-drama is to break through the inner spiral of anxiety,[175] through experiencing the awareness of trust, as expressed by acts of love.

---

[172] *Ibid.*, p. 771.
[173] See E. Drewermann, *Die Spirale der Angst* (1991⁴), p. 339.
[174] *Ibid.*, p. 341.
[175] See E. Drewermann, *Zeiten der Liebe* (1992⁴), pp. 7-37.

The Drewermann debate alerts pastoral care to the fact that psychology fails when it leaves people with their loneliness.[176] Theology becomes sterile when it does not consider the psyche and its pathology. It challenges pastoral theology to rethink the possibility of the psychological effect of grace and the presence of God in our lives.

This information makes a pastoral anthropology aware once again of the fact that the process of salvific concretizing cannot be fulfilled without human material. Faith also has a "psychic dimension," and there is a reciprocal link between faith actions, faith concepts and conditions of consciousness. Faith and the work of God's Spirit thus influence people in their depth consciousness. There are fields of contact in a person's depth consciousness which transcend the level of analytical reasoning and thought and point to the interaction between the human spirit and the Godly Spirit.

The link between human spirit and the transcendental focus of human existence creates a network of hidden dimensions, within which influences from "outside" affect life. The acknowledgement of this depth dimension of consciousness (unconsciousness) within religion was brought to the attention of the human scientific research mainly as a result of Jung's research. In his work, *A History of the Cure of Souls,* McNeill says that Jung's research has penetrated the materialistic and deterministic view of the psyche. His discovery of the collective dimensions of the unconscious with its symbols, once again brings the importance of religion to the attention of psychology. Jung's view that faith should be viewed as an important source for healing and therapy, underlines the considerable contribution that pastoral care could make in this field.[177]

---

[176] See K. Walter in Drewermann, *Zeiten der Liebe,* p. 8.

[177] See J. T. McNeill, *A History of the Cure of Souls* (1951), p. 322.

In contrast to Freud, Jung states that human basic faith needs are just as strong as sexual needs. In fact, the former needs are stronger, because sexual needs can be suppressed. In addition to faith needs, ambition also functions as a driving force in the ego, and often is stronger than sexual urges.

In his later works, Jung increasingly links this human drive and purposeful power to the "transcendental functions" of religious needs.[178] Transcendence allows one to soar to the level of a hero, a holy or a mythical figure. For Jung, transcendence is not related to a metaphysical factor, but to the process of symbol-formation.

In *Psychological Types*, Jung defines symbols as the expression of meaning concerning life's inexplicable dimension. He quotes Paul as an example:

> The way in which St Paul and the early mystical spectators handle the symbol of the Cross shows that for them it was a living symbol which represented the inexpressible in an unsurpassable way.[179]

Jung's approach can be described as purpose- and transcendence-oriented. Jung believes that the purpose of life and the symbols which express meaning are more important than the biographic causes of the human condition. An experience of meaninglessness develops as a result of a process of self-alienation: this means that consciousness has strayed too far from the unconscious. In order to conquer this self-alienation, a person should opt for self-fulfillment. By returning to the unconscious, the ego succeeds in healing its relation with the psyche.

Jung explains the concept "psyche" in *On the Nature of the Psyche*. He links archetype and psyche and describes the archetype

---

[178] On the connection between transcendental functions and religious needs in Jung's psychology, see C. Wilson, *Lord of the Underworld* (1984), p. 87.

[179] See C. G. Jung, *Psychological Types or the Psychology of Individuation* (1946), p. 602.

as "the authentic element of spirit, but a spirit which is not to be identified with the human intellect since it is the latter's *spiritus rector*."[180] Within the archetype, the human spirit displays a link with the element of faith that is present in religion and mythology. "The archetype is spirit of pseudo-spirit: what it ultimately proves to be depends on the attitude of the human mind."[181] The archetype is thus connected via the human spirit to the psyche. The archetype itself is not psychic, but manifests itself within the psychic dimension of human existence.[182] Jung's pronouncement means that the unconscious human factor is linked to a spiritual dimension which transcends the psychic capacities and creates a field of contact with the transcendental or religious dimension of meaning. Archetypes,[183] as potential in the human spirit and psyche, offer the opportunity for new life; they save one from isolation and introduce the relation: God and cosmos.[184]

Jung's linkage of the human spirit and the transcendental dimension of archetypes for a pastoral care which deals with the interplay between Spirit and spirit, is significant. Although Jung still describes the phenomenon "spirit" in terms of psychology, his acknowledgement of the value of religion in psychotherapy is of great importance to pastoral care. Psychology thus confirms a scriptural truth: God's Spirit teaches the human spirit. The difference between Jung's archetypal and scriptural transcendence is as follows: the former does not offer true freedom from anxiety. In

---

[180] See C. G. Jung, *On the Nature of the Psyche* (1973³), p. 125.

[181] *Ibid.*, p. 116.

[182] *Ibid.*, p. 125.

[183] In his study about Jung's psychology J. Jacobi (*The Psychology of C. J. Jung* [1968²], pp. 48-49) explains the archetypes as follows: "Thus for Jung the archetypes as a whole represent the sum of the latent potentialities of the human psyche — a vast store of ancestral knowledge about the profound relations between God, man and cosmos."

[184] See *ibid.*, p. 49.

contrast, when the human spirit contacts God's Spirit, one is liberated from anxiety and guilt. One's being is focused anew on a field of meaning that is not determined by archetypes, but by the symbols of eschatology. The link between pneumatology, spirit and human psyche remains important for a pastoral anthropology. The importance of this connection is emphasized in Paul's description of the *krupta kardia* as those hidden dimensions within which the human conscience is addressed by God's omnipresence.

A further important question in the design of an anthropology for a pastoral strategy is: what role does the human conscience play in a theological anthropology?

2.10 The Significance of the Human Conscience for Pastoral Anthropology

We have already pointed out that morality is not merely a moral category. Morality includes both the ethical dimension of norms and values as well as the existential dimension of "being functions." A person is profoundly moral, not only because one's life is determined by ethical norms, but because of God's claim to one's life. It has been pointed out that the conscious and unconscious dimensions of the human mind refer to symbols and a transcendence in which guilt and feelings of guilt play an important role. How should conscience be viewed as part of a pastoral anthropology?

The Greek concept *suneidésis* was originally used to describe the human capacity to get in touch with oneself, especially when forced to view one's past. This concept gradually attained a moral significance. The ability to look back and to justify oneself implies a good conscience; whereas feeling guilty implies a bad conscience.

In ancient literature, the conscience was increasingly seen as a kind of watchdog over human actions, or as the human's own inherent court of justice and critical power of discernment. In the Old Testament, the Israelite awareness of both the covenant and of God's presence was so strong that the concept "conscience," as such, did not function. Guilt was directly linked to an awareness of responsibility towards the Torah. The human heart functioned as the conscience (Ps 51:10).

According to Romans 2:15, the conscience operates critically to keep awareness of guilt alive. In his relationship with co-believers, Paul often mentions the conscience (2 Cor 4:2; Acts 24:16). The close association between conscience and God is thus an important scriptural perspective. 1 Peter 2:19 mentions the conscience before God. 1 Peter 2:21 points out the good conscience and the reality of resurrection. According to 1 Timothy 1:19 faith and a good conscience are inseparable: a good conscience is a characteristic of Christian life, which has been transformed and focused anew through faith. "In short, the conscience can be regarded as the place where the 'mystery of faith' is to be found (1 Tim 3:9)."[185] Hebrews 9:14 declares that Christ's blood cleanses "our consciences from acts that lead to death so that we may serve the living God." Hebrews 10:22 also refers to cleansing the conscience. Although the voice of the conscience itself is not ultimately normative, the conscience nevertheless functions sensitively and critically and results in an awareness of guilt. The human conscience should be transformed by faith. Only forgiveness in Christ can cleanse the conscience. The conscience is "good" nonetheless, because, in co-operation with faith, it convinces the new person of his/her new condition of life in Christ. The Word and knowledge of the salvific reality provide the conscience with a new orientation

---

[185] See H. C. Hahn, "Conscience (*Syneidesis*)" (1975), p. 351.

for its critical discernment. This new point of orientation is salvation in Christ and the reality of the new life's resurrection. The pain experienced within the conscience in moral issues functions like a red light, alerting people to the ethical implications of their actions and keeping them sensitive to the influence of the salvific reality.

The intention of this description of the conscience is not to imply that the conscience is localized in a specific organ or is a faculty of the human personality.[186] Several factors play a role in forming and sharpening the conscience.

Firstly, education and knowledge of norms and values, as well as the social context, all play an important role in forming the human conscience. Secondly, the conscience is further sharpened by the human memory and mind. Thirdly, a link also exists between the conscience and the unconscious dimensions in the human spirit. All these aspects underline the fact that the conscience is indeed a complex phenomenon. It is coincident to the human awareness of guilt, bound to norms and values, and provides the critical power of discernment between right and wrong.

Because it acts as a warning mechanism, the conscience also has a prohibiting function. The link between conscience and norms means that the conscience plays an important role in a theological anthropology. Nevertheless, real danger lies in regarding the conscience, with its prohibiting function, as a direct voice or as the will of God. When formulating a theological anthropology, we must be careful not to elevate the conscience to a medium of revelation. The human conscience is the voice of each individual's own internalized system of norms: the content of the conscience could thus be described as internalized values. The conscience

---

[186] See G. Peterson, *Conscience and Caring* (1982), p. 3 for a discussion of the problem how to describe the conscience.

also has a critical awareness which latches onto the remembering functions of consciousness.

A theological anthropology may assess the conscience — providing it regards it as an internalized system of norms, a warning mechanism and critical discerning organ — as a medium through which the Word of God works. Our Christian conscience is now sensitive to the fact that the Christian's entire life is determined by God's will, as this is revealed in Scripture. The conscience itself is not God's voice, but, through the work of God's Spirit, the human conscience is able to divert one from evil and to direct one toward God's ultimate meaning for human life.

The arguments and issues raised in this chapter, together with Paul's link between faith and the conscience, enable us to conclude that the conscience is regulatory in the process of faith development. The conscience directs knowledge of the Word to the human decision-making abilities and moral behavior. The conscience thus becomes critical in the process of decision-making. It warns one and serves as an early alarm. The conscience feeds not only the actual human consciousness, the *krupta kardia*, but also feeds the anticipatory consciousness of the new person. By "anticipatory consciousness" is meant the believer's pre-consciousness: that is, knowledge concerning the eschatological hope of the coming Kingdom of God. The conscience plays a constructive role in generating moral behavior. It is the task of pastoral care to influence the human conscience positively. In order to do this effectively, pastoral care should focus on the following three tasks:

• To feed the human conscience with knowledge and information of God's norms and values for the new life. Pastoral care encourages the new moral being in his/her focus on the new salvific reality. Hence, the importance of virtues for moral development.

• To liberate the conscience from a negative retrospection and introspection which imprisons people in their guilt and isolates them, as a result of their anxiety, from the future.

• To bind the conscience to positive promises which help the human spirit daily to anticipate the new life in hope, and to give expression to this new life by charitable deeds.

A good conscience creates an inner awareness of having been completely freed from guilt. This liberated conscience is "kept alive" by co-believers' admonition within the mutual and corporative fellowship of *koinonia*. The conscience and the body of Christ thus remain linked inextricably.

2.11 The Interplay between Pastoral Anthropology and Psychology of Religion: Design for a "Psychology of Grace"

This section attempts to overcome the dualistic model in which pastoral care only deals with faith and the spiritual dimension, while psychology deals solely with the mind, personality and behavior. Although their perspectives and focal points are not synonymous, faith and psychology do not exclude each other. The following questions arise in a bipolar approach: what is the effect of a theology of grace on psychology? What psychic effect does grace have on behavior? How does a theological transformation process change the human psyche and structure of personality? The question is equally important whichever way one considers it. How do psychic processes and a psychic predisposition influence the acceptance, realization and concretizing of grace? This raises other questions: is it possible to speak of a "psychology of grace"? What psychological reactions release grace in a person? What is meant by "faith

experience" and "faith behavior"? What connection exists
between the Christian faith and the more common phenomenon
of religious experience? These last few questions indicate the
problem of the so-called psychology of religion. This is a science which does not receive enough attention in pastoral care,
yet could play an important role for a better understanding of
the influence of theological concepts and symbols on human
experience and behavior.

"A psychology of religion" means the study of religion, rang-
ing from the biological basis of behavior to social psychological
factors which effect a change of attitude and behavior. The wide
scope of this field is mirrored in the diverse psychological
accounts of how religious behavior arises and how religious
beliefs and attitudes are formed. While debates continue about
what distinguishes religious from non-religious or irreligious
activity, the differentiation between institutional and personal
religion, which is attributed to William James,[187] is regarded as
"classic." To James, institutional religion concerns theology,
ceremony and ecclesiastical organization, while personal religion
concerns a person's inner disposition: conscience, helplessness,
and incompleteness.

This section deals more with the dispositional than the institutional components of religion. It is an attempt to describe the
experiential, personal and existential consequences of grace in
people's lives and their social context. Pastoral care should pay
attention to those studies conducted by human sciences, which
indicate the positive effect of religion on human behavior. In this
discussion, allowance should be made for the already classic

[187] William James (*Varieties of Religious Experience,* ed. M. E. Marty
[Harmandsworth, 1983], cited in M. A. Jeeves, "Psychology of Religion"
(1988), p. 543.

distinction between Freud and Jung concerning religion. Jeeves summarizes this distinction as follows:

> While for Freud, psychology pointed to religion as a neurosis which in time could be dispelled and the patient cured, for Jung religion is an essential activity of man and the task of psychology is not to explain away religion, but to try and understand how man's nature reacts to situations normally described as religious.[188]

While Freud views religion as an obsessional neurosis, Jung believes that the absence of religion was the chief cause of adults' psychological disorders. Jung's hypothesis gives rise to the following questions: what role could faith play in preventing pathology? What is the existential outcome of a Christian understanding of grace?

The connection between faith and experience is significant. It immediately implies that theological concepts and symbols remain abstract unless they affect, change and influence human psychic structure and behavior on an existential level. After all "faith" means: *I* believe. Faith affects how one understands oneself, thereby influencing one's self-esteem and identity. But "I believe" also means: I choose and I act. Thus, faith and behavior cannot be separated. Faith has a definite subjective component which is essential for pastoral practice. In order to obtain a better understanding of what could be called "faith experience" and "faith behavior," we will now turn our attention to the general field described as the psychology of religious experience and to the specific nature of faith behavior. Only after examining these areas, can we determine what negative components are hidden in theology which could cause disturbances on the psychic level, and vice versa. This will eventually lead us to the problematic field of the so-called "pathology of faith."

---

[188] See *ibid.*, p. 545.

The Psychology of Religious Experience

When approached scientifically, the field of religious experience is very complex. Because of its linkage to the human quest for transcendence, it is very difficult to deal with religion merely as an empirical phenomenon. "Religious experience" describes a part of human reality which cannot be dealt with totally at an empirical level. Nevertheless, because of its relevancy, this area cannot be ignored, least of all by pastoral theology.

Otto's work in the field of religious experience has been seminal. In a certain sense his work, *Das Heilige*, is a classic. Earlier attempts had been made to understand religious experience. Schleiermacher referred to the experience of transcendency as a feeling and subjective consciousness of ultimate dependence (*Gefühl schlechthinniger Abhängigkeit*). Calvin, when speaking of the so-called *semen religionis*, referred to religious experience as a primitive human sensing of the presence of God in creation. In Romans 1:19, Paul refers to a knowledge of God being available and within reach of all people.

> For since the creation of the world God's invisible qualities — his eternal power and divine nature — have been clearly seen, being understood from what has been made, so that men are without excuse (Rom 1:20).

While all these pronouncements are not quite the same as the hypotheses and findings of the more general psychology of religion, yet undeniably they deal with the same issue: the human awareness of transcendency. An awareness of transcendency is linked to the field of symbols and metaphors: these point to a reality beyond the level of general sensory perception. Rationality and empiricism do not have the final say here. Religious experiences refer to a field where people, influenced by their cultural tradition and religious past, give meaning to those symbols which focus on the human experience of transcendence. Empirical research nevertheless tries to understand and to describe the phenomenon of religious experiences, and the way in which these are connected to the attainment of holiness, their mystical power, and ability to instill awe in a believer. "The sacred power that is beyond man yet related to him and carries potent social implications."[189]

The attempt by humans to understand that which transcends one's own experience (that is, the transcendent factor) results in the use of symbols. This human capacity for symbolizing opens up an avenue for psychology to understand more about the self-exceeding process towards transcendency. Müller-Pozzi regards religious symbols as psychic representations of what lies beyond all inner boundaries. Symbols are the result of human imaginative contact with the influence of a reality external to the human sphere of power. In the symbols *the sacred are, phenomenologically speaking, embodied and enfleshed* (my translation).[190] The symbol "God" becomes a psychic representative for the experience of a transcendental reality.

Those studying the psychology of religion often seek the origin of this process of symbolizing in a child's development, especially in relationships towards parents. Belief in God and specific God-images gradually replace the child's parental dependence. The God-image thus attains negative or positive associations in the light of existing parental representations. Idealized parental traits are transferred to the God-image and are portrayed in further symbols. This explanatory hypothesis has given rise to various psychoanalytical theories, all of which offer interesting perspectives which can improve the pastor's understanding of the complexity of faith behavior.

---

[189] See L. B. Brown, *The Psychology of Religious Belief* (1987), p. 18.

[190] See H. Müller-Pozzi, *Psychologie des Glaubens* (1975), p. 147.

In a certain sense, Freud can be regarded as one of the pioneers in the field of research on religious experiences. He incisively subjected the religion of the Jewish-Christian tradition to intensive criticism. Freud's analysis of the influence of religion on the human psyche was mainly negative. He reduced religious experiences to the area of neurotic behavior.

> Belief in God is constructed from childhood feelings of dependence upon the strength and protection of one's human father. Freud concluded that religion is an illusion, meaning that its primary source, its basic authority, lies in our unconscious drives within.[191]

The influence of the super ego is such that religious norms and values, as transmitted by parents, can hamper the development of the ego.

In *The Birth of the Living God*, Rizzuto describes God as a "transitional object," established especially during childhood, and arising out of the child's quest for objects which represent security and intimacy.

> God is a special type of object representation created by the child in that psychic space where transitional objects — whether toys, blankets, or mental representation — are provided with their powerfully real illusory lives.[192]

A psychoanalytical study of faith explains religious experiences in terms of unconscious processes, psychic needs and neurotic behavior. Jung provides a more positive assessment of the value of religious experiences, regarding them as constitutive for the psyche. According to him, religious experiences latch onto the creative dimension of the human collective-unconsciousness and the process of symbolizing.

Current research in the psychology of religion leans increasingly towards a positive description of the value of religious experiences.

---

[191] See G. D. Weaver, "Psychology of Religion" (1986), p. 201.
[192] See A.-M. Rizzuto, *The Birth of the Living God* (1979), p. 177.

Brown comments: "Religion therefore appears to have a strongly supportive social role and it has been found to contribute to rated life satisfaction."[193]

Vergote focuses on the idea that religion is a social phenomenon with constructive value within a cultural context. He sees religion as part of human collective awareness, as well as providing subjective conditions of consciousness. Because religion is part of the human system of symbols, it cannot be completely explained and analyzed. "Religion is a symbolic system that belongs to what Popper calls the third world. It is present in humanity as an ensemble of languages, references and meanings, and prescriptions."[194] Vergote also contends that religious behavior should not be studied with regard only to its positive effects; studies should also include negative reactions like doubt, for example. Religious faith should thus also be understood from its possible antithesis: unbelief. Vergote's supposition is that phenomena like doubt, agnosticism and atheism should be studied for a better understanding of what factors play a role when people accept faith.

The psychology of religion is described as the examination of religious experiences, actions and structures associated with the human quest for transcendent meaning. James, the well-known researcher in this field, describes religious experiences as those events which exceed the experience of loneliness in relation to the Godly dimension — he calls this "overbelief." In his study, *Psychologie van de Religie*, Roscam Abbing describes a religious person as being open and receptive. *The open, receptive person indeed has an antenna focused on the supersensual* (my translation).[195] This area of the supersensual is linked to a field of reality

---

[193] See L. B. Brown, *The Psychology of Religion* (1988), p. 126.

[194] See A. Vergote, "Psychology of Religion as the Study of the Conflict Between Belief and Unbelief" (1985), p. 54.

[195] See P. J. Roscam Abbing, *Psychologie van de Religie*, (1981), p. 143.

or an object. Because this object results in faith, piety, and moral and cultural issues in both personal and public life, Rebell believes that the psychological base structure of these areas may be investigated.[196] The relation to this object and the human reaction within this relation form an important field of investigation for religious psychology. As a result of this relational dimension in religious experience, Roscam Abbing describes the religious person as *being aware of a relation to something supersensual to which he stands in awe* (my translation).[197]

The influence of a transcendental factor on the human being results in respect and awe: possibly the most distinctive characteristic of religious experience. Respect, awe and a form of fear and trembling are part of this reaction. But, on the other hand, religious experiences are also linked to human needs. *Because of a certain subjective destitution, people are in need of a God or something godly, in the hope that it will contribute to alleviating their distress, to satisfying their need* (my translation).[198]

This need may be conscious or unconscious, negative or positive. The role that needs play in religious experiences, means that religion can become a means towards an end or could be used to compensate for deficiencies. All these factors play a role in religious experiences.

Pastoral care, when attempting to guide people in their development of faith, must make allowance for the interaction between the content of faith in God and specific human needs. This interaction may be enriching, or it could hamper faith development. But when the value of religion is evaluated in terms of personal need-satisfaction and when emotional needs become normative,

---

[196] See Rebell, *Psychologisches Grundwissen für Theologen*, p. 152.
[197] See Roscam Abbing, *Psychologie van de Religie*, p. 160.
[198] *Ibid.*, p. 160.

then this excessive emphasis on needs may contribute towards negative religious development.

Need satisfaction and desires undeniably do play a great role in human expectations of religion. In order to understand faith behavior, pastoral care must make allowance for the fact that physical or psychic needs are often the filter through which people perceive God. For example, how Christians understand grace often depends on what emotional needs are dominant. Roscam Abbing identifies the following levels of needs as decisive for an assessment of the value of religion in life.[199]

• The human need to live. Believers expect that God will protect and preserve their lives, provide for their material needs and provide the strength to live. Religion should also guarantee no fear of death, and guarantee that life after death will be worthwhile and meaningful.

• Existential needs. People seek continuance, permanence and meaning in life in order to cope with life issues and succeed in accepting life as a challenge. They need a congruency which creates integration. They seek healing, health and intactness.

• Moral needs. Religion should help people to distinguish between good and evil. When confronted by their own guilt, people have a basic need for forgiveness and redemption.

Although human needs are most refined and complex, their scope has been well described by the above three levels. What is important is that these three levels of need play a valuable role in the significance of a specific religious tradition. An understanding or interpretation of people's religious experiences should thus always allow for interaction between people's needs and the transcendence factor in their lives. Phenomenologically speaking, religious behavior (also expressions of faith) manifests itself as a

---

[199] *Ibid.,* pp. 222f.

result of the interaction between human needs and life's transcendence.

The question arises: what is the difference between religious experiences and specific faith experiences?

In *Reiken naar Oneindigheid*, Weima uses the following basic aspects to clarify the components of religion. Firstly, religion needs an experience of the transcendental or absolute factor. The experience of transcendence can be described as a form of religious perception. Secondly, religion only becomes an issue when people enter into a relation with this transcendental factor. This relation develops contact with the absolute, via phenomena which may be perceived on an experiential level, such as symbols and rituals. Weima therefore describes the main task of a psychology of religion as *the study of the relation between the religious person and the transcendental object as made known through perception* (my translation).[200] Thirdly, religion results in ideological, philosophical or theological consequences. One of the most important consequences of religion is the formation of an ultimate value which imparts meaning and direction to life. Fourthly, religion has ethical consequences: it affects attitudes and behavior towards others. Finally, religion has institutional implications. It results, for example, in a religious community or church.[201]

Weima's description reveals the difficulty of distinguishing between religion and divine worship. Basically, both concern the same issue: the relation with transcendence. They can therefore be regarded as alternate terms. Nevertheless, the difference between religious or divine worship experiences on the one hand and faith experiences on the other, is still important. *Religious experiences are about the symbols, and are directed beyond the empirical*

---

[200] See J. Weima, *Reiken naar Oneindigheid* (1988), p. 21.
[201] *Ibid.*, p. 29.

world to the transcendental dimension. In contrast, it is through faith experiences that a person has a personal commitment to God (life's transcendental factor). Faith experiences bring to this relation a character of trust, reliability and personal devotion. God is perceived as reliable, and trustworthy. The transcendental factor is thus regarded as a source of comfort and inspiration. According to Roscam Abbing, a psychology of faith is about the religious person's need for safety and security.[202]

The psychology of religion applies variable factors which can serve as indicators for empirical research in this field. These indicators facilitate the identification and understanding of religious experiences. These indicators are also important for pastoral care because they promote a better understanding of spiritual experiences. Weima quotes Glock, who divides the variables into the following five groups:

• Religious views (*the ideological dimension*). These encompass the ideological and philosophical components of religious experience. For example, in certain situations religious views tend to allow people to act more conservatively (conservatism), while in others, religious views encourage people to think more liberally (liberalism). A conservative approach has the danger of reticence and rigidity; while a liberal approach has the danger of permissiveness.

• Religious practices (*the ritual dimension*). These are mainly measured in terms of church membership and church attendance.

• Religious feelings (*the experiential dimension*). These are experiences of the subjective or individual component of religion. Although the subjective factor encompasses tremendous variations, it is the easiest to measure.

• Religious knowledge (*the intellectual dimension*). This deals with specific contents which correlate with intellectual intelligence and understanding.

---

[202] See Roscam Abbing, *Psychologie van de Religie*, p. 144.

• Religious behavior (*the dimension of consequence*). This important variant concerns the question whether religious experiences, as such, transform personalities and behavior and whether this leads to change in socially accepted behavior.[203]

In order to get a better understanding of what is meant by "religious experiences," literature distinguishes between *extrinsic religiosity* (religiousness as traditional involvement in structures and rites; strongly dependent on the group or community) and *intrinsic religiosity* (the primary focus is on religious values, as well as on the experience of transcendence).[204] Some researchers describe this focus on values and the experience of transcendence as peak experiences; an intense awareness; sensing the holy/the numinous; an awareness of complete dependence; a disposition of satisfaction, happiness and aesthetic fulfillment; and contact with mysticism.

Freud's regression theory described mainly the extrinsic component of religious experience. In contrast, religious experiences are described today as a vitally important, constitutive factor, even despite their possible disintegrating effect on behavior. All forms of religious experience are regarded as an important part of growth and development of the personality.[205] Religion does not develop only out of regressive behavior. Religion is not the result of people suddenly seeking comfort during difficult circumstances;

---

[203] See Weima, *Reiken naar Oneindigheid*, pp. 40-43.

[204] The distinction between extrinsic and intrinsic religiosity has been criticized by several scholars (D. Hutsebaut, "Post-critical belief: A new approach to the religious attitude problem" [1996], p. 48). The impression has been created that the intrinsic is more mature than the extrinsic. In his study Hutsebaut distinguishes three types of religious attitudes: the orthodox believer who thinks in a rather literal way; the symbolic believer who thinks in a historical relativistic way; the unbeliever who is coloured by the external critique and who emphasizes human autonomy in opposition to God (pp. 62-63).

[205] *Ibid.*, p. 77.

or of extremely frustrated people in a crisis; or of unstable personalities, exposed to exceptional anxiety; or of socially suppressed groups, the deprived and victimized in society. On a positive level, religion could form part of a person's ability to adapt in a situation: mystic or peak experiences could indicate psychic health.

The claim to contact with a transcendental being is evaluated currently by the majority of religious psychologists as more than merely inner or subjective feelings or a mental condition. Otto describes contact with the holy as the numinous factor of our being. Otto also describes the nature of similar numinous experiences, thereby shedding light on the nature of faith experiences. We briefly discuss his view here, as expounded by Weima.[206]

Experience of the numinous possess the following dimensions:

• the *tremendum*. An experience of awe in fear and trembling. This fear is different from fear or anxiety. It implies a respect for the impact and immediate presence of the Other's uniqueness and holiness.

• the *majestus*. The uniqueness of the Other is experienced as majestic, implying superior power.

• a driving force, energy and motivation. Frankl describes this dimension as the *noödynamic* issue of existence. Contact with the numinous manifests in energetic will and drive because the Other is experienced as alive and real.

• the *mysterium*; the Other is experienced as totally different because this is beyond the human sphere and daily experiences.

• the *fascinans* — the Other has an appealing and irresistible effect, inspiring the imagination. The *fascinans* often encompasses religious bliss or peace. Such an experience of peace surpasses our rational faculties.

---

[206] *Ibid.*, pp. 105-109.

• the issue of *augustum*. The Other attains an indicative, objective meaning which calls for respect and results in commitment with specific implications or obligations (*obligatio*). The numinous now attains a meaning with absolute value.

Surrender; acknowledgement of the authority of the Other; commitment, responsibility and obedience; respect, value and esteem; trust; and the feeling of unity, integration and harmony are all essential for an understanding of religious experiences. Research in the psychology of religion has enabled pastoral care to gain a better understanding of the nature, structure and functioning of religious behavior. This enables the pastor to assess more accurately the quality of a person's experience of faith. It also allows pastoral care to realize anew that a theological anthropology cannot be practised in a vacuum: that theological contents (*e.g.*, grace) have a definite impact on faith experiences. Knowledge of religious experiences and the results of research being done by a psychology of religion thus help to build a framework for the development of a pastoral hermeneutics which aims to link people's life stories with the story of salvation.

The Psychological Implications of Faith Contents: a Psychology of Grace and Faith

Very little research has been done thus far by pastoral care on the possibility of a "psychology of faith." This can be ascribed to the fact that it is impossible to reduce the phenomenon of faith, within the context of the Reformed tradition, to a psychological phenomenon.[207] Yet, nobody can deny that faith has psychological implications and affects personal behavior.

---

[207] See Rebell, *Psychologisches Grundwissen für Theologen*, p. 151.

The reason why theology in general, and pastoral care in particular, has been wary of a psychology of faith can be ascribed to the relationship between *fides qua creditur* and *fides quae creditur*. *Fides qua creditur* usually refers to a personal or subjective experience of the content of our faith; it describes a human reaction to revelation and deals with the "how" of faith. In contrast, *fides quae creditur* denotes content: the "what" of faith in terms of God's salvific actions and the forensic character of salvation.

There is no doubt that faith has two sides: a subjective-existential component and an objective-juridical component. But can the relation between the "how" and the "what" of faith be described by means of an ontological paradigm? An ontological comprehension in terms of a metaphysical model implies that subjective reaction (A) and objective condition (B) are two separate and unique entities. Thus, in such a model, the involvement of A with B means that A can affect the nature of B to such an extent that B will be assimilated by A, thereby losing its uniqueness.

In contrast to the metaphysical understanding of ontology, the hermeneutic approach sees the relation between *fides qua* and *fides quae* in communicative, relational or personal terms. The hermeneutic paradigm is not about the relation between human reaction and objective content, but is an interpretation and understanding of salvation in terms of human existence and need. Salvation is accepted as an eschatological reality and as a deed of God's grace. The question is how salvation may be known, understood, interpreted and transmitted in such a way that a person can understand God's personal involvement with life. The relation between *fides qua* and *fides quae* should therefore be conceived more in terms of a hermeneutic, than a metaphysical model.

The same applies to the declaration: *gratia perficit naturam*. Reformed theology has avoided this declaration because the relation between nature and grace has been understood in ontological categories. Reformed theology feared that such a declaration could underestimate the sinfulness of human nature. When grace "influences" nature, the effect of such a contact between grace and nature could bring about an integration in which a person could become part of the Godly nature and, ultimately, be perceived as having contributed substantially to grace. This contact could result in a dangerous human deification and a disastrous humanizing of God. But, if nature and grace are understood in terms of a relation, then theology can look afresh at a declaration like: *gratia perficit naturam*. The framework for a psychological and existential hermeneutics of grace does not explain the nature of this relation ontologically, but understands this relation in the light of the behavioral and ethical implications of grace. Of course, such a hermeneutical approach cannot be viewed apart from a pneumatological understanding of the God-human relation. *Gratia perficit naturam* means that grace releases an immanent and inner power which changes a person's total outlook on life and ultimate function.

A "psychology of faith," and, more especially, "a psychology of grace," implies something other than merely the religious experiences described by the psychology of religion. It does not attempt to explain religious images and symbols within the framework of human behavior and psychic needs, as an empirical model would do. A psychology of grace is concerned with the transforming effect and consequence of grace on a person's psychic functions. Its aim is to describe the influence of God's undeserved grace on human conduct and relations.

Reformed anthropology has been dominated thus far by the more theoretical and ontic problem: a person as a sinner. This approach perforce raises the question about a person acting as a co-operating and contributing factor in the process of salvation and the accomplishment of grace. For reasons that can be easily understood, Reformed theology has always reacted negatively to this approach. The Reformed principle of "grace alone" has often been interpreted as a causal and explanatory factor for faith, thereby ignoring any effect this might have on human behavior. The possibility of an experience of faith has often been strongly opposed. The relationship between nature, sin and grace was introduced in this debate as a result of over-hasty reactions arising from the fear that a person could be regarded as being able to contribute towards salvation. All references to human creative functions were rejected as synergism.

A psychology of grace is not a disguised form of synergism. Instead, it encompasses a type of phenomenology which could promote the pastor's understanding of the complicated relation between personal identity, spiritual identity and a mature faith. A psychology of grace does not intend to practice an ontology of faith: its intention is not to declare the origin of faith only in terms of psychic and existential needs. It merely describes the context of faith experiences. After all, it is people who believe and personalities which should internalize faith.

The term "a psychology of grace" could also be understood as follows. A psychology of grace is not a discussion about sanctification or sanctifying grace. The sanctifying nature of grace is assumed as the theological context and background. A psychology of grace is more concerned about a secondary level: the effect of grace in human conduct and behavior. It examines psychic images and those structures within which sanctification emerges, thereby correlating the human psychic structure and the social context. Because it is based on the assumption that salvation in Christ has a healing effect, a psychology of grace, inter alia, involves the therapeutic effect of salvation on psychic functions.

Meissner formulates the problem facing the psychology of grace as follows: "The question that the psychology of grace poses is the question of human nature and of what changes may occur in it under the influence of grace."[208]

Meissner regards this interactionary link too much in ontological terms. Even though Meissner tried to avoid it, the following comment indicates this direction: "Under grace, man becomes a unified, integral existent whose existence becomes specifically supernatural."[209] Meissner's basic hypothesis is nevertheless important to a psychology of faith and grace.

> My basic conviction in this regard is that the action of grace must make a difference to the living of the Christian life. It must alter our experience and the course of our life cycle. This does not mean that the action of grace is itself immediately experienced, but it does mean that we are somehow changed and presumably spiritually assisted and advanced by its influence.[210]

What transforming effect does grace have on the human psyche, thereby causing spiritual identity to play a role in personal identity?

A psychology of grace attempts to describe the influence which the content of faith has on the human I and the issue of self-esteem. Because a person is a unity, the ego, as the center of conscious orientation (the acting, thinking, feeling and volitional ego), is the decisive factor in the process of concretizing faith. An interactionary link thus exists between spiritual and personal development, because both processes are exercised in and through the same ego functions. Although the sources of spiritual identity (grace) and personal identity (self-actualization) differ fundamentally, they can never be separated radically.

Meissner believes that the task and role of grace is to serve as an energy factor, dynamo or driving force. Grace becomes a

---

[208] See Meissner, *Life and Faith*, p. 5.
[209] *Ibid.*, p. 8.
[210] *Ibid.*, p. 7.

mobilizing factor, which actively integrates human behavior. "Grace is the energizing and relational principle on the spiritual level for the proper functions of the ego."[211] According to Meissner, the effect of grace on the psychic level results in an improved autonomous self-determination and control over needs and emotions.

A "psycho-spiritual identity" means a certain reorganization and restructuring of psychic functions in the light of ultimate values and norms. A psycho-spirituality describes a new form of commitment, devotion, and faithfulness. As a result of the influence of grace, the character of this commitment, can be described as *unconditional devotion*.

In order to understand the nature of psycho-spirituality, we need to regard the cognitive functions of the human mind as key factors for the realization of faith. Grace becomes operationalized because of the function of the following cognitive processes.

• *Semantic integration*: Cognitive skills are necessary to grasp, understand and know grace better. Grace is understood by means of existing concepts and the rational faculties of the human mind.

• *Internalization* describes a process through which those values and goals which are unique to the sphere of grace, become part of human daily orientation to life. By identifying with Christ's work, the person is able to accept the norms of the new life in Christ as criteria for personal actions.

• *Synthesis* is the process through which the ego's abilities and the effect of grace are meaningfully linked, thereby creating a condition of peace and harmony which offers tranquility and security to the ego.

[211] *Ibid.*, p. 58.

In addition to these three cognitive functions, the ego also has three general functions which determine the relation between personal and spiritual identity.[212]

• *The principle of reciprocal influencing*: Defects in the ego (for example poor self-esteem and feelings of inferiority) could hamper the influence of grace. Conversely, grace transforms the functioning of the ego by liberating people from selfishness to other-centeredness.

• *The principle of compensation and supplementing*: Grace compensates for the lack of the ego by supplementing the ego's source of energy with an external source, that is, with the power of the Holy Spirit.

• *The principle of epigenesis*: Grace is not detached from a person's organic growth through life's various stages. Meissner speaks of an epigenesis of spiritual identity. According to the epigenetic theory:

– The measure of trust/distrust in the ego structure feeds the character of faith and is directly linked to the problem of doubt.

– The degree of autonomy/independence/self-esteem of the ego influences the process of openness and critical self-examination. The latter is an important component of a constructive understanding of self-renunciation.

– The readiness for initiative and imagination feeds the processes of penitence through which the believer is forced to accept responsibility for his/her deeds.

– The principle of self-activity strengthens the process of self-control and dealing with pain.

- An established ego-identity promotes the acceptance of limitations and restrictions, as well as an attitude of humility.

– The experience of intimacy, creativity and integrity influence the character of Christian virtues. For example, intimacy influences

[212] *Ibid.*, p. 58.

the Christian understanding of love; and creativity influences the Christian application of the principle of service and sacrifice; while integrity strengthens the character of sympathetic charity. The importance of the epigenetic principle lies in the way it makes pastoral care aware of the connection between ego functions and needs during the various stages of life. The process of concretization of faith is clearly not isolated from ego functions. Grace has a threefold effect on ego functions:

– Grace helps the ego towards an internal ego-integration and ego-empowerment.
– Grace influences the ego by promoting the internalization of values, eventually determining the direction, course and priorities of meaningful conduct.
– Grace imparts a dimension of sensitive devotion which liberates the ego from an excessive focus on egoistic, personal needs.

This discussion of a psychology of faith at last raises the question regarding the unique character of faith as a psychic phenomenon. Meissner's basic ideas may be used to answer this question.[213] We have followed the broad outlines of his description, although a few alterations have been made.

• *The paradoxical character of faith*: Faith has a tendency towards regression, in which faith reaches back to the most basic and primitive needs of the human ego: to the level of desires and instinctive powers. Needs often are narcissistic and, according to Freud, latch onto infantile feelings of helplessness and a need for protection and love. But faith also has a tendency towards progression in which it reaches out beyond the transient to the infinite. Faith transcends the finite in hope and anticipation. It is part of the paradox of faith that, as it progresses beyond finitude, it simultaneously regresses to the most primitive level of that finitude.

---

[213] *Ibid.*, pp. 138f.

• *The steadfastness of faith*: Faith is a relation of trust which offers continuance, permanence and security. Faith implies a capacity for trust, receptivity and openness to God, and willingness to accept His Word. It displays confidence in His love and saving power.[214]

• *The commitment and fidelity of faith*: Faith implies fidelity and devotion. The process of surrender and making a commitment provides the believer with a feeling of belonging and identity.

• *The integrative function of faith*: Faith reorganizes and reactivates experiences, feelings and needs into a new psychic composition. This results in a condition of integration, peace and conciliation. Such inner harmony heightens the mature functioning of the ego. Thus, faith has an integrative function in the psychic economy. True faith is restorative, recuperative and effectively maturing.

• *The transforming and transcending effect of faith*: Faith helps to direct the process of indentity formation towards new norms and a reality independent of the limitations of the ego. In the light of what already has been said about the role of a pneumatology in pastoral care, faith directs the human I into a new direction: towards the coming Kingdom of God.

An important anthropological question now arises: does grace guarantee a better and a healthier psychic functioning? Does it necessarily effect a heightened measure of integration and stability? The perspective of grace does not imply that a believer will necessarily act with more stability than an unbeliever. There is even evidence of the contrary in practice. Development of a faith perspective could be accompanied by tension, conflict and doubt. As a result of the eschatological tension between the "already" and the "not yet," grace generates a struggle in the believer: between selfish interests (the old person) and the interests of the

---

[214] *Ibid.*, p. 142.

Kingdom (the new person). The important contribution of the perspective of grace for personal identity is thus not so much an improved psychic stability, but that it provides a fixed point of orientation which could integrate emotional instability and those human interests that have been torn apart. This fixed point of orientation is an external factor: God's faithfulness. Grace has a dual perspective. Firstly, it prevents mankind from becoming victims of their selfishness, guilt feelings and fear of death. Secondly, it offers a point of reference which provides stability and security, despite painful experiences and constant distress. Grace does not function as a panacea to all suffering. Nevertheless, grace does provide a God who can be addressed, and who can even be blamed in anger.

In summary: while a psychology of grace increases the ego's capacity to mobilize its inner resources and to perform more effectively, it also reveals the following perspectives on the understanding of faith:

a) *Motivation*: Grace acts as a dynamic dimension of faith. It provides a driving power and a source of energy which motivate human existence positively.

b) *Reintegration*: Grace offers external support which promotes both the integration of human behavior as well as a positive and constructive self-understanding. Grace thus provides a core of reintegration for behavior. This does not necessarily mean that a person acts with more stability as a result of a mature faith, but merely that the believer now has a point of reference which helps him/her to interpret life in a more coherent context of meaning.

c) *Normativity*: Grace brings about reorganizing and restructuring of ego functions in terms of a new system of values and ultimate meaning. Faith actions now attain an ethical dimension whereby human responsibility may be evaluated. This dimension of normativity promotes purposefulness.

d) *Anticipation*: Grace actualizes anticipation. As a result of the future dimension of faith and its stimulating effect on hope, the believer is able to transcend existing crises in the light of the promissory character of grace.

e) *Trust*: Grace provides a feeling of security and continuity during experiences of uncertainty, making people aware of endurance and permanence.

f) *Significance*: Grace stimulates the human experience of receiving and imparting meaning. Grace opens a dimension of meaning which influences life positively. Its psychological effect is a disposition of joy and gratitude, patience and endurance.

g) *Transformation*: Grace changes people's dispositions and attitudes towards life. It is a transforming power which influences people's way of thinking (cognitive restructuring) and how they adapt and daily orientate themselves (change in attitude).

h) *Koinonia*: Grace provides a support system. The congregation, as the body of Christ, creates a caring community. The *communio sanctorum* functions as a fellowship of believers on the basis of mutual love.

2.12 A Pathology of Faith

The current psychoanalytical assessment of faith is less negative than it was in the past. Psychology regards faith as less obstructive in the development of the child's personality. Nor is religion seen necessarily as the projection of unfulfilled desires. Religion does not develop merely as a result of idealized parental characteristics being transferred to certain religious symbols; faith cannot be described as infantile needs, dependent on parents. The fact that faith plays a positive role in people's development is increasingly being accepted within psychological circles. Faith does not only play a supplementary role with regard to people's values, but essentially is a constructive factor in the development of personality. But faith does become pathological when the focus on God and the interest in faith contents alienate people from their immediate reality, so that their faculties of discernment are blinded by either an artificial identification with God, or an obsessive, and thus unilateral identification, with God. It is extremely difficult to reduce a pathology of faith to a single component. We should rather examine it as a complex phenomenon with various aspects.

Pruyser points out the difference between a pathology of faith, which is a result of a psychiatric factor or a psychic dysfunction, and faith pathology, which results from a distorted interaction between the content of faith and faith behavior.

A distinction can be made between various groups of pathologies of faith.[215] Pruyser identifies the following groups:

a) *Narcissistic disorders* are distinguished by a conspicuously unrealistic self-regard, towards either over-inflation or towards self-deprecation. Delusions of grandeur (megalomania) or self-hatred could play a major role. Grandiosity may lead to attributing superhuman powers and divine or demonic qualities to oneself.

b) *Thought disorders* are coherent with religious delusions which are unrealistic. These include delusional ideas, paranoic schemes, and preoccupation with hyper-symbolic cosmic ideas.

c) *Mood and affective disorders* are uncontrolled emotions, or viewing events out of context. These manifest in unmodulated and immoderate emotions, which are out of proportion with precipitating events or stimuli.

---

[215] See P. W. Pruyser, "Psychopathology and Religion" (1990), p. 1015.

d) *Moral disorders*: The influence of ethics on religion makes people preoccupied with matters concerning right and wrong, virtue and vice, righteousness and sinfulness. This results in irrational feelings of guilt or an overactive or punitive conscience.

e) *Behavioral disorders* involve ritual acts that may resemble or abuse sacramental practices. Compulsive behavior is displayed in excessive ritualizing actions. It is often accompanied by perfectionism, fear of spoiling, and often with exhaustive preparatory movements and postures. A feeling of being torn apart emotionally is caused by excessive and extraordinary forms of doubt which obstruct the normal functioning of faith.

In his outline of faith pathology Rebell points out the following aspects of pathology which affect functioning as a result of excessive forms of doubt and faith behavior.[216]

a) Excessive forms of doubt and disharmony. The feeling of being torn apart emotionally could cause violent conflict concerning certainty and the content of faith.

b) Aggressive behavior. The person concentrates on the sins of others, merely diverting the focal point away from his or her own deficiencies.

c) An extraordinary fear of God's punishment.

d) Spiritual compulsion. This degenerates into unusual religious demands, and results in legalism.

d) Delusions regarding sin. This results from a loss of contact with reality and extreme fear of loss.

e) Masochism. This misuses religion in order to punish oneself and views suffering and pain as a necessary condition for faith.

---

[216] See Rebell, *Psychologisches Grundwissen für Theologen*, p. 159f.

f) A lack of flexibility and intolerance towards others. This results from rigid perceptions and unusually selfish actions.

g) Fanatical actions. This results from a loss of contact with reality, misrepresentations about eschatology, and delusions about future events.

h) Religious fanaticism. This is caused by hysterical traits.

i) Formalism. This results from an extraordinary view of the church as an institution. The person's actions are strongly authoritarian as a result of an overwhelming commitment to church doctrine and dogma.

j) Ascetic practices. This results in a despised life and an eventual degradation of the value of the human body.

k) "Ecclesiogenetic neurosis." Pietistic tendencies can lead to a person viewing the church as exclusive, and therefore practising religion in isolation from other church denominations.

When considering the problem of faith pathology, three important factors must be taken into account. These are:

• *A negative identity*: This is created in reaction to an inappropriate image of God. It is commonly accepted today that infantile father images influence the child's later interpretation and understanding of God. For example, the image of an aggressive, punishing father can be transferred to God so that He is viewed in terms of judgement and vengeance. This gives rise to a negative identity which is based on anxiety and fear of punishment.

• *A fear of resignation*: Faith, as a process of surrender, is rejected because of a fear of self-resignation. A refusal to relate oneself to infinity can give rise to a narcissistic self-assertion, which is based on an inherent fear to be oneself in relation to external factors. The effect of this on faith behavior is often despair, and a false sense of self: a self created out of relentless self-assertion.

• *Obsessive commitment and ideology*: Faith implies total commitment. Fixation takes place when only one aspect of the life of faith is emphasized, to the exclusion of others. When adherence to one issue in the Gospel becomes an obsession and results in over-commitment, there is the danger of ideology. One aspect is absolutized, excluding others. Such an obsession tends to be exclusive and causes intolerant behavior.

> The commitment to ideology tends to be exclusive, even as ideologies themselves tend to be intolerant of each other. The danger, of course is overcommitment ....[217]

In summary, religious pathology is concomitant with inflexible perceptions that have a strong moralistic undertone. A pathology of faith is also connected to: the misuse of religion (when God is used for selfish purposes or when religion is practised to manipulate God); fanatical actions, resulting in a loss of contact with reality; legalistic approaches which are strongly prescriptive and demanding; ascetic behavior which is damaging to life; artificial commitments and pietistic exclusivism. An analysis of these elements reveals that the following fundamental problem often lurks beneath all such pathologies: there is a continuous interaction between a neurotic personality structure and a false or inappropriate perception and image of God. It is extremely difficult, however, to determine whether an inappropriate image of God gave rise to the disorder, or vice versa.

People's concepts of God are an integral element of both their faith and their psychic structure. *God-images in people are internal components of our human psychic structure. They should therefore not be viewed separately or assessed as something apart* (my translation).[218] The close association between psychic structure

---

[217] See Meissner *Life and Faith*, p. 161.
[218] See Rebell, *Psychologisches Grundwissen für Theologen*, p. 165.

and God-images is an important factor which pastoral care should consider most seriously in the development of faith towards maturity. The pastor will thus have to work very carefully when attempting to change people's God-images. A theological correction immediately implies interference in a person's psychic structure. It does not merely alter concepts on a cognitive level, it also affects a person's experience of security and identity. Changes to God-images are thus a painful process, which could meet with strong opposition. This opposition could be accompanied by negative God-images, which have originated in childhood. Paternal and maternal symbols could provide an important source for religious concepts which, at a later stage, become the filters for an understanding of God. This process of formation is also affected by other factors, such as negative associations from catechism, or being exposed to excessive punishment and aggression in the parental home or within a Christian context. In order to alert people to the link between their disorders and God-images, they should be encouraged to describe the nature of their God-image and expectations. These are expressed in faith concepts. Sometimes it may be necessary for people to describe how authoritarian figures acted towards them during their childhood, as well as any traumatic experiences which evoke associations of God. People could also be asked to write a sketch about God or to draw their representation of God. The purpose of these tasks is to identify inappropriate God-images and then to proceed towards discovering appropriate God-images which could be linked to scriptural metaphors such as Father, Friend and Savior.

Care should be taken that any understanding or interpretation of God-images are controlled by careful hermeneutics and thorough exegesis. The purpose of a pastoral hermeneutics is to regard faith development as a dynamic and imaginative process of continual interpretation of God-images. The main function of such a pastoral

hermeneutics is to assess the significance of God-images within
the context of faith development and real life issues. A pastoral
hermeneutics needs a theological vision in order to perform this
diagnostic task. "Christian faith can be characterized accordingly
as faithful imagination — living in conformity to the vision rendered by the Word of God in the Bible."[219]

2.13 Consequences for Theory in Pastoral Ministry

"A praxis of pastoral care" describes how pastoral care works
in the practice of ministry. As such, a praxis of pastoral care needs
to be based on a theory which takes cognizance of three very
important components of pastoral care: human functioning, communication and conversation, and the relationship between pastoral care and psychology. These three components determine the
eventual therapy and practice in pastoral care. The first component
deals with the quest for a model which could promote the pastor's
understanding of how a person functions. This model should also
apply to a theological understanding of persons. On a practical
level, it should reflect our argument concerning a pneumatological
stance. The second component deals with the unique and distinctive character of pastoral counseling. The third touches on a crucial issue: the relationship between theology and human sciences.
Hence, the attention to:
  a) the different dimensions of our being human and its impact
     on a pastoral model;
  b) discourse;
  c) the relation between pastoral care and psychology (psy-
     chotherapy).

---

[219] See G. Green, *Imagining God* (1989), p. 134.

a) Different Dimensions of our Being Human and the Impact on a Pastoral Model

Scripture combines three dimensions: the heart, the reason and the body. Pastoral care is thus obliged to treat a person as a unity, and to ensure that all three dimensions are taken into consideration when designing a model for pastoral care. This model will also be affected by the interplay between Christology and pneumatology. But a fourth dimension to our understanding of persons has now become apparent: the dimension of normativity, and the notion of a person as a moral being endowed with a conscience. When designing a practical model, the four dimensions should be taken very seriously. They should play a decisive role in structuring the counseling processes, for example, and the objective of pastoral therapy. In order to link these four dimensions to this chapter's exposition of a psycho-pastoral model, we must take note of the following four anthropological components: the affective, cognitive, conative and normative. The bodily dimension is not viewed separately in an integrative approach: it should be viewed as the basic instrument through which the four components are exercised and operationalized. Besides the four basic components, very brief reference will be made to two more components — the physical and the koinonic — without discussing them in detail.

• *The affective component*: This gives access to the immediate human reactions and disposition. Emotions and feelings provide information about the immediate inner experience and the effect which events have on a person. Insight into feelings and emotions thus helps pastoral care to understand something of the immediacy of a person's experience. Making use of the affective component through sensitive listening and empathetic identification with the position of another, strengthens the elements of immediacy, concreteness and personal closeness.

• *The cognitive component*: The human *nous* tells pastoral care more about human standpoints, perspectives, opinions and vital perceptions. Knowledge about thought content helps a pastoral encounter to assess a person's aims, basic priorities and stance in life. Faith consists of a reasonable and rational knowledge regarding God and the Gospel which should be explored in counseling. Transmission of information by means of comprehensible concepts helps to explain the goals and aims of the pastoral encounter in rational categories. The pastoral encounter focuses on the transformation of human thinking: "to be made new in the attitude of your minds" (Eph 4:23).

• *The conative component*: Human passion and needs are part of the conative dimension. Analysis of needs and wishes plays an important role in the pastoral encounter because it promotes a better understanding of human motives behind deeds.

In decision-making processes, human thought and volition both play an important role. In Christ's approach to people, he points out that human motives are an important factor in behavior. For example, he turned discussion about behavioral issues away from external action to the level of motives and volition: "But I tell you that anyone who looks at a woman lustfully has already committed adultery with her in his heart" (Mt 5:28).

• *Normative component*: Norms and values form the point of integration between the human I, with its conscience and affective, cognitive and conative components. Norms and values label people as moral beings and impart an ethical dimension to their lives. It is our hypothesis that norms and values determine the significance and purpose of human existence. They could, therefore, be a source of integration or disintegration.

The goals which people choose to pursue and their value systems profoundly determine the quality of human existence. Pastoral care aims to effect a change within the human normative component so that the person, as a moral being, can focus on God's ultimate goal for life. The telic dimension plays a decisive role in human behavior. Normativity and purposefulness provide a link between conscience and values, thereby enabling human existence to attain a focus which influences the process of imparting and accepting meaning.

• *The physical component*: A person's attitude manifests itself visually in bodily reactions. The body also is the concrete medium through which God makes known his presence on earth through the Holy Spirit. The human body, as temple of the Holy Spirit, becomes a medium through which God operationalizes the effectiveness of salvation in behavioral reactions.

• *The koinonic component*: The element of group ministry plays an important role in the pastoral encounter. The corporative dimension of the *communio sanctorum* and the principle of being there for one another, become important elements in concretizing the comforting function of the message of salvation.

A theory regarding a pastoral anthropology for ministry could be presented diagrammatically as follows:

The Pneumatic Person

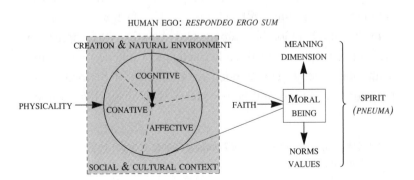

b) The Character of Pastoral Conversation, Discourse and Counseling: A Trialogue

Pneumatology adds another dimension to the pastoral conversation: it becomes more than a dialogue — it is a trialogue. Klein Kranenburg's exposition of the "third factor" in the pastoral conversation leads to this valuable insight: *pastoral communication should be rephrased so that it becomes a trialogue.* Communication and empathetic sustaining is of real importance to the pastoral conversation. Yet the actual identity of the pastoral conversation is not dependent on the quality of the relationship. The identity of the pastoral conversation is derived from the fact that God wishes to be a conversational partner and that God speaks in our midst.[220] Therefore the proprium of the pastoral encounter should be sought in its trialogic character.[221]

Klein Kranenburg's standpoint regarding the pastoral conversation's trialogic character has the following consequence for a pastoral anthropology: in the Christian faith, fostering and protection of the *humanum* is not situated in clarifying the being, but in saving the being through an encounter and dialogue with the addressing and communicating God.[222] Because of the pastoral conversation's trialogic character, the pastoral encounter serves the God-human encounter. It is not the person and his/her communication and counseling skills who is the third factor in the pastoral conversation, but God, in dialogue and operating via Scripture and creation. The pastor fulfills a hermeneutical function with regard to the third factor. This explicit interpretation of Scripture is the proprium of the pastoral conversation. This distinctive character

---

[220] See E. S. Klein Kranenburg, *Trialoog* (1988), p. 36.
[221] *Ibid.*, p. 38.
[222] *Ibid.*, p. 43.

distinguishes the pastoral encounter from all other helping professions and communication skills.[223]

c) *The Relation: Pastoral Care and Psychology (Psychotherapy)*

In summary: within the context of the principle of a bipolar
mutuality,[224] one must admit to the difference in perspective
between anthropology in pastoral care and anthropology in psychology. The difference should be understood in terms of *perspectivism* and not in terms of dualism. Pastoral care regards people pneumatologically, and regards the revelation in Scripture as
an important basic source of knowledge. Psychology seeks the
highest measure of self-realization and congruency of the personality, whereas pastoral care seeks the highest measure of faith
development and reconciliation. In psychological anthropology,
the field of tension is between self and ego, person and environment. Disturbances within this field lead to dysfunctional behavior. In a theological anthropology, the field of tension is the tension between God and people as a result of the bipolarity:
creature-Creator; sin-grace; death-life. Disturbances within this
field lead to guilt, despair, anxiety and complete meaninglessness.

The difference in perspective between pastoral care and psychology could also be formulated as follows. Pastoral care
approaches people from an eschatological perspective and deals

---

[223] *Ibid.*, p. 141.

[224] See also R.Sons, *Seelsorge Zwischen Bibel und Psychotherapie*, p. 110.
He advocates an integrative model: "Biblisch-therapeutische Seelsorge steht für
ein erweiterten Seelsorgebegriff, der psychotherapeutische Erkentnisse bewusst
integriert, ohne auf herkömmliche Formen und Methoden der Seelsorge zu
verzichten. Sie behält ihr Proprium als geistliches Geschehen, insofern sie in der
Wahrnehmung der Wirklichkeit Gottes geschieht ... . Es kommt auf diesem Weg
zu eiener 'cooperatio' ... ."

primarily with the transcendental dimension of meaning; psychology approaches people from an intra- and inter-psychic perspective and deals primarily with the empirical dimension of communication and behavioral patterns. From their unique perspectives, psychology and pastoral care both make an important contribution. Each deals with the entire person within all concrete relations. A perspective does not imply fragmentation of the human, but a unique approach to promote total human welfare in conjunction with other perspectives. Therefore a multi-disciplinary team approach is necessary.

As a result of its unique perspective, pastoral care does not operate from the notion that there is a natural point of departure in a person; a kind of natural inner knowledge about grace and salvation. The dialogical character of the God-human encounter becomes trialogical as a result of the indwelling Spirit. The indwelling Spirit thus becomes the point of departure between God and the human being. The Spirit creates a point of address (responsibility and obedience) and a point of contact (*metanoia* and focus on God). Within the pastoral encounter, salvific mediation is envisaged by the pastoral trialogue. This does not mean that communication does not play a role or mediate the Gospel. Communication does indeed influence the effect, functionality and consequences of the Gospel in the sense that it contributes towards a concretizing event and the effectiveness of the Gospel. The hermeneutic event is a process through which the truth of the Gospel is interpreted and declared within a process of understanding human existence in the world. Interpretation, which has the development of a mature faith as its goal, takes place. The pastoral encounter, as a symbol and metaphor of God's presence, does not fulfill salvation; salvation has already been fulfilled. The pastoral encounter interprets, testifies and proclaims salvation within the field of a unique phenomenon: faith. It also operates with a unique anthropology: the identity of people as determined by grace and our having been created in the image of God.

A pastoral anthropology differs from a personality theory in psychology. The distinctive features could be described as follows:

• *Methodology.* Psychology mainly uses psychotherapy, correlating with a specific personality or behavioral theory. Pastoral care mainly uses promissiotherapy, correlating with a specific theory regarding the theological character of faith. The conversational technique in psychotherapy is mainly dialogic and communication-oriented; the conversational technique in pastoral care is mainly trialogic and covenant-oriented. Psychotherapy is viewed as an occupation and is exercised by appointment in a consulting room. Pastoral care is viewed as a vocation and is linked to the office and calling of believers within the fellowship of the *communio sanctorum.*

• *Anthropological presupposition.* In its base theory psychology applies the anthropological presupposition that a person is an autonomous being with an inner potential for self-realization. In its basic theory, pastoral care makes use of the anthropological presupposition that the human, having been created by God, is dependent on God. Man's autonomy is receptive. Faith is viewed as a gift, while the human deepest potentialities are regarded, not as mere traits or virtues, but as gifts received from the Spirit.

• *Intention and purpose.* Psychotherapy focuses on healing human self-esteem within relations, with a view to fostering adulthood and maturation. Pastoral care focuses on transforming the human being within koinonic relations, with a view to nurturing a mature faith and spirituality.

• *Effect.* The effect of psychotherapy is psycho-physical well-being and personal stability. The effect of promissiotherapy is salvation, wholeness and stability, undergirded by God's faithfulness. This stability is linked to the objective dimension of salvation: Christ's mediating work (justification); and is strengthened and built up through the truth of fulfilled scriptural promises. Hence, the notion of promissiotherapy. Stability becomes concrete and visible through an operationalized faith — sanctification by means of the Spirit.

• *Context.* The context of psychotherapy is the communication network established between a counselor and a client. The context of promissiotherapy is the communication network established by the *communio sanctorum.*

The difference between pastoral care and psychology can be summarized as follows. (The reader should keep in mind that the difference is related to perspective and matter. It should not be considered in terms of a dualism.)

Focal Point of Pastoral Care	*Focal Point of Psychology*
1. The revelational and therefore invisible dimension of faith is primary (trans-psychic dimension).The confessional component is central. (Prescriptive analyses of faith.)	The phenomenological dimension of the human potential is primary. The empirical component is central. (Descriptive analyses of behavior.)
2. The content is important in the communication process. It is determined by Christology and pneumatology.	Skills are important in the communication process. They are determined by the counselor's attitude and by different theories about personality and behavior.
3. Being human is determined by creatureliness and salvation. Charismatic potential (gifts of grace) determines human conduct, disposition and behavior.	Being human is determined by personality, behavior and relationships. Conscious and unconscious processes are important.
4. The core factors leading to obstruction are sin (guilt),	The core factors leading to obstructions are: the neurotic and

transience (death) and despair (meaning).	psychotic components (psychopathology and disorders).
5. Growth takes place through radical change (conversion) and a qualitative transformation of existence. The basis for this growth is Christology and pneumatology.	Growth takes place by means of personality development (development of potential). The basis of this growth is a specific personality theory.
6. Edification within relations involves: *koinonia*. Empathy and sympathy are determined qualitatively by *agapé*.	Edification within relations involves group therapy. Empathy is determined by communication skills.
7. The disclosure of human potential is determined by the eschatological perspective.	Communicating techniques lead to self-disclosure, and result in self-realization.
8. Pastoral care as a science is not wholly empirical and should reckon with the dimension of revelation.	Psychology, as an empirical science, is content with a phenomenological analysis of human existence.

This diagram should not be interpreted antithetically and dualistically. For example, the revelationary character of pastoral care is not in opposition to the components of communication and relation. The creational character of a pastoral anthropology and the content of the eschatological perspective, which includes both Jesus Christ (the *Eschatos*) as well as created things (*eschata*), make a watertight separation impossible. The truth is inclusive: psychology's field of truth is not separate from the field of truth of eschatology. Continual interaction (interdisciplinary model) takes place between the two neighboring sciences of pastoral care and psychology. Each works with the total human being, within the unity of body, soul and spirit, thereby making fragmentation and compartmentalizing impossible. The various perspectives broaden the field of knowledge concerning the human being. Combining the various perspectives in a multi-disciplinary team approach greatly increases the effectiveness of those who are concerned about the development of identity, maturity and humanity in all aspects of life.

Summary

This chapter pointed out the following factors as integral components in the design of a theological anthropology. In a pastoral theology, people should be understood, hermeneutically speaking, from their dependence and focus upon God. Structurally speaking, a person, as God's creature, is dependent on God for the design of meaning in life. Creatureliness implies, inter alia, that human existence has a responding character. *Respondeo ergo sum* signifies that a person is a responsible/responding being. Responsibility is an ontic qualification, which is fulfilled within relations. The covenantal character of human relations is expressed in the togetherness of love, a basic trait of human existence. *Respondeo* places life within the normative context of "having been addressed." The pastoral encounter is exercised within these dialogic events, in which the *respondeo* component emphasizes the existential tension that exists between "ought" (ethical dimension) and "may" (charismatic dimension). The dynamic tension resulting from these two dimensions latch onto the fact that parishioners are continuously busy transcending themselves towards the future. As moral (ethical) and pneumatic (charismatic) beings, parishioners continuously anticipate the future in hope. The quality of this transcending process and the anticipation of events, are determined qualitatively by the eschatological perspective. The result of this perspective is a qualitative transformation of the human ontic condition. In terms of the eschatological perspective, a person focuses on the coming Kingdom of God. This eschatological focus provides humankind with a telic dimension.

This telic dimension in a pastoral anthropology correlates with the unique reality of faith. The new person is not understood phenomenologically, in the light of an empirical analysis only, but eschatologically, in the light of theological hermeneutics. An empirical analysis should therefore be supplemented by an analysis of salvation. This "salvific analysis" operates from the phenomenon of faith. On an existential level, the criterion for the effectiveness of faith is the nature and character of human gratitude.

Spirituality and maturity in faith can be assessed. In a pastoral diagnosis the assessment should be made in terms of the quality of Christian joy, gratitude, love and hope. In a mature faith the basic disposition is a positive manifestation of joy: this is a result of grace on an existential level. Humility, faith, love, hope, gratitude and joy may be viewed as the most basic virtues of Christian faith. They describe and define the basic Christian stance in life.

Continuance, permanence and purposefulness do not reside in a person but in the faithfulness of God. A Christian anthropology is therefore determined by theology: God's faithfulness to his promises. These promises create a transcendental point of continuance, which results in security and meaning. The process of disclosing meaning takes place in a pastoral anthropology, within the horizon of God's fulfilled promises. Because of this promissiological horizon of meaning, a person should not be addressed, primarily, in terms of an awareness of sin, guilt and feelings of anxiety. This approach is negative and one-sided. In the pastoral encounter, people should be addressed rather in terms of their creatureliness and God's grace. Doxology thus becomes the focal point of a theological anthropology.

A pastoral anthropology is determined essentially by Christology. Yet Christology is not completely commensurate with an
anthropology. Although Christology does include anthropology
and cosmology, it embraces even more. Christology focuses on
soteriology. The implication that this focus has for an anthropology is the promise of the new type of person: the pneumatic person. Faith is developed in the pneumatic person, and this affects all
relationships. This process of faith development implies sanctification: a process within which the new person is continuously transformed in his/her total thinking and behavior and is exposed to the
reality of eschatology. In order to be transformed, influenced and
renewed, the new person is dependent on the immanence and indwelling of the Holy Spirit. The formation of the new person is
thus essentially a pneumatological event. Inevitably, normativity
(norms and values) becomes most important for a pastoral anthropology. A person is essentially an ethical being, who is endowed
with a conscience and with the responsibility for making decisions.

As a result of pneumatology, pastoral anthropology presupposes a
dynamic interplay between faith and personality. In a psycho-pastoral
model, the affective (emotions and feelings); the cognitive (reason
and the mind); and the will (volition and motives) play a decisive role.
A developmental approach is important regarding the stages involved
in the formation of identity and the process of maturity. In this regard,
Erikson's exposition of the eight basic strengths or virtues is helpful:
hope, will, purpose, competence, fidelity, love, care and hope.

A psycho-pastoral model cannot avoid the issue of a psychological interpretation of scriptural texts. The notion of a "psychology
of grace" sheds light on the following dynamic issues in the development of faith: motivation, integration, normativity, anticipation,
trust, significance and transformation. It also prevents faith from
becoming pathological. This happens when inappropriate images
of God are connected to selfish purposes and result in hypocrisy.

CHAPTER III

HERMENEUTICS AND THE UNIQUE CHARACTER OF A PASTORAL DIAGNOSIS: ASSESSING FAITH AND GOD-IMAGES

The last sentence in the previous chapter refers to the fact that inappropriate images of God are connected to selfish purposes which often result in hypocrisy. The underlying assumption of such a statement is that if a pastoral anthropology is designed in terms of faith and is, therefore, essentially a theological matter, pastoral care deals with the impact of people's understanding of God within relationships and systemic contexts. Spiritual direction in pastoral care is, therefore, about assessing God-images and helping parishioners to grow in faith and to discover significance in the light of appropriate images of God. *Cura animarum*, the care of the souls, then exceeds the limitations of personality theories. It probes into the realm of the transcendent dimension of our human soul trying to interpret the so-called "signals of transcendence."[1] In theological terminology the dimension of transcendence is connected to our Christian understanding of God. We can even toy with the idea that our understanding of God determines our self-understanding (affirmation of creaturehood). Vice versa, it is also true that our self-understanding (self-esteem) influences our understanding of God.

Our hypothesis for this chapter is that spiritual direction is linked to the process of making a pastoral diagnosis. The latter

---

[1] See Berger, *A Rumor of Angels*.

should not be understood in terms of classification strategies. A pastoral diagnosis is about an assessment of the appropriateness/inappropriateness of parishioners' understanding of God (God-images) and the application of the Christian faith to those life-issues dealing with our quest for meaning and significance. Christian spiritual formation, guidance and direction are engaged in one's search for meaning within the realm of our basic fear of death (death anxiety); experiences of loneliness, isolation, depression and despair; our constant experience of guilt and shame.

3.1 Diagnosis in Pastoral Care and Counseling

A pastoral diagnosis involves a dynamic process of understanding and analysis of information and is focused on the integration of data concerning faith. Such integration takes place in the presence of God, against the background of the Scriptures and the person's existing experiences and perceptions of God. A pastoral diagnosis is thus a process within which the events taking place in a person's life are understood from a perspective peculiar to the Christian faith: eschatology. A pastoral diagnosis also adopts the character of an existential hermeneutics within the framework of a parishioner's belief system. A pastoral diagnosis does not attempt a purely existential analysis whereby it tries to understand human behavior merely in terms of choices and relations. Nor does it focus mainly on psychoanalysis, attempting to understand human behavior merely in terms of conscious or unconscious events. Rather, a pastoral diagnosis focuses primarily on an assessment of faith in terms of God-images and life's ultimate meaning.

This focus on faith does not mean that a pastoral analysis ignores emotions and experiences, but that it attempts to place these within a theological framework. Taylor describes this process as "a theological assessment." "Theological assessment is the art of thinking theologically about beliefs that undergird parishioners' feelings and actions."[2]

During the last two decades, people have developed an antipathy towards theological terminology and themes. The time has come now for the church to return to its own therapeutic resources and to utilize them better in pastoral counseling. The effective development of pastoral resources for counseling means that the question of diagnosis should be examined anew.

Pruyser is convinced that diagnosis is a substantial part of pastoral counseling. He believes that Rogers's negative evaluation gave an uncalled-for unilateral and negative connotation to diagnosis.[3]

According to Pruyser, diagnosis was misused by a moralistic type of theology, which aimed at a prior classification of the parishioner on moral principles. In this approach, the pastor often used only the field of the conscience to obtain knowledge about human behavior, thereby not doing justice to the person as a total being. Guidance was frequently so specific and so authoritative that the person received no hearing. This type of pastoral counseling was more prescriptive than truly hermeneutical (understanding and clarification).

Pruyser contends that every professional counselor should first obtain clarity about all the client's problems before deciding about any form of treatment. He defines diagnosis in any helping profession as:

> ... the exploratory process in which the troubled person is given an opportunity to assess and evaluate himself in a defined perspective, in which certain observations are made and specific data come to

---

[2] See C. T. Taylor, *The Ethics of Authenticity* (1991), p. 61.
[3] See P. W. Pruyser, *The Minister as Diagnostician* (1976), p. 39.

light, guided by conceptual or operational tools, in a personal relationship with a resource person.[4]

The importance of a pastoral diagnosis is confirmed by the research of De Jongh van Arkel.[5] He points out that diagnosis can help the pastor in the process of organizing and connecting relevant data. It can also generate hypotheses, in the light of which both pastor and parishioner can apply the truth of Scripture more effectively to a certain area of the parishioner's life. Diagnosis intensifies the quality of a pastoral assessment because it sheds light on all relevant data. It helps the pastor to summarize in order to attain integration. Assessing, summarizing and eliciting are skills which help the pastor to obtain all the facts and beliefs that are part of the key feelings and actions which constitute parishioners' problems and joys.

It is not far-fetched to claim that diagnosis and pastoral counseling are inextricably linked. Allowance should nevertheless be made for the following statement: *a diagnosis does not focus on a procedure of classification through which human behavior is categorized and typologized in advance. Diagnosis is simply the interpretation of a person's total existence. It focuses on clarification, establishing connections, organizing data and interpreting behavior in terms of the quest for meaning. Focus on the organizing, summarizing and interpretation of data enables a pastoral diagnosis to establish links between faith and life; between God-image and self-understanding; between scriptural truth and existential context.*

The pastoral diagnosis focuses on the interplay between "faith and life" in all its dimensions. Pastoral care is concerned about the

---

[4] *Ibid.*, p. 58.

[5] See J. T. de Jongh van Arkel, "A Paradigm for Pastoral Diagnosing" (1987), p. 20.

effect which faith has on a person's emotional processes and feelings (*affective dimension*). The association between faith and personal motivation is also important (*conative dimension*). Faith is a form of knowledge of God, which includes a rational component (*cognitive dimension*). Faith is formulated by means of existing concepts, ideas and perceptions (*experiential dimension*). The connection between faith, reason and experience is thus also important for a hermeneutical process of understanding. Conscience and norms play an integral role in behavior. Hence, the important link between faith and ethics (*ethical dimension*). Human life is embedded in a network of relations and structures. A pastoral diagnosis thus cannot ignore the connection between faith and the socio-political dimension of a parishioner's life (*contextual dimension*). A pastoral diagnosis thus focuses on the interplay between faith and its fields of application within the whole spectrum of anthropological data: the affective, conative, cognitive, experiential, ethical and cultural dimensions of human behavior. All this data is interwoven into the parishioner's language of faith. It is therefore important for a pastoral diagnosis to analyze and understand faith metaphors, in order to determine exactly what the parishioner means by faith in God and how he/she applies it in concrete situations.

A diagnostic approach in pastoral counseling should thus consider the following criteria:

• *Problem thinking and problem behavior.* The immediate personal reality can be assessed by determining its ego strength, identity, maturity and responsibility. Reality is related to certain presuppositions, assumptions and concepts, which can be subjected to a rational analysis. Problem thinking strongly influences behavior and people's self-esteem.

• *History context and life story.* Determining the influence of past events within the context of all the facts can enable one to understand more about a person's history or life story. The person's family history, values gained and internalized during the person's upbringing as well as interactional patterns within family ties, all provide important material for the understanding of the distinctiveness of various faith patterns.

• *Ego-strength and purposefulness.* The person's capacity to deal with impulses, feelings, needs and significant decision making. Value systems, goals and their ethical context play a major role in developing discernment and responsible decision making.

• *Social analysis.* The social milieu, community structures and the nature and character of all existing relations should be analyzed for a better understanding of faith behavior.

• *Coping skills and temporal events.* The time dimension is important. There is a link between past, present and future. The person's mechanisms to anticipate future-oriented behavior and goals should be studied to determine to what extent faith has a regressive (infantile), or progressive (creative) function.

• *Interplay between motive, need and expectation — vocation.* The person's level of motivation, as well as his/her basic needs, role expectations and tasks, should be analyzed.

• *Ethical dimension.* The role which norms play within the level of a person's moral awareness and conscience. The important role played by the ethical dimension is often underestimated and neglected in many diagnostic models. Since it is true that a mature faith is linked to the content of an issue (a person is a moral being), it is almost impossible to ignore the ethical dimension of growth of faith in a pastoral diagnosis.

Browning pointed out the necessity of norms and values in pastoral care and the influence of ethical codes on human behav-

---

⁶ See D. Browning, *Normen en Waarden in het Pastoraat* (1978).

ior in his book, *The Moral Context of Pastoral Care*.[6] Metaphors, specific obligations, particular personal needs, the prescriptions of a specific social milieu and regulations all play an important part in influencing human behavior. A pastoral diagnosis should thus try to determine in what way faith is influenced by these existing laws or prescriptions and obligations of a social milieu, a political context and a family system. The following questions can play an important role in any pastoral diagnosis:

• What are the most important metaphors and symbols which dominate the parishioner's field of language?

• What is his/her moral code of behavior, life-style and daily pattern of living?

• What themes and means does the parishioner use to satisfy his/her basic needs?

• What social and cultural factors play a dominant role in his/her immediate context?

• According to what rules does the parishioner live? What role expectations determine his/her daily pattern of living?

Two concepts have been used thus far which could be confusing: diagnosis and analysis. Both terms are closely associated with the psychological context in which they are usually used. What is meant by a pastoral diagnosis and a pastoral analysis?

3.2 Pastoral Hermeneutics and a "Substantial Model" as Supplement to a "Functional Model"

Both a pastoral diagnosis and a pastoral analysis are essentially concerned with a pastoral hermeneutics. The objective of this hermeneutics is to apply the salvation in Christ in such a way that it enables a person to discover meaning in life, and also fosters growth in faith. Heuer speaks of "hermeneutics of application to life."[7] He states that the application of faith-truths at the level of human behavior does not mean that a new type of psychology is being enforced on theology. Heuer refers to Jung's declaration, taken up by Paul Tillich: "There is no revealed psychology." A pastoral hermeneutics does not attempt an analysis of God's nature in order to apply this to the human personality by means of psychoanalysis. Rather, pastoral hermeneutics attempts to clarify the significance and existential implications of the encounter between God and humankind, thereby focusing its attention on the discovery of meaning and on fostering the growth of faith. In a somewhat different vein, but along the same lines, Heuer comments about pastoral hermeneutics: "It is a badly needed application of the Christian Scriptures to the problems of being human and behaving in a growthful manner."[8]

The concepts "pastoral analysis" and "pastoral diagnosis" refer to the same issue: the understanding, interpretation and clarification of faith within the context of existential questions regarding the meaning of life. *In both an analysis[9] and diagnosis, what is at stake is the significance of salvation, and how this is expressed in God-images and faith behavior.*

As already indicated, both an analysis and diagnosis refer to the same subject matter, *i.e.*, a mature faith and significant experiences

---

[7] See A. C. Heuer, *Pastoral Analysis* (1987), p. 16.

[8] *Ibid.*, p. 21.

[9] The concept "analysis" refers to perception and interpretation. "Therefore the work of the analyst is involved with observing the activity of God in the individual's experience and relating this encounter to the goal of wholeness as the person's ultimate need. That is why this particular function is referred to in pastoral analysis as diagnostic theology" (*Ibid.*, p. 8).
By "ultimate need" Heuer implies the human "soul" in relation to God. We prefer to use the term "salvation" instead of "ultimate need" and "wholeness." A pastoral analysis is thus concerned with the procedures of analysis and interpretation regarding growth in faith in both spirituality and maturity.

of God. Nevertheless, it is possible to differentiate between the two in order to gain more clarity regarding the function of a pastoral hermeneutics. *A pastoral diagnosis concerns the process of evaluating and assessing faith processes in the light of all role-playing factors regarding our disposition, conduct and social context. The "what" of a pastoral diagnosis is the quality of mature faith. Pastoral analysis concerns a more specific factor which plays a role in the development of a mature faith. In a pastoral analysis (as a subdivision of pastoral diagnosis) three factors may be identified: faith, religion and God-images.*

In summary, a pastoral diagnosis concerns the process, mode and significance of faith, while a pastoral analysis, as a more specific component of the process of assessment, concerns the what and content of faith. Our understanding of a pastoral diagnosis and a pastoral analysis has an implication for our pastoral hermeneutics. The fact that we link pastoral diagnosis to faith, religion and the concept of God, means that we prefer a more *substantial approach* in pastoral counseling rather than merely a *functional approach.*

In *Assessing Spiritual Needs,* Fitchett distinguishes between a *functional* and a more *substantial* approach.[10] Fitchett describes his model as a functional approach.[11] "This approach focuses more on *how* a person makes meaning in his or her life than on *what* that specific meaning is." His model is known as the "7 × 7 model for spiritual assessment." It consists of two main dimensions: a holistic and a spiritual dimension.[12] He divides the holistic dimension into seven subdimensions: medical, psychological, psycho-social, family system, ethnic and cultural, social and welfare, and spiritual. He divides the spiritual dimension into seven

---

[10] *Ibid.,* p. 40.
[11] *Ibid.,* p. 40.
[12] *Ibid.,* pp. 42-43.

subdimensions: faith convictions and meaning; vocation and ethical consequences; experience and emotion; courage and growth; ritual and religious practices; community systems; and authority and guidance.

The value of Fitchett's model lies in the way in which it integrates the various components of an assessing process. By "assessing" he implies: "both a statement of a perception and a process of information gathering and interpreting."[13] His model focuses on improving the quality of the processes in pastoral counseling. Fitchett believes that the value of such a "spiritual assessment" lies in the fact that it serves as a basis for effective and purposeful pastoral action; it is part of a more profound process of communication; it provides clarity about contracting and program designs/plans of action; it founds personal responsibility and accountability; it deepens the quality of our capacity and sensitivity for discernment; it is more cost-effective; it offers a scientific basis for better control of research data in pastoral care; it influences the pastoral view of health and the pastor's feeling of professional identity and competence.[14]

We have discussed Fitchett's functional model here because it should be viewed as a supplement to a more substantial model. Some may agree with Fitchett that the greatest value of a pastoral diagnosis lies in the way it helps the pastor to move from a subjective level of reflection to a more objective level, thereby achieving a greater measure of planning and structure in counseling. Making an accurate diagnosis helps the pastor to listen and understand with greater sensitivity, and to combine this effective listening with purposeful action planning. The greatest value of a pastoral diagnosis is that it helps to direct faith specifically to the

---

[13] *Ibid.*, p. 17.
[14] *Ibid.*, pp. 20-22.

problem and growth areas of people's lives. A pastoral diagnosis also uses Scripture organically, thereby making it relevant to parishioners' dealing with crucial problems.

In order to develop a more substantial approach in a pastoral diagnosis, a diagnostic chart has been drawn up which could enhance the pastor's understanding of faith behavior. The diagnostic chart has three analytical components:

a) *An analysis of faith*: the character of a parishioner's faith is examined with regard to adulthood and existential events. The strength and quality of a person's faith may be assessed by employing the following structural model: the factor of suffering (how does the person react to experiences of pain?); the factor of guilt (to what degree is guilt present and how are feelings of guilt dealt with?); the quest for meaning (what is the nature of a person's goals and priorities in life within the framework of norms and values); the factor of maturity (the correlative connection and congruency between ego strength and spiritual identity); the belief factor (the quality and content of faith and connection between biblical thinking, God-images and life issues).

b) *An analysis of religion*: determining the nature of a parishioner's religion. The purpose of a religious analysis is to distinguish an extrinsic form of faith behavior (legalism, being bound to tradition, dogmatism) from the intrinsic value of religion (already discussed in Chapter 2 under "The interplay between a theological anthropology and the psychology of religion"). A religious analysis is particularly interested in the character of a true commitment which is manifested in devotional acts and practices and an integrated consciousness of God.

c) *A theo-logical analysis*: assessing parishioners' understanding of God. This concentrates on an analysis of God-images or God-concepts, which could either play a constructive role in faith behavior (adequate/appropriate images), or constitute a disrupting factor, resulting in irrational images of God (inadequate/inappropriate images).

3.3 Spiritual Direction and the Making of a "Theo"-logical Assessment: God-Images

It is problematic to speak of a "theo"-logical analysis. The purpose of a "theo"-logical analysis is not to evaluate God's being in terms of his characteristics, but to assess parishioners' understanding of God by determining the content of their God-concepts. God-images are linked to parishioners' experiences of God within specific contexts. They do not reflect the essence of God in terms of an ontological paradigm, but reflect God's actions and style (his mode) as experienced by believers according to real life events. God-images are also determined by a general theological hermeneutics: the understanding and reading of scriptural texts.

The quest for criteria for identifying and assessing God-images must be undertaken with extreme care. God-images are a complex issue, within which important roles are played by cultural concepts, ecclesiastical confessions and dogmas and questions about philosophical and anthropological concepts. This complexity means that no "pure" concept or image of God exists which could communicate God credibly and meaningfully. A pastoral diagnosis should thus consider these guidelines:

• Each pastor has a unique image of God which reflects his/her own experience of God and what He means to him/her personally. Subjective and existential factors influence both the pastor's and the parishioner's understanding of God.

• The pastor's ecclesiastical tradition and dogma influences his/her evaluation. For example, the following images are possible, depending on the particular ecclesiastical tradition: a Reformed concept of God, emphasizing a revealing and proclaiming God; a Roman Catholic and Anglo-Saxon concept of God emphasizing an incarnated God; a Lutheran concept of God, emphasizing a suffering God; a Third World concept of God, emphasizing a liberating Exodus God.

• The pastor should display great sensitivity towards each parishioner's concept of God. Particular reserve and reticence is required here. The large variety of discourses and metaphors about God should help the pastor to realize that each parishioner's image of God is unique. It can be extremely painful and traumatic to alter a concept of God. Great sensitivity and care should be exercised in this process.

• A pastoral diagnosis should not make an ethical issue of a "*theological analysis.*" It should not moralize, nor should it be concerned with the question whether it is a good or bad, right or wrong concept of God. The main focus of a pastoral diagnosis concerns how a certain image of God is associated with scriptural metaphors and life experiences. An inappropriate understanding of God can give rise to dysfunctional or pathological faith behavior. Once again, it should be borne in mind that challenging God-images is a very sensitive issue.[15]

Bassett and others, in "Picturing God: A Non-verbal Measure of God-concepts for Conservative Protestants", contends: "Perceptions of God are important to researchers interested in religious issues."[16] This study was based on the technique of getting a

[15] See C. Lindijer (ed.), *Beelden van God* (1990^2), p. 9. He poses the following important question: What is the norm for criticizing and challenging? His view is that an image of God is problematic if it makes a person rigoristic, feel trapped, inhuman or anxious and if it creates delusions.

[16] See R. L. Bassett *et al.*, "Picturing God" (1990), p. 73.

group of people to reflect on God, by instructing them to draw a picture portraying their individual image of God. These pictures were divided into categories according to age groups. They were then shown to new groups of believers, who were members of Protestant churches. Each person chose a picture with which he/she wished to identify. This exercise provided insight into people's images of God. Butman refers to various other methods of evaluating people's faith behavior and God-images as a complicated task, particularly because a complex myriad of factors are at stake.[17] "Obviously, spiritual maturity and well-being are multiply-determined by a complex interaction of biological, cognitive, psychosocial, sociocultural and transcendental processes."[18]

The analysis and assessment of God-images become even more complex in modern society where there is an ongoing process of transforming traditional images and role models. For example, within the context of the traditional family, God-images have been influenced highly by parental images. A. Vergote refers to the parental role in people's experience of God when he says that his empirical research confirms the fact that God-images often reflect influence from both parents.[19] For example, the father image represents authority and discipline,[20] while the mother image represents affection and availability.[21] A shift in role functions immediately affects God-images.

Van Gennep points out the importance of metaphorical theology and the impact of metaphorical language such as God's

---

[17] See R. E. Butman, "The Assessment of Religious Development" (1990), pp. 14-24.

[18] *Ibid.*, p. 14.

[19] See A. Vergote, *Religie, Geloof en Ongeloof* (1984), p. 203.

[20] *Ibid.*, p. 200.

[21] *Ibid.*, p. 198.

fatherhood on God-images.[22] God-images should, therefore, not be understood in terms of ontology (categories of being), but in terms of a parable. Ontological speech implies direct, unmediated communication, while speaking in symbols and parables implies an indirect or mediated way of speaking. For example, ontologically speaking, God cannot be our Father. Nor should his Fatherhood be based on a patriarchal model of power. In metaphoric theology the Fatherhood of God tells us the story in which God, in his love, becomes involved in human history and in our human suffering.[23]

Recent research in both theology and human sciences points towards a metaphorical approach. Hence, the reason why pastoral care should face the challenge of how to deal with the notion of God-images in spiritual direction. Without a clear understanding of the appropriateness of one's God-image, our Christian faith can even become a confusing matter rather than playing a helpful and healing role. Assessing God-images is thus about the functionality of religious experiences and our perceptions of God.

The objective of a "theo"-logical analysis is to determine how people perceive God in order to enable the pastor to help them develop from inappropriate God-images (infantile faith) towards appropriate God-images (mature faith). This process is based on the assumption that an appropriate God-image promotes more constructive and purposeful actions, instills hope and contributes towards the eventual therapeutic effect of pastoral ministry.

In a pastoral hermeneutics three kinds of theological analyses could be identified. The first is concerned with the function and understanding of God within parishioners' life stories. By making

---

[22]   See F. O. van Gennep, *De Terugkeer van de Verloren Vader* (1990[4]), p. 358.
[23]   Ibid., p. 362.

use of a method of story analysis, the listening process can be enhanced. Different kinds of stories give rise to different experiences of God. Hence, the link between God-images and story analysis.

The second is more engaged in the metaphorical and symbolic meaning of different concepts used to portray God. A metaphorical model tries to trace back the meaning of different images of God as they are embedded in cultural and social contexts as well as painful experiences of suffering and meaninglessness.

The third is more complex and sophisticated. It could be applied by the more professional pastor in a clinical setting or counseling room. It is called a Pastoral Semantic Differential Analysis. A Semantic Differential Analysis makes use of different opposing adjectives which depict an abstract concept like God, in terms of four different dimensions of religious experiences: probable — improbable (the reality dimension of God); empowering — hampering (the evaluative dimension regarding the character of God in connection with life experiences); strong — weak (the dimension which describes the potency of God); active — passive (the dimension which touches the efficiency and activity of God).

All three of these methodological analyses can be used by the professional pastor in a counseling setting to determine the character of a mature faith and the quality of a parishioner's relationship of faith with God. It is obvious that these analyses can only be exercised and applied to situations where people do believe in God and are motivated to reflect critically on different God-images. It is not applicable to situations of severe distress, depression and confusion where painful emotions and severe suffering are at stake. It should be used in counseling when the parishioner feels free to take responsibility for his/her situation and is willing to make new decisions and to identify new significant goals.

a) God-Images and Story-Analysis

A *"theo"*-logical analysis may be done using the method of story analysis. Various elements of a story[24] are considered: the context with its prelude; all facts and events; the coherency and all relevant relations or associations; the intrigues and core problem or crisis; the dénouement and eventual solution or healing. The pastor should listen to where the God-image is strongly emphasized, the extent of its role, or whether it was completely lacking when the story was told. Mention of the name of God or related themes (*e.g.* God's will, providence, punishment, or grace) as well as the various elements of the story, could indicate the character of the parishioner's commitment to God, and dependence on Him.

The way in which the name of God is mentioned in storytelling will now be analyzed further. Six types of stories can be distinguished:

– *Comic stories* focus on the relation between God and humor. This type of story often indicates a realistic and constructive understanding of God. The connection between God and life awakens pleasant associations, in spite of contrasts which cannot be understood or solved. Funny stories strengthen the perception of the living God as Partner, Friend and Father. They also allow for paradoxes, without trying to resolve them. Humor could be described as a "comic" understanding of God.

– *Tragic stories* focus on the connection between God and suffering. Here the question of theodicy is at stake. A tragic story can be meaningful, especially when combined with an understanding of the "crucified God" (*i.e.,* his identification with human suffering

---

[24] On the practical and therapeutic value of storytelling, see I. Baumgartner, *Pastor — Psychologie* (1990), pp. 596-600.

through Christ's suffering, as Mediator). But a tragic story can become problematic, especially when feelings of powerlessness and helplessness are projected onto God in such a way that He is experienced as far away and disinterested. The notion of God's defenselessness in Christ will be emphasized in communicating faith in tragic experiences.

– *Romantic stories* focus on the connection between God and a person's personal needs and desires. God is portrayed as the ideal solution to all human problems; religion is an instant solution to all problems and faith has an answer to all questions. This strong emphasis on the victorious dimension of faith often denies the reality of sin, and does not make allowance for impairment and contingency.

The value of a romantic story is that the person usually is able to distinguish between the positive and negative so that he/she can concentrate on constructive solutions.

– *Ironic stories* have a strong focus on the experience of injustice largely because of the use of contrasts and ambiguities, for example, between what is believed of God and what is experienced in reality. Concepts like the omnipotence of God usually figure very strongly and an appeal is made to God's justice. Within the context of ironic stories pastoral care can concentrate on the concept of God as Judge, focusing on the maintenance of justice and salvation for all.

– *Dramatic stories* focus on the relation between God and evil elements, particularly concentrating on conflict and struggle. Dramatic stories allude to destructive powers, which often exceed personal capacities and potential. The question of theodicy arises within dramatic, ironic and tragic stories. People seek to understand and justify God in the light of existing evil. In dramatic stories, there may be a strong emphasis on the resurrection and God's faithfulness.

– *Therapeutic stories* focus on the connection between faith in God and the quest for meaning. They concentrate upon the nature of God's caring and compassionate involvement in our lives. In these stories, the person tries to find practical solutions for problems by using his/her faith. Therapeutic stories therefore focus on peace and forgiveness in situations of conflict. God, as Savior and Redeemer, could figure strongly in such stories.

b) The Metaphorical Model

McFague believes that theology can only use metaphors to speak about God. "Metaphor" is a term which is not used literally (therefore not aptly) to make certain associations. "It is an attempt to say something about the unfamiliar in terms of the familiar, an attempt to speak about what we do not know in terms of what we do know."[25] Without a precise definition, a metaphor aims to stimulate a creative process of imagining. "Metaphor always has the character of 'is' and 'is not': an assertion is made but as a likely account rather than a definition."[26] McFague thus concludes that all talk about God is indirect: "no words or phrases refer directly to God, for God-language can refer only through the detour of a description that properly belongs elsewhere."[27]

In contrast to the monarchic model in Western theology in which God is spoken of as a ruler or king,[28] McFague prefers a

---

[25] See McFague, *Models of God,* p. 33.

[26] *Ibid.,* p. 33.

[27] *Ibid.,* p. 34.

[28] G. D. Kaufman's book (*God-Mystery-Diversity* [1996], p. 100) argues that the depiction of God and our human awareness of God did not actually arise out of direct perceptions or experiences of the divine Being itself. Rather, they emerged in connection with cultural contexts and philosophical issues. Hence,

sacramental model.[29] For McFague, God as monarch, ruler and patriarch are all metaphors with an imperialist connotation that creates distance. She does not regard the world as God's kingdom, but as his "body." She therefore chooses the following metaphors:

> I will suggest God as mother (father), lover, and friend. If the world is imagined as self-expressive of God, if it is a "sacrament" — the outward and visible presence or body — of God, if it is not an alien other over against God but expressive of God's very being, then, how would God respond to it and how should we?[30]

McFague answers this question with the suggestion that God is parent, "lover" and friend of the earth. Her model may be adapted

---

the configuration of such images/concepts as king, creator, father, lord — all drawn from everyday human language and experiences, but now put together in a conception believed to represent the all-dominant power in the universe. Kaufman (p. 101) poses a very important question. "A principal question that must be faced in theological reflection today is whether a notion of God constituted largely by anthropomorphic political and familial metaphors such as father, lord and king can continue to function effectively as a focus for the sort of world-pictures — conceptions of the universe and our human place within it — which most of us now take for granted." He argues that the symbol "God" leads us to attend to and reflect on the ultimate mystery of things and their connection to enhancing human existence. "'God' is the name ordinarily used to designate that reality (whatever it might be) that grounds and undergirds all that exists including us humans; that reality which provides us humans with such fulfillment or salvation as we may find; that reality toward which we must turn, therefore, if we would flourish."

[29] See McFague, *Models of God,* p. 63. The reader should take note of the fact that in a pastoral diagnosis, different models come into play. Whether you opt for God as Father or Mother, the assessment is interested in the influence and implication of a God-image on human conduct and the meaning question. For example, for some authors the Fatherhood of God is still a very useful metaphor. See J. McGrath & A. McGrath, *The Dilemma of Self-Esteem* (1992), pp. 105-106 on the Fatherhood of God and self-esteem. God's fatherly care for his children meets their deepest needs, such as nurture, acceptance, setting of clear standards, teaching.

[30] See McFague, *Models of God,* p. 61.

for use in assessing God-images in a pastoral diagnosis as follows:

- the *monarchic model* perceives God as ruler, king, governor, and judge;
- the *family model* views God as parent (father/mother);
- the *covenantal model* portrays God as friend, partner and confidant;
- the *personal/love model* views God in terms of love, as beloved or intimate lover (see the bridegroom-bride metaphor).

While McFague's model deals with a metaphorical concept of God, Van der Ven's model is an empirically-based experience of God metaphors in a situation of suffering.[31] In other words, the metaphor is adapted to fit people's experience[32] of God during suffering, within the broader context of a theodicy.

Van der Ven's empirical model uses various symbols in theological literature which deal with the problem of theodicy (apathy, retribution, providence/counsel, therapy, compassion, substitution, mysticism).[33] He reduces them to the following four diagnostic criteria for assessing human experience of God during suffering:

- apathy,
- retribution,
- pedagogy and
- solidarity.

This reduction provides the pastor with a good framework whereby to assess people's experience of God in their quest for

---

[31] See J. A. van der Ven, *Entwurf Einer Empirischen Theologie* (1990), p. 197.

[32] Van der Ven (*ibid.*, p. 33) regards "experience" as much more than merely sensual experience: it is an all-encompassing event which includes an intense awareness of God in the world. Hence, his argument for an "empirical theology." He is convinced that in an empirical theology, the object of theology is not God but our human experience of God and our reflection on Him. God is only indirectly the object and goal of theological reflection.

[33] *Ibid.*, p. 179.

meaning during suffering. The pastor may consider the possibility that apathetic and retributive symbols create a greater distance between God and the sufferer, while the pedagogic symbol may create some tension. Solidarity symbols are intent on closeness and stimulate security.

It becomes clear that the assessment of God-images opens up various metaphors and different approaches. Not one correct mode or metaphor necessarily exists.

K. Depoortere deals with the problem of theodicy and discusses three acquittals of God: God is a fair Judge, God as supreme Educator[34] and the inscrutability of God. He tries to schematize the theodicy question in terms of A. Gesché's sketch: *contra Deum, pro Deo, in Deo, ad Deum,* and *cum Deo.*[35] Indeed, it can be most helpful to assess whether the naming of God in suffering refers to a plea on behalf of God; a complaint against God; an effort to relate to God and to suffer *in Deo*, in God's name; the courage to make an appeal to God and the possibility to suffer together with God.

Of importance is Depoortere's finding that we cannot accept an image of God which paralyses the fight against suffering and leads to passivity or fatalism.[36] Because of the fact that Jesus is our Fellow-Sufferer, Depoortere views the notion of the defenseless supremacy of love[37] as the best option for a variety of God-languages[38] especially for that language which will empower the sufferer to attain an

---

[34] See K. Depoortere, *A Different God* (1995), pp. 28 and 36.

[35] See A. Gesché, Topiques de la Question du Mal (1995), pp. 102-103.

[36] See Depoortere, *A Different God*, p. 25.

[37] *Ibid.*, p. 103.

[38] Some common God-perceptions have been identified by M. E. Cavanagh ("The Perception of God in Pastoral Counseling" [1992], pp. 76-78): God is vengeful; God is needy; God is our caretaker; God is our tutor. See also M. Sarot "Pastoral Counseling and the Compassionate God" (1995), p. 189. It is indeed the case that the conception of God as co-suffering is psychospiritually more helpful than that of God as blissfully impassible.

"inspirational meaning" in suffering where suffering is integrated with life issues and the quest for meaning. "The inspirational attribution of meaning must tell us something about life's ultimate horizon ... . Inspiration ... involves the courage to persist in the face of the divide between the theoretical attribution of meaning and the concrete praxis ... ."[39] It helps the sufferer to move in the light of the resurrection of Christ from "Why?" to "With Whom?" It contributes to a spirituality of confidence and resistance[40] and opens our eyes to care for the poor and the suffering.

The following diagram is an attempt to merge the different accents in a metaphorical approach. The diagram indicates how an integrated model enables pastoral diagnosis to have a substantial and material approach. For example, the first block of the diagram illustrates how a monarchic metaphor, through the principle of authority and an understanding of God's mode of involvement (omnipotence), can influence an experience of suffering and can give rise to a better self-examination and -understanding. The family metaphor could have a most supportive effect on parishioners' experience of suffering; the covenantal metaphor could motivate parishioners to active self-responsibility, while the personal/love model has a liberating effect, which is manifest in gratitude, joy and hope.

[39] See Depoortere, *A Different God* (1995), p. 58.
[40] *Ibid.*, p. 118.

GOD-METAPHOR				
Metaphor	*Monarchic* King Judge	*Family* Parent Father/Mother Confidant	*Covenant* Friend Partner for Life	*Personal* Lover
Principles	Authority	Care Support	Fellowship	Liberation Unconditional love
Mode	Omnipotence	Consolation	Faithfulness Grace	Reconciliation Mercy
Human experience of suffering and understanding of God	Apathy Retribution	Pedagogy Empathy	Solidarity Identification	Service Vicariousness
Psycho-physical influence and consequence	Awareness of guilt Awe Devotion	Support Change Development Growth Obedience	Responsibility (ethical) Commitment Empowerment	Gratitude Joy Hope

This diagram does not imply that the different metaphors and principles can be classified, nor that the principle, mode, human experience and psycho-physical influence mentioned under each column can be isolated from the others. Metaphors have different meanings under different circumstances. They are even associated with each other: principles and modes mentioned under one category are relevant for, and applicable to, other categories as well. Human experiences and psycho-physical influences and consequences are much more complex than portrayed in our diagram. They are all interrelated. The diagram's object is to help us to understand the interplay between metaphor, principle, mode, experience and personal consequences in a much more schematized manner.

c) The Pastoral Semantic Differential Analysis (PSDA)

In addition to the method of story analysis mentioned above, a semantic differential analysis may also be employed. Osgood designed this analysis in order to study the semantic processes involved in the different meanings given to concepts.[41] The semantic differential now provides a method whereby to assess the connotation of a given concept and the emotional impact of this concept.

According to Osgood such a method comprises:

> (a) the use of factor analysis to determine the number and nature of factors entering into a semantic description and judgement, and (b) the selection of a set of specific scales corresponding to these factors which can be standardized as a measure of meaning.[42]

Standardization is made possible because of the general hypothesis that concepts have an affective and thus also an existential meaning. The affective power of a word has a dimensional structure which may be researched. It is divided into three main dimensions: 'evaluation, activity and potency.'[43] This measuring of meanings should be viewed within the psychological and existential impact of concepts against the background of a process of

---

[41] See C. E. Osgood, "The Nature and Measurement of Meaning" (1969), p. 4.
[42] *Ibid.,* p. 36.
[43] See C. E. Osgood & G. J. Suci, "Factor Analysis of Meaning" (1969), p. 130.

symbolizing. It should not be regarded as a final classification of the linguistic meaning of a concept.[44]

Fishbein and Raven's research identifies a fourth dimension: the dimension of probability.[45] This dimension refers to the component of reality. Hence, their proposal to change the Osgood scale. They identify the following five experiential belief items: "probable — improbable; possible — impossible; likely — unlikely; existent — nonexistent; true — false."[46]

Fishbein and Raven's finding could be used to amplify a pastoral semantic differential analysis. Applied to God-images and belief items, it touches the problem of the probability and likelihood of God. Is God real or not, existent or nonexistent?

A PSDA has value for pastoral theology because it enables people's understanding of God to be assessed. Semantic differential (SD) thus promotes the process of understanding in communication. In order to determine the meaning of concepts, opposite meanings should be identified. In this way a general group of contrasting concepts may be identified and then applied to all concepts. For example, the *evaluation category* has the following pairs of contra-adjectives: beautiful — ugly, pleasant — unpleasant, clean — dirty, nice — disgusting. *Potential category*: strong — weak, large — small, heavy — light. *Activity category*: immediate — delayed, active — passive, quick — slow. *Probability category*: possible (real) — impossible (unreal, imaginary), likely — unlikely, existent — nonexistent, true — false.

Osgood's model could be adapted for a pastoral analysis as follows.[47] Experiences associated with God's actions in the salvific

---

[44] *Ibid.*

[45] See M. B. Fishbein & B. H. Raven, "The AB Scales" (1967), p. 184.

[46] *Ibid.*

[47] Osgood's model has been applied by P. J. van Strien & N. C. A. Meyer ("Semantisch onderzoek van religieuze begrippen" [1969], pp. 541-550) to

history can be identified through their opposite values. According to Osgood's model, these can be divided into three categories: value, potential and activity. The central concept (in this case God) can be assessed on a seven-point scale. This evaluation may clarify a person's processes of understanding, as well as give the pastor insight regarding the association between cognitive understanding and existential experience. The difference between Osgood's initial model and the revised model resides in the fact that a pastoral semantic differential analysis (PSDA) focuses more on the cognitive associations of the parishioner's understanding of the concept "God," than on the affective associations. This focus does not mean that such a cognitive understanding (belief system) necessarily excludes affective associations.

A PSDA consists of the following dimensions:

a) *The probability dimension.* It signifies whether or not parishioners regard God as real. It should be taken into consideration that an assessment of this dimension includes associations with positive and negative life experiences. It is linked to situations of pain and suffering which are often an indication whether God is conceivable or inconceivable within parishioners' experiential framework. The probability dimension reflects the classical problem of theodicy.

b) *The evaluating dimension.* This concentrates on the value of concepts. This value or meaning may tend to be more affective or more cognitive. In the case of a PSDA it will be mixed, with a strong tendency towards a more dogmatic presentation and wording. (In the case of PSDA a Reformed approach would be followed.) The value of concepts on the

examine the semantic value of religious concepts such as "God as Father." Their research showed that the correlation of the concepts "God" and "Father" increased with intensified religiosity. The method appears to be useful for studying the structure of individuals' religious semantic space.

seven-point scale could either edify and provide security, or could hamper and disrupt existing associations and identifications.

c) *The dimension of potential.* This concentrates on the ability hidden in the relevant concept. In a PSDA, this ability or potential is associated with contrasting concepts, indicating strength or weakness.

d) *The activity dimension.* This focuses on action. In a PSDA, God's actions and deeds would predominate. The associations can move either in the direction of doing or towards passivity and uninvolvement.

An analysis of the seven-point scale (numbered either from 1 to 7 or from +3 to -3) will indicate whether the person's understanding of the central concept is appropriate or inappropriate. It will thus indicate directly whether or not the person has an efficient association.

When the semantic differential analysis is applied to the God-concept, it is possible to identify the following pairs of contra-adjectives. The dimension of probability (quest for reality): real — fictitious; knowable — unknowable; conceivable — inconceivable; personal — general idea. The evaluating dimension has the following pairs: just/fair — unjust/unfair (biased); faithful/trustworthy — unfaithful/untrustworthy; loving — hostile/enemy; steadfast — inconsistent; approachable/merciful — unapproachable/merciless. The ability component has omnipotent — powerless; sympathetic/compassionate — unsympathetic; revealed (will) — concealed. The activity dimension has: presence (intimacy) — distance (afar); redeemed by (saved) — rejected by; blessed (gifts) — accursed (withholding gifts, isolation); help (assistance) — withdrawal.

The score obtained using this semantic differential analysis provides the following information. A positive tendency in the scores of (a), (b), (c) and (d), indicates a positive identification between the parishioner and God. A score tending to fluctuate around nil indicates a possible neutral attitude towards God. This could result either from deficient knowledge or from a lack of interest and commitment. A score tending towards the negative provides insight into the possible crisis levels which a person experiences and how this influences his/her experience of God. When the score reflects a neutral position, this could indicate deficient growth or a superficial identification with God. Constructive confrontation or challenging could be applied to alert the parishioner to the curbing effect which a neutral understanding of God has on the growth of faith. If the negative score is accompanied by painful emotions, then the pastor may encourage the person to communicate these emotions honestly to God through lamentation formulas. The person should also be encouraged to take note of the association between his/her emotional condition and his/her negative reaction to crises or problematic situations.

The pastor could use a PSDA in the following way. Parishioners are asked to evaluate the concept "God" against the designated scale. They should be encouraged to reflect on their immediate experience of God first, and then to concentrate on their association between God and events during the past. It should be explained to them that appropriate (positive) — inappropriate (negative); probable — improbable; empowering — hampering; strong — weak; active — passive are not ethical categories that reflect good or bad. Since both appropriate and inappropriate interpretations of God could play an important role in parishioners' development of spirituality, they should not attempt to avoid remembering negative associations of God. Parishioners must answer honestly. They should also not feel obliged to recall exemplary associations with God, in an attempt to make these fit the expectations of the church or dogmatics. Each person's immediate association and experience of God is important.

Pastoral Semantic Differential Analysis (PSDA)

Appropriate   God   Inappropriate
                                  Reality

a) Probable	+3	+2	+1	0	−1	−2	−3	Improbable
Real (possible)								Fictitious (impossible)
Knowable								Unknowable
Conceivable								Inconceivable
Personal								General idea

Evaluation

b) Empowering	+3	+2	+1	0	−1	−2	−3	Hampering
Just/fair								Unjust/ unfair (biased)
Faithful/trustworthy								Unfaithful/ Untrustworthy
Loving								Hostile/enemy
Steadfast								Inconsistent
Approachable/merciful								Unapproachable/ merciless

Potential

c) Strong	+3	+2	+1	0	−1	−2	−3	Weak
Omnipotent								Powerless
Sympathetic/compassionate								Unsympathetic
Revealed (will)								Concealed (will)

Activity/Efficiency

d) Active	+3	+2	+1	0	−1	−2	−3	Passive Uninvolved
Presence (nearness)								Distance/absence (afar)
Redeemed by								Rejected by
Blessed (gifts)								Accursed (withholding gifts)
Help (assistance)								Withdrawal

*   *
*   *

What is important is that the whole process of diagnosis and assessment should be understood in terms of our attempt to design a pneumatological anthropology of pastoral care. God-images deal with experience, perception and imagination. We can say that God-images are the outcome of a process of imagining God. And it is right here that the indwelling work of the Spirit comes into play. The Spirit is the "work-out" of God who influences our understanding of Him. The dynamics of God-images and the assessment of their appropriateness have everything to do with what can be called the "imaginatory work of the Spirit." McIntyre observes: "Imagination is the medium which the Spirit employs in enabling men and women to understand, interpret and appropriate Scripture."[48]

The unravelling and imaginatory work-out of the Spirit bridges the so-called abstract transcendency of God. It brings about the immediacy of God within existential and social contexts. It saves us from a purely rationalistic approach and opens up avenues to explore new ways of God-language and the naming of God. Within a pneumatology the reference to Braaten in the introduction should be valued: pastoral care is a theology from "below" — the existential locus of God-language.[49]

The implication of the proposed assessment models is that diagnosis in pastoral care should concentrate less on God-images that refer to attributes which try to describe the character of God in terms of Western metaphysics: God as *Logos*; God as the Ultimate Being, God as the Ground of Being. Such a description easily leads to speculation (*e.g.*, the *impassibilitas Dei*). God is less understood in substantial categories (*naturae rationalis individua substantia*)[50]

---

[48] See McIntyre, *The Shape of Pneumatology*, p. 271.

[49] See Braaten, "The Problem of God-language Today," p. 19.

[50] See Boethius in J. A. van der Ven, "De Structuur van het Religieuze Bewustzijn" (1996), p. 57.

than in functional categories: the indwelling presence of the Spirit of God in the world.[51]

Our assessment model is not about a *metaphysics of God's being*. Rather, it focuses on attributes which reflect God's function or doing activities. Such a model is indeed *functional*; *i.e.*, it tries to assess the value of God-experience within contexts of suffering. It could even be identified as an *experiential* model; *i.e.*, how people experience God (religious experiences) and its connectedness with the quest for humanity and meaning.

3.4 The Structure of God-experiences and the Quest for Contextualization and Inculturation

Diagnosis in pastoral care introduces the need for empirical research. Because it deals with God-experiences, it should ask the question about possible different structures and the interplay between structures and different cultural contexts.

The following different structures for empirical research have been identified by J. A. van der Ven.[52]

The *ecclesiological structure*. In such a structure the value of God-images is assessed in terms of the question whether people participate in the religious activities of the church or not. The problem with such a structure is that the meaning dimension of God-images is often attached to experiences that deal with people's

---

[51] Such a functional model does not deny the value of a description of God's possible different attributes. The naming of God does not exclude an essential or substantial description of God. See G. van den Brink & M. Sarot (eds.), *Hoe is uw Naam?* (1995). A functional model tries to assess the value of a relational model which links God's actions with our human quest for meaning. "Functional," in a pastoral model, refers to the functions of comforting, caring, helping, sustaining, guiding, reconciling, nurturing, empowering and assessing.

[52] See Van der Ven "De Structuur van het Religieuze Bewustzijn," pp. 40-45.

involvement in secular relationships. Church-going is not an indication of the value of people's religious awareness and divine consciousness. The ecclesiological structure could even be misused to hide very hostile feelings towards God.

The structure of a developmental approach. Another option is to identify different stages in our human development and to look at the different structures which experiences of God can take on. The undergirding hypothesis, for example, of J. Fowler's stage model[53] is that the development of human self-consciousness passes through various stages which eventually influence the development of a person's faith.[54] Nevertheless, it remains an open question whether our religious experience is always necessarily an outcome of developmental stages. The structure of religious experiences is often shaped more by suffering than by developmental issues.

The generation structure. Such a structure is linked to life issues reflecting the philosophy of life. It is attached to a specific generation within social and cultural contexts. For example, the generation before World War II and thereafter; the older generation and the younger generation with, in between, the "generation gap."

The problem is that generational issues are intertwined with philosophical issues, which surface from cultural and life issues. The influence of the paradigm shift from premodernity through modernity to postmodernity, is a good example of this.

The philosophical structure. It is possible to compare the influence of different philosophies of life on God-images. Modernity

---

[53] See J. W. Fowler, *Stages of Faith* (1981), p. 14.

[54] By "a developmental model" J. W. Fowler (*Faith Development and Pastoral Care*) does not mean a development in terms of the theological content of faith: "These are not to be understood as stages in soteriology" (p. 80).

and its emphasis on rationality indeed make a difference in reflections on God. The paradigm shift from metaphysics to functionality has deeply influenced God-experiences. Still, it is a very difficult task to identify the exact influence of different philosophies on religious experiences.

The experiential structure and functional differentiation of God-images. This model is an attempt to assess the function of God-images and their "performance" value within different roles and relationships. Van der Ven interprets performance in terms of social and professional role fulfillment; *i.e.,* the intra-personal character of different God-images for a person connected to different social circumstances.[55] God-images are influenced and shaped by people's performance within social roles.

Our proposal for the assessment of God-images is not to assess the social performance value of God-images, as such, but merely to help both the pastor and parishioner to reflect on the intra-personal structure and character of God-images and their relatedness to different interpretations of faith and social/cultural contexts. What I have in mind is a *hermeneutical model* which brings about a *consciousness* and *awareness of God* within contexts of suffering, as well as the possible correlation between different perceptions of God and our self-understanding within the dynamics of different contexts. The aim of such a model is the enhancement of a pastoral discourse about God.

The further underlying assumption is that such a discourse about different experiential awarenesses of God can help people to gain more clarity on what their personal needs are, what exactly they expect from God and are hoping for. In the pastoral conversation it also reveals the dynamics and interplay between personal needs, social contexts and vital expectations about the meaning of life.

---

[55] See Van der Ven, "De Structuur van het Religieuze Bewustzijn," pp. 47-48.

The intention of our model is to enhance the interconnectedness of *fides quaerens intellectum* (faith seeking understanding) and *fides quaerens verbum* (faith seeking ways of discoursing). In such a discourse appropriate God-images should bring about *an awareness of the presence of God* (spirituality) and *growth towards a more mature faith.* Hence, the task of the pastoral caregiver to foster a mature faith and to instill hope.

The implication of our model for making a *theo*-logical analysis is that pastoral care should try to overcome the dualism between God's transcendence and immanence. In a pastoral diagnosis the issue at stake is the *immediacy* and *presence* of God: what is the will of God within this context? An assessment is, therefore, predominantly about a true discernment of God's involvement in our lives. To do this one needs an understanding of God in terms of "panentheism"[56] — the penetrating perichoresis of God's Spirit within people (*inhabitatio*) and cosmos.

The implication of a pneumatological model is that a pastoral assessment concentrates more on personal images of God (metaphors within either the monarchic, family, covenant or personal tradition) than impersonal images of God (metaphors referring to cosmic elements or metaphors within contemporary society). Hence, our attempt to seek our point of departure for a *theo*-logical assessment of God-images in the content of the Christian faith: *i.e.,* God's faithfulness, vulnerability and friendship.

Before moving on to a discussion concerning the naming of God in spiritual direction, attention must be paid to the dynamics and interplay between structures and cultural contexts. It has been mentioned that social contexts do play a role in the pastoral

---

[56] By "panentheism" is meant what Van der Ven (*Ibid.,* p. 50) calls "the bipolarity of God," both transcendent and immanent. For more detail on the theological implication of a pneumatological understanding of "panentheism," see 3.5.

conversation and assessment of God-images. Structures are connected to different roles and relationships. They are embedded in cultural environments which influence people's understanding of themselves and God. No anthropology, not even a theological anthropology, can be designed without taking the cultural context and influence into consideration.

It is impossible to make a valid pastoral diagnosis without dealing with the interplay between anthropology, cultural contexts and experiences of God. Thus, the reason for a deeper probe into this area. The reader should gain a more balanced perspective on what a hermeneutics of pastoral care and counseling is about. The encounter with people is inevitably an encounter with cultural belief systems which shape expectations regarding the presence and will of God.

The Pastoral Encounter and Contextualization/Inculturation

"Encounter" does not describe a relationship between a personal God and an isolated individual. When seen in terms of the Gospel's covenantal framework, "encounter" implies a network of relationships, reciprocal interaction and associations. The pastoral encounter implies "connectedness."

Graham, referring to Augsburger's use of the term "interpathy," is convinced that a systems approach is important when pastoral care moves into a cross-cultural situation.[57]

> Interpathy is an intentional cognitive envisioning and affective experiencing of another's thoughts and feelings, even though the thoughts rise from another process of knowing, the values grow from another frame of moral reasoning, and the feelings spring from another basis of assumptions.[58]

---

[57] See L. K. Graham, *Care of Persons, Care of Worlds* (1992), pp. 19-20.
[58] See Augsburger, *Pastoral Counseling Across Cultures*, p. 29.

Bosch also refers to the importance of the process of incultura-tion.[59] Inculturation does not focus on accommodation or adaptation to a certain culture, but on a "regional or macrocontextual and macrocultural manifestation."[60] Inculturation implies an inclusive, all embracing comprehensive approach.[61] In a certain sense, inculturation aims at being a form of incarnation: "the gospel being 'en-fleshed,' 'embodied' in a people and its culture ... ."[62] This process of inculturation implies further that different theologies and approaches enrich each other within a systemic approach to the pastoral encounter. Bosch claims that we are not only involved with inculturation (the contextual manifestation), but also with interculturation (the interdependent relationship between different cultures for mutual enrichment).[63] In the light of the recent development of ethnopsychology, Hesselgrave advocates that the area of missionary work needs to be re-thought in terms of "enculturation" and "acculturation," using what he calls a "cross-cultural missionary psychology."[64]

[59] See D. J. Bosch, *Transforming Mission* (1991), p. 452.

[60] *Ibid.*, p. 453.

[61] J. M. Waliggo *et al.* (eds.) (*Inculturation: Its Meaning and Urgency* (1986), p. 11) point out the different concepts used to describe the process of identification between Christianity and different cultures. *Adaptation* implies a selection of certain rites and customs, purifying them and inserting them within Christian rituals which have any apparent similarity. Then *indigenization*: this refers to the necessity of promoting indigenous church ministers. *Reformulation* refers to the Christian doctrine and understanding of God in the thought and language that are understood by local people. *Incarnation* is used to reveal the humane character of the Gospel and Christ's identification with cultural issues. According to Waliggo, *inculturation* underlines the importance of culture as the instrument and means for realizing the incarnation process of the Christian religion and the reformation of Christian life and doctrine in the very thought-patterns of different cultures.

[62] *Ibid.*, p. 454.

[63] *Ibid.*, p. 456.

[64] See D. J. Hesselgrave, *Counseling Cross-culturally* (1984), p. 39.

In future, the pastoral encounter and diagnosis must take note of a systemic and cultural context. For instance, a systems approach would be important in a situation where group bonding (family, tribe) is a primary value.

Graham, believes that a systems approach in the pastoral encounter implies a new way of thinking.[65] He calls this "systemic thinking" which is a view about the universe, or a picture of reality, affirming that everything that exists is in an ongoing mutual relationship with every other reality. For Augsburger, a systemic perspective means an inclusive process of relationships and interactions:

> System is a structure in process; that is, a pattern of elements undergoing patterned events. The human person is a set of elements undergoing multiple processes in cyclical patterns as a coherent system. Thus a system is a structure of elements related by various processes that are all interrelated and interdependent.[66]

Two factors should be considered during the pastoral encounter in order to understand human problems. Firstly, problems are embedded in cultural contexts in which attitudes, values, customs and rituals play an important role. Secondly, problems may correlate with the position and status which people adopt and hold within a certain network of relationships.

Friedman draws attention to the fact that a systems approach focuses less on the *content* and more on the *process*: "less on the cause-and-effect connections that link bits of information and more on the principles of organization that give data meanings."[67] Systemic thinking means that the pastoral encounter not only takes note of the person and psychic composition, but notices especially

---

[65] See Graham, *Care of Persons, Care of Worlds*, p. 40.

[66] See Augsburger, *Pastoral Counseling Across Cultures*, p. 178.

[67] See E. H. Friedman, *Generation to Generation* (1985), p. 14.

the *position* held by a person within a relationship. "The components do not function according to their 'nature' but according to their position in the network."[68]

Graham lists four characteristics of a systemic view of reality.[69]

- It affirms that all elements of the universe are interconnected in an ongoing reciprocal relationship with one another.
- It affirms that reality is organized. The universe is an organized totality, the elements of which are interrelated.
- It emphasizes homeostasis, or balance and self-maintenance. Balance is maintained by transactional processes such as communication, negotiation and boundary management.
- It emphasizes creativity in context, or finite freedom. Although systems are self-maintaining, they are also self-transcending.

In Graham's terms, the implication of a systems approach is that a human being is a "connective person."[70]

> The self is not only a network of connections, it is an emerging reality eventuating from those ongoing connections. By definition, the self is the qualitative and unique expression of the psyche, which emerges from reciprocal transactional processes within individuals and between individuals and their environments.[71]

It would seem that a systems approach has implications for a pastoral anthropology. During pastoral encounters, a person is approached as an open system, not as an isolated individual. "The soul is both *activity* of synthesizing and creating experience, and the *outcome* of the process of synthesis and creation."[72]

It is gradually becoming clear that the pastoral encounter involves both our spiritual and our existential life. It involves a

---

[68] *Ibid.*, p. 15.
[69] See Graham, *Care of Persons, Care of Worlds*, pp. 39-40.
[70] *Ibid.*, p. 73.
[71] *Ibid.*, p. 78.
[72] *Ibid.*, p. 42.

complex network of relations which should be assessed contextually. The pastoral encounter is a contextual event within a systemic setting.

Cross-cultural Communication

It is important that when the pastoral encounter is applied in a situation of cross-cultural communication, it should be free from the unilateralisms of an "individualistic" and "private" understanding of human problems.[73]

An example of a more holistic and systemic way of thinking is the African philosophy of life. For the African, life is a continuum of cosmic, social and personal events. When one breaks society's moral codes, the universal ties between oneself and the community are also broken. This factor may be the main issue in a person's experience of suffering. It also brings a new dimension to recovery and cure. It is not the individual who has to be cured: it is the broken ties and relationships that need to be healed.

Ancestors play a decisive role within the African societal order and network of relationships. It is often stated, erroneously, that Africans *worship* their ancestors. This is not so. The latter are not

---

[73] In *Pastoral Care to the Sick in Africa*, ([1988], p. 5) A. A. Berinyuu, writes: "In Africa there is no division and/or differentiation between the animate and inanimate, between the spirit and matter, between living and non-living, dead and living, physical and metaphysical, secular and sacred, the body and the spirit, etc. Most Africans generally believe that everything (human beings included) is in constant relationship with one another and with the invisible world, and that people are in a state of complete dependence upon those invisible powers and beings. Hence, Africans are convinced that in the activities of life, harmony, balance or tranquility must constantly be sought and maintained. Society is not segmented into, for example, medicine, sociology, law, politics and religion. Life is a liturgy of celebration for the victories and/or sacrifices of others."

gods, but are part of the systemic network of relationships. Ancestors are the protectors of life and of the community. "Africans do
believe strongly in the presence and influence of ancestors in daily
life, so much so that they do things, often unconsciously, to reflect
such a belief, but they do not worship them as gods."[74]

Pastoral care should view an African primarily as a social
being who is intimately linked to his/her environment. Systemic
concepts have important *anthropological implications*. For example, personality is not a purely psychological concept. In Western
psychology, personality usually refers to the self-structure of a
person. It is part of the I-nucleus with its conscious and unconscious processes. Personality thus becomes an individual category which reflects the constant factor of typical behavior and
personal characteristics. The human being is autonomous and
independent.[75]

In contrast, within an African context, personality refers to a
dynamic power and a vital energy which allow a person to come
into contact with ancestors, God and society. For example,
Berinyuu, refers to an Akan tribe who have their own unique view
of a person. "The *ntroro* spirit is the energy which links him/her
to the ancestral lineage."[76] The human spirit is not regarded as an
identifiable self, but as a personal consciousness of powers which
is associated with the concept of "destiny." This destiny can be

---

[74] *Ibid.*, p. 8.

[75] Within African life, the community counts for almost everything. The individual is absorbed in the community. The relationship between the two is somewhat like that in a living organism: the single persons are like the limbs of a living
body (E. Ackermann, *Cry, Beloved Africa!* [1994], pp. 43-44). The constitutive
community in African society consists of a relatively autonomous extended family which depends on marriage and blood relatives. It ties together three to four
generations and ancestry. The special duties and rights in every aspect of life are
determined by ancestry and the degree of relationship.

[76] *Ibid.*, p. 10.

modified, so that one can adapt within circumstances and within a social context.

The above facts shed more light upon Africans' non-analytical approach to life. They do not practise Western-style introspection. Life, with its pain and problems, is accepted without questioning. This approach to life demands much patience and adaptability. As such, it differs vastly from a Western model. The West regards (clock) time and the manipulation of the environment as important. (This does not mean that African rhythm does not also manipulate and often abuse life and nature.) The point to grasp is that, within an African model, time is an *event* and life is an interplay of powers. Life and personality possess dynamic energy within societal relationships. Myth and symbol, ritual and rhythm determine everyday life, and not structures, analyses and solutions.[77] In terms of this view, a person can never be an isolated entity, but is embedded within social and other powers within which the individual has a role to play. A person's role in society determines identity. This is of greater importance than personal qualities and individual needs. Role fulfillment[78] becomes more important than personal self-actualization.

The previous outline of contextualization and inculturation makes it very clear that the assessment of a mature faith and the impact of different God-images on different religious experiences cannot be made without making a social and cultural analysis. A model for pastoral anthropology should therefore

[77] On the meaning of African spirituality, see A. Bellagamba, "New Attitudes towards Spirituality," (1987), p. 108: "African spirituality is spirit-inspired, life-centered, Gospel-based, creation-celebrating, hope-oriented, people-affirming, joy-filled. It is an incarnated, cosmic and global spirituality."

[78] A role does not indicate social position as a result of skills, possessions and professional status, but is a behavioral pattern based on society's expectations. A role is not a matter of choice. The view of the community/tribal community determines the person's role. Social identity therefore creates the person's role.

always try to determine the interplay between cultural values and God-images. The cultural context will determine contemporary views on being human. A good example of this is the individualism attached to the achievement ethics of postmodern materialism and capitalism. Another example to prove our argument is the brief sketch of an African view on life and the human being.

The following diagram (p. 280) could help the pastor to refine his/her pastoral diagnosis. It functions as a guideline to pose different questions and to control whether the diagnosis deals with the immediate context and reality.

For clarity on the interplay between a social-cultural context and an understanding of our being human, the following structural components should be dealt with. In a cultural[79] and social analysis, these structures shed light on vital questions which should be posed in order to obtain a better profile of those factors which influence the process of making a pastoral and anthropological assessment. They are the following:

a) *Existential questions within environmental settings.* These questions embrace issues regarding the meaning of one's life. What are the driving forces and motivational factors behind people's behavior? What are the main objectives and how are they linked to major life issues and philosophical

---

[79] In the various disciplines, there is, generally, little consensus on the meaning of "culture." For example, culture could refer to the "social practice" of activities and attitudes. It could even refer to the symbolical level denoting rites, traditions, myths, language, etc. In a more technical sense, it refers to technology and the transformation of creation into a human environment or "Heimat." It could even include the human attempt of understanding him-/herself within the processes of self-realization in the world. It includes knowledge or the act of knowledge. On the notion of culture as self-realization, see A. R. Crollius, "The Meaning of Culture in Theological Anthropology," (1986), p. 52.

questions? What causes anxiety and what kind of suffering determines a person's outlook? These questions should try to probe painful events which shape current attitudes and important processes of decision-making. Existential questions should also try to obtain clarity regarding the link between our human suffering and the destruction/pollution of our environment.

b) *Belief systems.* Questions should be asked in order to determine how a person, or a group of people, view the quest for the ultimate. The transcendental dimension refers to the important factor of spirituality and religiosity. Belief systems reveal the cultural background of God-images and refer to norms, values and customs which shape basic religious needs and expectations. They also give an indication of concepts used to express experiences of faith.

c) *Societal and communal structures.* An analysis should reveal those structures which determine social and communal behavior. Politics and economics play a crucial role in defining and determining the character of these structures. For example: whether one deals with a democratic, communist, socialist, bureaucratic or autocratic system should be questioned. Are the economics oriented towards an open market system (free enterprise) or are they dominated and regulated by a nationalistic or socialistic ideology? Other important factors are technological development, the communication network, the education system, and the legal system.

d) *Language and symbols.* Communal stories should be investigated in order to come to grips with possible existing myths which shape attitudes and thinking. A narrative analysis and linguistics could be of great assistance in this regard. Symbols in language and metaphoric expressions often reveal a culture's "inner soul" and its influence on anthropology.

e) *The dynamics of relationships.* Another area is the important influence of marriage and family structures on human behavior. For example, monogamy has a different influence on sexual values than polygamy. An important area which should be investigated, is that of sexuality (norms and values) and its influence on marriage structures, role fulfillment and family life. Whether one deals with an extended family system or a modern family unit (the private family), will determine the outcome of personal identity (interconnectedness versus privatization and individualization).

f) *The existing ethos.* Ethos refers to morals and basic attitudes regarding diverse life issues. A culture's dominating ethos influences anthropology because it reflects the values and norms which determine personal identity and self-image. The ethos deals with questions relating to what is right or wrong. It also mirrors the influence of long-standing traditional values (the impact of tradition on anthropology).

g) *Philosophy of life.* The undergirding view of life, as expressed in different philosophical models, should be determined: for example, whether one deals with a premodern, modern, or postmodern society. What is the existing approach to life: is it religious, rationalistic, scientific, socialistic or capitalistic?

h) *Passages of life and rituals.* Throughout the various stages of life, rituals occur which help people to pass through difficult phases. Rituals are embedded in cultural views and indicate how a person or cultural group deals with important life issues such as birth, festivity, death and grief.

DIAGRAM FOR MAKING A SOCIAL AND CULTURAL ANALYSIS

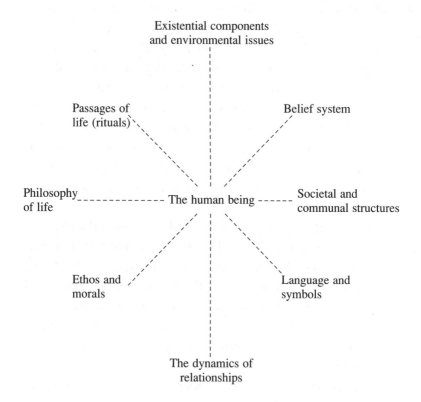

Remark: The diagram should be used together with the various models for making an assessment of God-images and the character of religious experiences. The whole notion of understanding our being human and the processes of developing a mature faith and growth in spirituality must be interpreted within the components and structures of the above-mentioned diagram. It helps the pastor to gain a more realistic insight regarding the dynamics of spirituality and contextuality (a care for life). The value of such a systemic approach to anthropology and spirituality is that it contributes to developing a pastoral hermeneutics of care and counseling which operates within systems and contexts rather than merely with isolated individuals and privatized religiosity.

3.5 Towards the Naming of God in Spiritual Direction and Pastoral Counseling: God as our "Soul Friend" and "Parner for Life"?

Throughout the tradition of spiritual direction, the main emphasis has been on discipline, contemplation, meditation and different exercises to mold spirituality in terms of personal identity and devotion.[80] Prayer and awareness exercises shape worship and personal piety. Central to the understanding of spiritual direction is a way of togetherness, presence, silence and peace where pastor and parishioner share a mutual fellowship with God.[81]

---

[80] It is even possible to speak of a psychology of spirituality which refers to a process of mental thinking in which different ideas regarding an object are being experienced (H. F. de Wit, *De Verborgen Bloei* [1993], pp. 90-97). Such experiences can lead to wisdom, prudence — a contemplative mode of knowledge. Contemplative psychology refers to a process of inner growth/flourishing which brings about experiences of spiritual empowerment and deep joy/happiness. The inner peace and rest create an openness towards life, filled with a mysterious stability.

[81] Togetherness and presence (immediacy) in spiritual direction has been described by J. Fentener van Vlissingen in *Het Pad van de Geestelijke Begeleiding* (1980), pp. 75-114. He sees listening and silence as the two dynamic poles of spiritual direction. Empathy (p. 92) is the key word for what he calls an "a-verbal" form of communication (p. 74). Body language and trust are both ingredients of such a way of communication.

In a very extensive volume, C. E. Kunz, (*Schweigen und Geist* [1996], pp. 4-5) develops what she calls "a theology of silence" — the art of how to keep quiet. The event of incarnation compels the theologian to be silent and to meditate within a liturgical awareness of the presence of Christ. She connects the silence with experience. Both create a spirituality where the presence of Christ is linked with the Spirit. "Erst Logos und Pneuma bilden auch den theologischen Kontext

It is clear that world-wide there is a new interest in spirituality. Although it has been predicted that secularization means the end of Christianity, it seems that modernity, with its emphasis on rationality, functionality, and economic achievement, is looking anew for some form of transcendence and spirituality. Modern human beings still attempt to escape a materialistic world view by trying to make contact with the realm of transcendency and mystic experiences.[82] An example of this is the interest in oriental meditation techniques and the experimentation with drugs by teenagers and pop groups.

Despite the fact that many mainline churches experience a decline in membership and interest in worship, religiosity still prevails. In this regard the remark of H. Cox in his new book, *Fire from Heaven*,[83] is quite remarkable: "If God is really dead, as Nietzsche's mad man proclaimed, then why have so many billions of people not received the news? Nearly three decades ago I wrote a book, *The Secular City*, in which I tried to work out a theology for the 'postreligious' age that many sociologists had confidently assured us was coming. Since then, however, religion — or at least some religions — seems to have gained a new lease on life. Today it is secularity, not spirituality, that may be headed for extinction."

Although this might not be true of Europe, the question still prevails whether secularization is not the luxurious byproduct of a

des Schweigens" (p. 16). Word (*Logos*), silence and *Pneuma* — those three are the constitutive elements of true spirituality. The anthropological consequence of a theology of silence is faith (p. 758). "Das Schweigen in der Begegnung trägt mehrere Gesichter; das menschliche Antlitz dieser Begegnung heisst theologisch 'Glaube.' Glaube ist jenes Gesamtverhalten, jene Gesamtbefindlichkeit, worin der Mensch durch die Kraft der Gnade der Offenbarungsanrede Gottes entspricht" (p. 758).

[82] On the issue of spirituality within the context of modernity, see M. Légaut, *Vie Spirituelle et Modernité* (1992), p. 65.

[83] See H. Cox, *Fire from Heaven* (1995), p. xv.

wealthy and affluent society and a church which has become so identified with the values of a materialistic world view that it suffers from role confusion. The positive outcome of secularization is that the flirtation between church and state has been broken down. If this is not true of other countries in the world, it is rather true of contemporary developments in South Africa. Secularization can even open up new avenues for Christian spirituality and the engagement of the church with social issues such as poverty, racism, classism, sexism and economic discrimination.

Nevertheless, the conviction still prevails that our postmodern culture should be assessed as a challenge to the church to reflect anew on the meaning of God-language within a secular world.[84] The naming of God should, therefore, lead to a pastoral hermeneutics which is essentially heuristic.[85] The question at stake in "postmodern spirituality" is not whether one believes in God or not, but in which god one believes.[86] In his book, *Geloofscrisis als Gezichtsbedrog*, D. Tieleman[87] envisages a new task for pastoral theology, *i.e.,* to uncover the still hidden quest for meaning. A hermeneutics which is heuristic should challenge postmodernity and try to reflect anew on the meaning of God-language. And this is precisely what spiritual direction in a postmodern society should be about.[88] Hence, Tieleman's proposal for a spirituality of dialogue

---

[84] See D. Tieleman, "De Pastor als Grenzganger" (1996), pp. 6-7.

[85] *Ibid.,* p. 12.

[86] *Ibid.,* p. 17.

[87] See Tieleman, *Geloofscrisis als Gezichtsbedrog*, 171.

[88] J. C. Noordzij (*Religieus Concept en Religieuze Ervaring in de Christelijke Tradisie* [1994]) remarks that spiritual direction indeed includes the correction of God-images. His attempt is to reflect on the process character of spiritual development towards an awareness of reality and self-realization. The latter is not contradictory to an understanding of God's presence. The reciprocity between knowledge of God and knowledge of self is important for an understanding of a developmental model of Christian spirituality (p. 123). He concludes: Christian spirituality includes

which takes into consideration the following five elements of spirituality:[89] the contemporary way of thinking; living and the prevailing philosophy of our time; the norms and values which serve as a source of inspiration (Leidmotiv); the mutuality between personal existence and personal functions in society; a center of meditation where one can be directed regarding how to concentrate and reflect on essential life and religious matters; a mystical experience where one becomes aware of the ultimate.

One should bear in mind that the spiritual direction which deals with God-images, does not exclude meditation, contemplation and mystical experiences. What it tries to illuminate is an important aspect, namely, the influence of an understanding of God on human conduct and experience (life issues). This accent indeed brings a difference when one compares it, for example, with what has been called "orthodox spirituality" with its focal point on the ascetic and mystic tradition.

An orthodox spirituality is much more focused on a transforming union between the soul and God. "The transforming union or spiritual marriage is described both by those who conceive spiritual life as a deification (theosis) and by those who lay stress on the nuptial relationship between the soul and her Lord."[90] Contemplation has been identified with perfection — which denotes charity (love). "But a contemplation which would be the utmost exercise of charity, *culmen caritatis*, would also be the acme of perfection, *culmen perfectionis*."[91] In this process the three ways

both self-knowledge and knowledge of God. Both are ingredients of a spiritual direction (p. 124) which wants to create an expansion of an awareness of reality (p. 127). The spiritual way becomes a metaphor for development. Within the stages along the path in which the process of change occurs, different phases can be distinguished: crisis, sensibilization and breakthrough to a next stage (p. 225).

[89] See Tieleman, *Geloofscrisis als Gezichtsbedrog*, pp. 119-120.

[90] See Monk of the Eastern Church, *Orthodox Spirituality* (1980[2]), p. 29.

[91] *Ibid.*, p. 30.

— purgative, illuminative and unitive — have become classic.
One should therefore develop from the practice of virtues (*praxis*);
then to contemplation (*theoria*) and the suppression of passions
(*apatheia*); to the last *teleios* (perfectness) which is connected to
an experiential knowledge of God (*theologia*). Within these stages
three essential moments in spiritual life have been distinguished:
the rituals of baptism, confirmation (*chrisma*) and the Eucharist.
They all contribute to a process of unfolding sanctification.

Because of modernity, contemporary spirituality is more
involved in social and contextual issues. At stake is more the relevancy of the presence of God within experiences of suffering
than contemplative exercises which foster a perfect union and fellowship with God.

A clear distinction between the sacred and the profane no
longer exists. Nevertheless, the quest for meaning prevails. A new
interpretation of spirituality and spiritual direction could help pastoral care to be engaged with those life-issues where the question
about our human significance and purposefulness surfaces: "la
principale fin de la vie humaine" (Calvin). The quest for meaning
equals our quest for humanity. Perhaps the answer is no longer the
straightforward one put forth by Calvin: to glorify God. In a postmodern context the answer is more complex: to interpret God in
terms of contexts.

I. Baumgartner's proposal for spirituality is an attempt to link a
contextual spirituality with an understanding of the diaconic function of the church.[92] The pastoral intervention should, therefore,
reveal the meaning of the concept "God" in such a way that people will start experiencing God as their Friend of Life and Love.[93]
Contextuality is then shaped by an understanding of God which

---

[92] See I. Baumgartner, *Pastoralpsychologie* (1990), p. 332.
[93] *Ibid.*, p. 333.

reveals the diaconic engagement of God with vital life and cosmic issues.

S. Hauerwas warns against the conventional image which perceives God as "a transcendent watchdog, a bureaucratic manager — by the assumption that we must control our existence by acquiring the power to eradicate from our lives anything that threatens our autonomy as individuals. Instead, theology should deal with the friendship of God."[94]

The notion of the "friendship and partnership of God" should then become an indication of that kind of identification between God and the cosmos (ontology of communion) which reveals a cosmic spirituality and reflects a cosmic understanding of reconciliation. The "friendship and partnership of God" can even lead to a reinterpretation of what was traditionally known as "panentheism."

Towards a Theological Reinterpretation of "Panentheism"

Empirical research underlines the need for a fresh theological paradigm, interpreting God in terms of relationships and human experiences; that is why theology should reframe the concept: panentheism.

Anthropomorphisms, i.e., speaking appropriately and metaphorically about God in human terminology, and existential modes of being, are inevitable. From a pneumatological perspective we can even risk the following: panentheism as an indication of the indwelling presence of God in this world and the cosmos. The indwelling presence of the Spirit (inhabitatio) forces one to move further than the traditional understanding of a relational model: God and human being/cosmos. In a pneumatology one should go

---

[94] See S. Hauerwas, Naming the Silences (1990), pp. 60 and 83.

further and admit: God *in* human being/cosmos. Panentheism, then, is a metaphor for God's immediacy and presence in the cosmos through the penetrating work of the Holy Spirit.

J. A. van der Ven's empirical research investigated the appropriateness of the three classic models in theology: theism, deism and pantheism.[95] The survey reveals that the pantheistic interpretation of God (the unity of all existing beings with God as a driving force, a transcendent factor rather than a personal entity)[96] has a profound influence on the modern human understanding of individual and social autonomy.[97]

The outcome of Van der Ven's empirical research indicates that theology should re-interpret panentheism: the simultaneous experience of God's immanency and transcendency.[98] Panentheism then reflects the beauty of creation; the ecstasy of love within human relationships; the awe for the complexity of nature and the energetic force of imagination and creativity. All these elements within a cosmology should then be interpreted in terms of the dynamics of pneumatology — *a critical pneumatology of perichoresis*: the notion of God *in* humanity (not humanity *is* God, but humanity as a metaphor for the love of God).

J. Moltmann latches onto this notion of panentheism.[99] God and creation cannot be separated metaphysically. Within a web of reciprocal relationships, God's "in" is a pneumatological reality. "In this network of relationships, 'making,' 'preserving,' 'maintaining'

---

[95] See J. A. van der Ven, "Autonom vor Gott?" (1997), p. 301.

[96] *Ibid.*, pp. 301-302.

[97] Van der Ven, "Autonom vor Gott?", p. 311: "In sieben von zehn Fällen zeigt sich dass der pantheistische Glaube Einfluss auf die individuelle und soziale Autonomie ausübt, einmal beeinflusst der theistische Glaube die soziale Autonomie, und zweimal liegt kein einziger Einfluss des Glaubens an Gott auf die individuelle und soziale Autonomie vor."

[98] *Ibid.*, p. 317.

[99] See J. Moltmann, *God in Creation* (1993), pp. 13-14.

and 'perfecting' are certainly the one great *one-sided* relationship: but 'indwelling,' 'sym-pathizing,' 'participating,' 'accompanying,' 'enduring,' 'delighting' and 'glorifying' are relationships of *mutuality* which describe a cosmic community of living between God the Spirit and all his created things."[100] By panentheism is then meant the principle of mutual penetration: "... that all relationships which are analogous to God reflect the primal, reciprocal indwelling and mutual interpenetration of the trinitarian perichoresis: God in the world and the world in God."[101] Panentheism, understood in the light of pneumatology, does not exclude the transcendence of God. Within a metaphorical understanding, it means: the transcendence of God then is the preeminent or primary Spirit of the universe. It means that nothing exists outside God, "... though this does not mean that God is reduced to things."[102]

The penetrating effect of a pneumatological perichoresis of God *in* humanity has the following implication for a pastoral anthropology: the essence of our being human is determined by the pneumatological principle of love and grace (the charismatic fruit of the Spirit; the pneumatic person as a metaphor of God's love for and in the world).

God-images and the friendship, companionship, partnership and faithfulness of God

The issue of God-images in theology is closely linked to different models of interpretation. A hermeneutics of pastoral care should, therefore, reckon with the following schemata of interpretation:

[100] *Ibid.*, p. 14.
[101] *Ibid.*, p. 17.
[102] See McFague, *Models of God,* p. 73.

- The *hierarchical schema*. God is then interpreted in terms of dominionship. Such a schema often leads to a very authoritarian and autocratic interpretation of God. Within an imperialistic paradigm, God, as King or Lord, becomes a Monarch. Inevitably, this leads to the tension between superiority and inferiority. In a hierarchical model, this often happens to be the case: God is everything (theocentrism) and human beings are nothing.
- *The metaphysical schema*. Metaphysics should still be a very important matter for theology and could not be disregarded. Metaphysics addresses the very important question of matter and the "What?" One cannot forever brush aside metaphysics in a pragmatic and functional society. Ontology remains an important philosophical issue and should not be ignored, not even in theology.

The theological problem surfaces when a speculative and very rationalistic and positivistic interpretation of metaphysics is used to interpret and explain God's "beyondness," "otherness" and "transcendence." The danger then is that one disconnects God from his relatedness to creation and from the important event of the encounter between God and human beings. As such, metaphysics cannot be projected onto the being of God. This easily leads to speculation when one runs into the danger of portraying God as the prototype of being: Being. The further problem with such a model is that, instead of his proximity, God becomes disengaged from our human misery.

- *The Hellenistic schema*. Here God is interpreted in terms of an ontological principle of immutability. This leads to the notion of the impassibility of God. Human suffering does not affect a disinterested God (apathy).

The Hellenistic schema reveals several of the tendencies, attached to the ontologies of the Greco-Roman world.

> (1) In their highest expressions, as in Stoicism, Platonism, and Aristotelianism, they press toward systematization and theoretical abstraction. (2) They search for universals, whether as "real"

(Plato) or "conceptual" (Aristotle), that explain and transcend all particulars. (3) They tend to identify "the really real" with intangible, spiritual being, which is either limited or positively distorted by material embodiment. (4) They tend accordingly to classify existing entities in a hierarchic manner, with those possessing the greatest potentiality for spirit/reason having precedence over those more subject to their physicality. (5) They tend therefore to consider being substantially, that is, as comprised of qualities or attributes (such as spirit, mind, body) whose presence or absence in existing entities determines their nature and worth.[103]

- *The romantic schema.* In terms of our human need to strive for "happiness" and to seek peace, God easily becomes the prototype of a romantic understanding of love (cheap grace: the "yes," without the "no"). Then love is an indication of God's identification with humanity in terms of the incarnation. Our being human and relationships become a medium for a direct revelation of God. The implication is that love becomes an unqualified "yes" without the "no" (resistance and judgement). God becomes the embodiment of a love that is not associated with pain and evil. Negation is thus ignored. The further implication of such a "nice God," to be found all over creation ("incarnational embodiment"), is that everything is "okay" and acceptable.

- *The rationalistic, positivistic schema.* The attempt to describe God in terms of his attributes, easily ends up with mere rationalistic speculation. Attributes are then an indication of substance and disclose "the essence of God." Attributes become a substantialistic description of God (his intrinsic Being) in such a way that human beings can define, comprehend and determine God totally. The problem with such a model is that it does not take the metaphorical meaning of God-language and the function of anthropomorphism into consideration. Attributes are then estimated as *essential*

---

[103] D J Hall, *Professing the Faith* (1993), p. 318.

characteristics and not as a depiction of God in terms of his condescending involvement with human beings and his concrete actions of salvation. Instead of being merely modes and functions, they acquire the status of ontological indicators. "The key to the whole discussion of the divine attributes is relationship, that is, the ongoing encounter between God and human beings that is characterized by trust and truth."[104]

- *A relational model.* In a relational model the being of God is understood in terms of "being-with." It reckons with the fact that biblical theology operates with an epistemology based upon faith and revelation. In a revelational model, *relation*, rather than *essence/substance* is important. In a relational model the key concepts which are used to describe the truth, point towards an ontology of communion. They do not describe substances, qualities, or endowments.[105] Moreover, when they are deployed to describe the latter, they are torn from their biblical context and are badly distorted.

Faith, grace hope, repentance, gratitude, praise — these words do not connote substances or qualities that may be acquired. To "have faith" as though it were a possession, is a misconception. Faith is *trust* and presupposes another in whom faith is placed. To trust God is not to possess God or to comprehend the character of his very Being, but is to rely on his faithfulness. Trust functions and operates within the ontological assumption of the interrelatedness — the integrity — of all that exists.

In theology there is always the danger of connoting substance to God, rather than relation and faithfulness. "*Theos, Christos, Pneuma* and *anthropos* do not name beings who possess being to a greater or lesser extent and can be arranged on a scale of being

---

[104] *Ibid.,* p. 155.
[105] *Ibid.,* p. 321.

accordingly. Salvation does not refer to the triumph of a 'higher' substance, soul, or a 'lower,' body. Christology does not consist in the harmonious admixture of seemingly antithetical substances, humanity and divinity. The Trinity does not describe a deity capable of containing transcendent and immanent qualities."[106] All of these categories do not exclude the notion of *reality;* but then a reality connected to God's faithfulness and directed towards the restoration of broken relationships. Because of "being-with" and *koinonia*, God-language should reflect an image which views God, not "all alone" as an entity, a being "greater than whom none can be conceived,"[107] but rather as the center and source of all relatedness. And it is to this center that the notion of God as Soul Friend, Companion and Partner for Life refers. A center which is determined by faithfulness, servanthood, sacrifice, suffering and vulnerability.

The implication for a Christian and pastoral anthropology is that humanity should then be defined in terms of the law of inter-communion. When human beings seek to defy this law of intercommunion, interrelatedness, interconnectedness (cohumanity) and integrity in order to acquire an autonomy built upon selfish self-centeredness, despite other human beings, freedom becomes distorted and "inhumanity" sets in.

> What humanity "is" is cohumanity — is inconceivable apart from the companionship, both human and extrahuman, that constitutes its original condition. Being truly human in God's intention is being in relationship with the counterparts of our being. Human existence is co-existence.[108]

"Being-with" and God's friendship declares that being human, as intended by God, is reciprocal being. "It is characterized by

---

[106] *Ibid.*, p. 321.
[107] *Ibid.*, p. 322.
[108] *Ibid.*, p. 323.

mutuality, interdependence, communion, dialogue, cooperation, sympathy, sharing, concord."[109]

Within a pastoral anthropology, the friendship of God should inevitably lead to the ethical principle of sacrifice and servanthood (love). Theologically speaking, both humanity and an ethics of love/servanthood (sacrifice) is not merely based upon the incarnation (God became human in order that we might become truly human), but upon "inhabitation" and "interpenetration": God interpenetrates our very being and creation by the indwelling presence of the Spirit in order that we might be empowered to act in a humane manner. Because of *inhabitatio*, God is *in* us and *in* creation ("panentheism"). This *in* is not to be assessed substantially, but relationally. It becomes a metaphor for healing, restoration, peace and integrity.

The argument to view the relationality of God in terms of friendship, companionship, partnership and faithfulness, hinges on the following basic assumptions.

• Ontology, in theology, should deal with communion, interconnectedness, relationality and mutuality, rather than with abstract substance. Transcendent otherness should therefore be understood in terms of communion with that in relation to which it is, indeed, "wholly other."

• Because of human beings' need for intimacy (the need to be accepted unconditionally without the fear of rejection) in a post modern era, *solidarity* becomes an important issue in theology.

• Although different, the Christian tradition operates with a *Theos* who is "other-centered," rather than "beyond-centered." The living God is a faithful God and his presence is an interpenetrating, pneumatological event within the whole of creation. Grace, in a theonomous model, means that the living God is *geocentric* and *anthropocentric* rather than theocentric.

---

[109] *Ibid.*, p. 325.

• To understand God, a theological hermeneutics inevitably leads to the notion of a suffering God and to the paradigm of a theology of the cross (*theologia crucis*). The power of God is not linked to immutability, but to vulnerability (weakness). "A Theology that maintains the image of a deity based on a power principle that can only comfort the comfortable is a flagrantly disobedient, not merely a doctrinally distorted, Theology."[110] A theology of the cross should replace the romantic image of an "efficient," "prosperous" God within an affluent society. A theology of the cross deals with the darkness in the light, the no within the yes.

• A very unique ethos correlates with communion, companionship and friendship: sacrificial servanthood. Humanity is thus fostered by servanthood and selfless stewardship. Attached to the notion of humanity and identity in a pastoral anthropology, are the notions of representation, embodiment, enfleshment, vocation and stewardship. A Christian is a person who, because of his/her communion with a suffering God, should display an ethos of sacrificial servanthood. Christians should express the presence of God chiefly in the language of gratitude, thanksgiving and praise. Why? Because God *is* love.

In an article on the nature of divine love, V. Brümmer advocates the concept, "God as Love," as an indication of a relationship of reciprocity and mutuality.[111] The freedom of God is expressed by the concept love, because God is in need of our love. Thus God's love should be reciprocated. According to Brümmer the *amicitia Dei*, the friendship of God, is not a new concept in the Christian tradition and mysticism.[112] Bernard of Clairvaux even stressed the point that the unity between God and humans is not an essential identification but a voluntary identification. Hence, the

---

[110] *Ibid.*, p. 134.

[111] See V. Brümmer, "The Nature of Divine Love" (1995), pp. 1 and 7.

[112] See V. Brümmer, "God, Geen Persoon?" (1996), p. 11.

notion in the Christian tradition of the enjoyment of God: *Deum glorificare eodemque frui in aeternum.*[113]

A. Matti is convinced that our God-images should be revised in terms of contemporary issues.[114] She, too, utilizes the love paradigm and proposes "God as Lover." As Lover, God is the source of love and a mystical experience of devoted friendship.[115]

V. Brümmer describes friendship and a relationship of love in terms of the following five characteristics.[116]

a) A relationship of love and friendship is concerned with the importance and interest of the other. It banishes every form of self-interest and selfishness.

b) The partners in a relationship of love are unique and irreplaceable.

c) It reflects a mutual freedom which is maintained in terms of reciprocity, and not in terms of plight or demand.

d) A relationship of love and friendship makes both partners vulnerable. Love always implies a risk and the possibility of suffering.

e) Love and friendship presuppose a relationship which is personal. Hence, Brümmer's attempt to portray the friendship between God and human beings in terms of the love paradigm.

Our choice for introducing the metaphors, God as our "Soul Friend," and "Partner for Life" latches on to the love paradigm and the notion of God's faithfulness. This reflects the current need for acceptance, fellowship, intimacy and continuity. It should be borne

[113] *Ibid.,* p. 212.

[114] See A. Matti, *Of Zoek naar God als Minnaar* (1996), p. 106.

[115] It seems that there is a new interest in God-language and the naming of God. See C. den Hertog, *Het Zonderlinge Karakter van de Godsnaam* (1996); P. Vardy, *Het Raadsel van God* (1997); R. Adolfes, *De Afwezigheid Gods* (1997); R. E. Friedman, *The Disappearance of God* (1995); N. Ter Linden, *Het Verhaal Gaat* (1996); J. Miles, *God: A biography* (1995).

[116] See Brümmer, "God, Geen Persoon?", pp. 212-214.

in mind that the naming of God is an existential matter and exposed to relationality and relativity.[117] Many different metaphors for God exist and should be applied to different religious experiences. Indeed, God is still our "Shepherd," our heavenly "Father," our "Lord" and "King." But all of these metaphors become more and more exposed to a theological inflation as our experience of shepherds in a postmodern society vanishes, and our perception of existing fathers, lords and kings becomes blurred. With regard to spiritual direction in an age void of meaning, perhaps the metaphor God as Soul Friend can help to instill hope and the metaphor God as Partner for Life can help to discover significance and meaning. And hope is central to what pastors do. This is the reason why D. Capps reframes the distinctiveness of pastors among the other helping professions in terms of the category of hope.[118] Pastors thus are "agents of hope." "... Pastors can help to instill hope in other persons."[119]

The reasons for choosing the metaphors God as Soul Friend and Partner for Life within spiritual direction (the formation of a mature faith) can be summarized as follows:

[117] Kaufman (*God-Mystery-Diversity*, p. 107): "The symbol 'God' holds together two motifs. On the one hand as the irreducible mystery of things, God is understood to transcend everything human. On the other hand, God is regarded as having a significant connection with our humanness and our struggles for humanness." The problem with Kaufman's approach is that the symbol "God" becomes a substitute for our need for order, security and consistency. God becomes a sustaining power for life. "God is not thought of here as a particular being but rather as a particular form of ordering activity going on in the world, namely that serendipitous ordering which has given rise (among other things) to the evolution of life on our planet" (p. 109). But, and this is the challenging question, if we are employing the name "God" to designate that creativity, that mystery, which undergirds our human existence in all its complexity and all its diversity (p. 109) — are we not then committing ourselves to projecting our wishful thinking for a humane world? What about the existence of God as a personal being? It is understandable why Kaufman refers to Christ in a symbolic mode rather than as some sort of immediate physical presence (p. 111).

[118] See D. Capps, *Agents of Hope* (1995), pp. 2-3.

[119] *Ibid.,* p. 2.

a) It conveys God's vulnerability in terms of his identification with human suffering. God's friendship led towards sacrifice — his pathos as conveyed in Christ's cross. The friendship of God is the pastoral consequence which stems from the theological notion, the crucified God.

b) It creates a sense of intimacy and belonging. As Soul Friend, God has accepted human beings unconditionally. The metaphor creates a re-interpretation of the contemporary quest for meaning and humanity in postmodernity. It opens up avenues to explore a fresh understanding of spirituality which transcends the "metaphysical paradigm" (the God beyond) in the direction of a "panentheistic paradigm": the God "with-in"; *with* our being human, *in* our suffering.

c) It solves the gender issue in the contemporary debate about the question whether God should be understood in terms of masculinity (God as Father) or femininity (God as Mother).

d) It communicates partnership, companionship, stewardship, deputyship and fellowship (*koinonia*).

e) It prevents God-images from becoming interpreted merely in terms of helplessness, vulnerability and weakness. Friendship points to faithfulness and trust. As a Soul Friend, God is faithful to his promises.

f) Friendship brings about honesty and spontaneity. It describes our relationship with God in terms of different emotional experiences, such as joy, gratitude, anger, disappointment and depression. Within the framework of the lament in the Old Testament, the friendship of God opens up avenues to even accuse and blame God. God's friendship can take our anger and rage.

g) Partnership reflects Israel's covenantal tradition. It, therefore, portrays God's engagement with his suffering people and describes God's salvific involvement in our history.

h) Within a situation of cross-cultural communication, the metaphors of God as Soul Friend and Partner for Life opens up new ways of understanding and interpreting foreign religious values in other cultures.

i) It does not assess persons in terms of an achievement ethics. What is of importance within a loving relationship, is not our knowing or doing functions. As a Soul Friend and Partner for Life, God is interested in our "being functions." Who we are is more important than what we know and achieve.

j) Friend is linked to a metaphor used by Christ in John 15:13-15. We are no longer slaves. Our human dignity is expressed by the fact that Christ called us his friends. James 4:4 also refers to friendship with God, while Abraham, in James 2:23, was called a friend of God.

L. T. Johnson gives an exposition of the meaning of friendship (*philia*) in the letter of James.[120] He mentions the fact that "friend" was not used lightly in the Greek world. Epicurus included it among the highest of goods available to humans. For Plato it was the ideal paradigm for the city-state. Even Aristotle considered friendship the prime metaphor and motive for society.

In the Greek world, friendship was not considered simply a casual affection. "On the contrary, it was regarded as a particularly intense and inclusive kind of intimacy, not only at the physical level but, above all, at the spiritual. Already in the *Orestes* friends are called 'one soul' (*mia psuchés),* and Aristotle quotes this among other proverbial expressions of the sort by means of which the Greeks typically expressed their deepest perceptions."[121]

---

[120] See L. T. Johnson, "Friendship with the World/Friendship with God" (1985), p. 173.

[121] *Ibid.,* p. 173.

To be "one soul" with God means to share the same purpose in life: the transformation and empowerment of human beings in terms of the realm of grace and reconciliation. It indicates that God and humans share the same spiritual value: unconditional love. The sharing of love and friendship which emanates from the reciprocity between persons and God is expressed in fellowship (*koinonia*). The *koinonia* in the body of Christ (the church) enfleshes friendship on the basis of equality. This is the reason why humanity stems from the discovery of intimacy: *i.e.,* the experience that one is accepted both in spite of who you are, as well as because of who you are.

A mature faith is the anthropological consequence of the theological principle: we have been saved by grace and unconditional love. It gives birth to a hope which is founded in the faithfulness of God and has been shaped by the vulnerability and suffering of God. It transcends the limitations of our human misery. Because of the penetrating perichoresis of the Spirit, a mature faith is, pneumatologically speaking, determined by the fruit of the Spirit (Gal 5:22-23). Spiritual direction is the result of the empowering presence of the Spirit and its main purpose is to promote growth in love, joy, peace, patience, kindness, goodness, faithfulness, gentleness and self-control (Life and wholeness).

BIBLIOGRAPHY

E. Ackermann, *Cry, Beloved Africa! A Continent Needs Help* (Munich-Kinshasha: African University Studies, 1994).

J. E. Adams, *More than Redemption* (Grand Rapids: Baker, 1979).

R. Adolfes, *De Afwezigheid van God* (Baarn: Ten Have, 1997).

R. S. Anderson, *On Being Human: Essays in Theological Anthropology* (Grand Rapids: Eerdmans, 1982).

H. Andriessen, *Oorspronkelijk bestaan: Geestelijke Begeleiding in Onze Tijd* (Baarn: Gooi & Sticht, 1996).

David W. Augsburger, *Pastoral Counseling Across Cultures* (Philadelphia: Westminster, 1986).

K. Barth, *Die Lehre von der Schöpfung,* Kirchliche Dogmatik III/2 (Zollikon-Zürich: Evangelischer Verlag, 1948).

K. Barth, *Die Lehre von der Versöhnung*. Kirchliche Dogmatik IV/1. (Zollikon-Zürich: Evangelischer Verlag, 1953).

R. L. Bassett *et al.*, "Picturing God: A Nonverbal Measure of God-concepts for Conservative Protestants," *Journal of Psychology and Christianity* 9, no. 2 (1990) 73-81.

I. Baumgartner, *Pastor — Psychologie: Einführung in die Praxis Heilender Seelsorge* (Düsseldorf: Patmos Verlag, 1990).

I. Baumgartner, *Pastoralpsychologie* (Düsseldorf: Patmos Verlag, 1990).

H. L. Bee, *The Journey of Adulthood* (New York: Macmillan, 1992[2]).

E. J. Beker & J. M. Hasselaar, *Wegen en Kruispunten in Dogmatiek: Deel 4, Over de Heilige Geest en de Sacramenten* (Kampen: Kok, 1987).

A. Bellagamba, "New Attitudes towards Spirituality," *Towards African Christian Maturity*, eds. A. Shorter *et al.* (Kampala: St Paul Publications, 1987).

D. G. Benner (ed.), *Psychotherapy and the Spiritual Quest* (Grand Rapids: Baker, 1988).

L. Benze, *Die Kirche als Kommunikation* (Zsambek: Ungarn, 1996).

P. L. Berger, *A Rumor of Angels: Modern Society and the Rediscovery of the Supernatural* (New York: Doubleday, 1969).

A. E. Bergin, "Values and Issues in Psychotherapy and Mental Health," *American Psychologist* 46, no. 4 (1991) 394-403.

A. A. Berinyuu, *Pastoral Care to the Sick in Africa: An Approach to Transcultural Pastoral Theology* (Frankfurt: Peter Lang, 1988).

H. Berkhof, *Christelijk Geloof* (Nijkerk: Callenbach, 1973).

G. C. Berkouwer, *De Mens het Beeld Gods: Dogmatische Studien* (Kampen: Kok, 1957).

G. C. Berkouwer, *Geloof en Rechtvaardiging* (Kampen: Kok, 1975²).

J. H. Billington, "Education and Culture Beyond 'Lifestyles,'" *Virtue — Public and Private*, ed. R. J. Neuhaus (Grand Rapids: Eerdmans, 1986).

L. C. Bishop, "Healing in the Koinonia: Therapeutic Dynamics of Church Community," *Journal of Psychology and Theology* 13, no. 1 (1985) 12-20.

G. L. Borchert & A. D. Lester (eds.), *Spiritual Dimensions of Pastoral Care* (Philadelphia: Westminister, 1985).

D. J. Bosch, *Transforming Mission: Paradigm Shifts in Theology and Mission* (Maryknoll: Orbis, 1991).

W. J. Bouwsma, "Christian Adulthood", *Adulthood*, ed. E. H. Erikson (New York: W. W. Norton, 1978).

Braaten, C. E. "The Problem of God-language Today," *Our Naming of God: Problems and Prospects of God-talk Today*, ed. C. E. Braaten. (Minneapolis: Fortress, 1989) 11-33.

J. Brinkerink, "Ontstaansgeschiedenis van het Begrip Verantwoordelijkheid," *Nederlands Theologisch Tijdschrift* 30, no. 3 (1976) 207-220.

C. Brown (ed.), *The New International Dictionary of the New Testament* vols. 1, 2, 3 (Exeter: Paternoster, 1975, 1976, 1978 respectively).

L. B. Brown, *The Psychology of Religious Belief* (London: Academic, 1987).

L. B. Brown, *The Psychology of Religion: An Introduction* (London: SPCK, 1988).

L. B. Brown (ed.), *Religion, Personality and Mental Health* (New York: Springer, 1994).

D. Browning, *Normen en Waarden in het Pastoraat* (Haarlem: De Toorts, 1978).

D. Browning, "Images of Man in Contemporary Models of Pastoral Care," *Interpretation* 23, no. 2, (1979) 144-156.

D. Browning (ed.), *Practical Theology* (San Francisco: Harper & Row, 1983.)

V. Brümmer, *Liefde van God en Mens* (Kampen/Kapellen: Kok/Pelckmanns, 1993).

V. Brümmer, "The Nature of Divine Love," *South African Journal for Philosophy* 14, no.1 (1995) 1-8.

V. Brümmer, "God, Geen Persoon?" *Collationes* 26 (Juni 1996) 211-219.

R. E. Butman, "The Assessment of Religious Development: Some Possible Options," *Journal of Psychology and Christianity* 9 no 2 (1990) 14-26.

J. Calvijn, *Institutie* (translated by A. Sizoo) (Delft: Meinema, *s.a.*).

D. Capps, *Deadly Sins and Saving Virtues* (Philadelphia: Fortress, 1987).

D. Capps, *The Depleted Self: Sin in a Narcissistic Age* (Minneapolis: Fortress, 1993).

D. Capps, *The Poet's Gift: Toward the Renewal of Pastoral Care* (Louisville, Kentucky: Westminister, 1993).

D. Capps, *Agents of Hope: A Pastoral Psychology* (Minneapolis: Fortress Press, 1995).

M. E. Cavanagh, "The Perception of God in Pastoral Counseling," *Pastoral Psychology* 41, no. 2 (1992) 75-80.

J. K. Chamblin, *Paul and the Self: Apostolic Teaching for Personal Wholeness* (Grand Rapids: Baker, 1993).

H. J. Clinebell, *Basic Types of Pastoral Care and Counseling: Resources for the Ministry of Healing and Growth* (Nashville: Abingdon, 1984).

E. H. Cousins, "What is Christian Spirituality?," *Modern Christian Spirituality: Methodological and Historical Essays,* ed. B. C. Hansan (Atlanta: Scholars Press, 1990).

M. Cox, *Handbook of Christian Spirituality* (San Francisco: Harper & Row, 1985²).

H. Cox, *Fire from Heaven: The Rise of Pentecostal Spirituality and the Reshaping of Religion in the Twenty-first Century* (Reading: Addison-Wesley, 1995).

A. R. Crollius, "The Meaning of Culture in Theological Anthropology," in *Inculturation: Its Meaning and Urgency,* eds. J. M. Waliggo *et al.* (Kampala: St Paul Publications, 1986).

J. W. Crossin, *What are They Saying about Virtue?* (New York: Paulist, 1985).

G. Dautzenberg, "Seele (*Naefaes — Psyche*) im Biblischen Denken sowie das Verhältnis von Unsterblichkeit und Auferstehung," *Seele,* Hrsg. K. Kremer (Leiden/Köln: EJ Brill, 1984).

J. T. de Jongh van Arkel, "A Paradigm for Pastoral Diagnosing" (Unpublished dissertation: Pretoria" University of South Africa, 1987).

W. J. de Klerk, *Pastorale Sensitiwiteit* (Johannesburg: Perskor, 1975).

H. F. de Wit, *De Verborgen Bloei: Over de Psychologische Achtergronden van Spiritualiteit* (Kampen: Kok Agora, 1993).

J. Delumeau, *Une Histoire du Paradis* (Fayard: Libraire Arthéme, 1992).

C. den Hertog, *Het Zonderlinge Karakter van de Godsnaam: Literaire, Psychoanalytische en Theologische Aspecten van het Roepings*verhaal *van Mozes* (Zoetermeer: Boekencentrum, 1996).

K. Depoortere, *A Different God: A Christian View of Suffering,* Louvain Theological & Pastoral Monographs 17 (Louvain: Peters Press/W. B. Eerdmans, 1995).

M. Dombeck & J. Karl, "Spiritual Issues in Mental Health Care," *Journal of Religion and Health* 26, no. 3 (1987) 183-197.

D. Dorr, *Integral Spirituality: Resources for Community, Justice, Peace and the Earth* (New York: Orbis, 1990²).

E. Drewermann, *Die Spirale der Angst* (Freiburg: Herder, 1991⁴).

E. Drewermann, *Tiefenpsychologie und Exegesen*, Band 2 (Freiburg: Olten, 1992³).

E. Drewermann, *Zeiten der Liebe* (Freiburg: Herder, 1992⁴).

J. H. Ellens, "Sin and Sickness: The Nature of Human Failure," *Counseling and the Human Predicament: A Study of Sin, Guilt and Forgiveness*, eds. L. Aden & D. G. Benner (Grand Rapids: Baker Book House, 1989).

E. H. Erikson, *Identity and the Life Cycle: Psychological Issues*, vol. I, no.1 (New York: International University Press, 1959).

E. H. Erikson, *Youth: Change and Challenge* (New York: Basic, 1963).

E. H. Erikson, *Identity. Youth and Crisis* (London: Faber & Faber, 1974²).

E. H. Erikson, "Reflections on Dr. Borg's Life Cycle," *Adulthood*, ed. E. H. Erikson (New York: W. W. Norton, 1978).

J. Fentener van Vlissingen, *Het Pad van de Geestelijke Begeleiding: Van Praatpaal tot Waarborg* (Den Haag: J. N. Voorhoeve, 1980).

J. Firet, *Het Agogisch Moment in het Pastoraal Optreden* (Kampen: Kok, 1977³).

M. B. Fishbein & B. H. Raven, "The AB Scales: An Operational Definition of Belief and Attitude," *Readings in Attitude, Theory and Measurement*, ed. M. B. Fishbein (New York: John Wiley & Sons, 1967).

G. Fitchett, *Assessing Spiritual Needs: A Guide for Caregivers* (Minneapolis: Augsburg, 1993).

P. Foot, *Virtues and Vices and Other Essays in Moral Philosophy* (Berkeley: University of California Press, 1978).

J. W. Fowler, *Stages of Faith: The Psychology of Human Development and the Quest for Meaning* (San Francisco: Harper & Row, 1981).

J. W. Fowler, *Faith Development and Pastoral Care* (Philadelphia: Fortress, 1987).

M. Fox, "Introduction: Roots and Routes in Western Spiritual Conscience," *Western Spirituality*, ed. M. Fox (Santa Fe/New Mexico: Bear & Co., 1981).

M. Fox, *Creation Spirituality: Liberating Gifts for the Peoples of the Earth* (San Francisco: Harper, 1991).

R. W. Franklin & J. M. Shaw, *The Case for Christian Humanism* (Grand Rapids: Eerdmans, 1991).

E. H. Friedman, *Generation to Generation: Family Process in Church and Synagogue* (New York: Guilford, 1985).

R. E. Friedman, *The Disappearance of God: A Divine Mystery* (New York: Little Brown & Co., 1995).

G. Friedrich, "'Eusebes,'" *Theological Dictionary of the New Testament*, vol. 7 (Grand Rapids: Eerdmans, 1971).

W. A. Galston, "Introduction," *Virtue Nomos XXXIV*, eds. J. W. Chapman & W. A. Galston (New York University Press, 1992).

B. Gareis, "Entwicklung und Lebenslauf," *Handbuch der Psychologie für die Seelsorge* Band I: Psychologische Grundlage, Hrsg. J. Blattner *et al.* (Düsseldorf: Patmos, 1992).

C. Gerdes, "Rypheid," *Die Ontwikkelende Volwassene*, eds. C. Gerdes *et al.* (Durban: Butterworth, 1981).

C. V. Gerkin, *The Living Human Document: Re-visioning Pastoral Counseling in a Hermeneutical Mode* (Nashville: Abingdon, 1984).

A. Gesché, Topiques de la Question du Mal. *RTL* (1986) 393-418.

A. D. Goldberg, "Hillel's Maxim: Framework for Psychological Health," *Journal of Religion and Health* 31, no. 2 (1992) 107-111.

L. Goppelt, *Theologie des Neuen Testaments* (Göttingen: Vandenhoeck & Ruprecht, 1980³).

C. Graafland, *Van Calvijn tot Barth: Oorsprong en Ontwikkeling van de Leer der Verkiezing in het Gereformeerd Protestantisme* ('s-Gravenhage: Boekencentrum, 1987²).

L. K. Graham, *Care of Persons, Care of Worlds: A Psychosystems Approach to Pastoral Care and Counseling* (Nashville: Abingdon, 1992).

G. Green, *Imagining God: Theology and the Religious Imagination* (San Francisco: Harper & Row, 1989).

W. Günther, "Godliness, Piety (*Eusebeia*)," *Dictionary of New Testament Theology* vol. 2, ed. C. Brown (Exeter: Paternoster, 1976) 90-95.

D. Guthrie, *New Testament Theology.* (Leceister/Illinois: Inter-Varsity, 1981).

O. Haendler, *Grundriss der Praktischen Theologie* (Berlin: Alfred Töpelmann, 1957).

H. C. Hahn, "Conscience (*Syneidesis*)," *The New International Dictionary of New Testament Theology* vol. 1, ed. C. Brown (Exeter: Paternoster, 1975).

D. J. Hall, *Professing the Faith: Christian Theology in a North American Context.* (Minneapolis: Fortress Press, 1993).

A-G. Hamman, *L'homme Image de Dieu: Relais-Études* 2 (Paris: Desclée, 1987).

S. Hauerwas, *Naming the Silences: God, Medicine and the Problem of Suffering* (Grand Rapids: Eerdmans, 1990).

D. H. Heath, *Fulfilling Lives: Paths to Maturity and Success.* (San Francisco: Jossey-Bass, 1991).

F. Heinemann, *Filosofie op Nieuwe Wegen* (Utrecht: Aula, 1963).

G. Heitink, *Pastoraat als Hulpverlening: Inleiding in de Pastorale Theologie en Psychologie.* (Kampen: Kok, 1977).

D. A. Helminiak, *Spiritual Development: An Interdisciplinary Study* (Chicago: Loyola University Press, 1987).

E. Herms, "Virtue: A Neglected Concept in Protestant Ethics," *Scottish Journal of Theology* 35 (1982) 481-495.

D. J. Hesselgrave, *Counseling Cross-culturally* (Grand Rapids: Baker, 1984).

A. C. Heuer, *Pastoral Analysis: Introductory Perspectives* (The Institute for Pastoral Analysis S.A., University of Durban-Westville, 1987).

J. A. Heyns, *Teologiese Etiek* deel 1 (Pretoria: NG Kerkboekhandel, 1982).

J. Hick, *The Metaphor of God Incarnate: Christology in a Pluralistic Age* (Louisville, Kentucky: Westminister, 1993).

S. Hiltner, *Preface to Pastoral Theology* (Nashville: Abingdon, 1958).

L. R. Hubbard, *Dianetics: The Modern Science of Mental Health* (Surrey: New Era, 1986).

P. E. Hughes, *The True Image: The Origin and Destiny of Man in Christ* (Grand Rapdis: Eerdmans, 1989).

D. Hutsebaut, "Post-critical belief: A new approach to the religious attitude problem," *Journal of Empirical Theology* 9, no. 2 (1996) 8-66.

J. Jacobi, *The Psychology of C. J. Jung* (London: Routledge & Kegan Paul, 1968²).

M. A. Jeeves, "Psychology of Religion," *New Dictionary of Theology*, eds. S. B. Ferguson & D. F. Wright (Leicester: Inter-Varsity Press, 1988) 543-547.

P. K. Jewett, *Who We Are: Our Dignity as Human (Humans?): A Neo-Evangelical Theology* (Grand Rapids: Eerdmans, 1996).

L. T. Johnson, "Friendship with the World/Friendship with God: A Study of Discipleship in James," *Discipleship in the New Testament*, ed. F. F. Segovia (Philadelphia: Fortress Press, 1985).

W. D. Jonker, *Christus, die Middelaar* (Pretoria: NG Kerkboekhandel, 1977).

W. D. Jonker, "Die Eie-aard van die Gereformeerde Spiritualiteit" (Unpublished Paper, Faculty of Theology, University of Stellenbosch, 171 Dorp St., Stellenbosch, S. Africa, February 1989).

S. M. Jourard, & T. Landsman, *Health Personality: An Approach from the Viewpoint of Humanistic Psychology* (New York: Macmillan, 1980⁴).

C. G. Jung, *Psychological Types or the Psychology of Individuation* (London: Kegan Paul, Trench, Trubner, 1946).

C. G. Jung, *On the Nature of the Psyche*. The Collected Works of Jung, vol. 8, Bollingen series 20 (Princeton: Routledge & Kegan Paul, 1973³).

E. Jüngel, "Der Menschliche Mensch: Die Bedeutung der Reformatorischen Unterscheidung der Person von Ihren Werken für das Selbstverständnis des Neuzeitlichen Menschen" (Unpublished Paper: University of Stellenbosch, 171 Dorp St., Stellenbosch, S. Africa, August 1987).

G. D. Kaufman, *God-Mystery-Diversity: Christian Theology in a Pluralistic World* (Minneapolis: Fortress Press, 1996).

E. S. Klein Kranenburg, *Trialoog: De Derde in het Pastorale Gesprek* ('s-Gravenhage: Boekencentrum, 1988).

M. Klessmann, *Identität und Glaube* (München: Kaiser-Grünewald, 1980).

F. H. Klooster, "The Uniqueness of Reformed Theology: A Preliminary Attempt at Description," *Calvin Theological Journal* 14 (1979) 32-54.

H. Köhler, *Theologische Anthropologie: Die Biblische Sicht des Menschen und der Mensch der Gegenwart* (München: Ehrenwirth Verlag, 1967).

P. Kreeft, *Back to Virtue* (San Francisco: Ignatius, 1986).

K. Kremer, *Seele: Ihre Wirklichkeit, Ihr Verhältnis zum Leib und zu Menschliche Person* (Leiden: Brill, 1984).

C. E. Kunz, *Schweigen und Geist: Biblische und Patristische Studien zu Einer Spiritualität des Schweigens* (Freiburg/Basel/Wien: Herder, 1996).

K. Leech, *Spirituality and Pastoral Care* (London: Sheldon, 1986).

M. Légaut, *Vie Spirituelle et Modernite* (Paris: Duculot/Centurion, 1992).

B. H. Lemme, *Development in Adulthood* (Boston: Allyn & Bacon, 1995).

C. Lindijer (red.), *Beelden van God: Orientaties op het Denken en Spreken over God in Onze Tijd* ('s-Gravenhage: Meinema, 1990[2]).

H-G. Link, "Eschatos," *The New International Dictionary of the New Testament* vol. 3, ed. C. Brown (Exeter: Paternoster, 1978).

H. Löhr, *Umkehr und Sunde im Hebraerbrief* (Berlin: Gruyter, 1994).

R. B. Louden, "On Some Vices Of Virtue Ethics," *American Philosophical Quarterly* 21, no. 3 (1984) 227-236.

D. J. Louw, "Spiritualiteit as Bybelse Vroomheid in die Teologie en die Gemeentelike Bediening," *Praktiese Teologie* 4, no 2 (1988) 1-17.

S. Macedo, *Liberal Virtues* (Oxford: Clarendon, 1991).

A. MacIntyre, *Der Verlust der Tugend: Zur Moralische Krise der Gegenwart* (Frankfurt: Campus Verlag, 1984[2]).

D. D. Martin & J. van Engen, *Carthusian Spirituality: The Writings of Hugh of Balma and Guigo de Ponte* (New York: Paulist Press, 1997).

A. Matti, *Of Zoek naar God als Minnaar* (Baarn: Ten Have, 1996).

S. McFague, *Models of God* (Philadelphia: Fortress, 1987).

J. McGrath & A. McGrath, *The Dilemma of Self-Esteem: The Cross and Christian Confidence* (Wheaton/Cambridge: Crossway Books, 1992).

J. McIntyre, *The Shape of Pneumatology: Studies in the Doctrine of the Holy Spirit* (Edinburgh: T. & T. Clark, 1997).

J. T. McNeill, *A History of the Cure of Souls* (New York: Harper & Row, 1951).

G. C. Meilaender, *The Theory and Practice of Virtue* (Notre Dame, Indiana: University of Notre Dame Press, 1984).

W. W. Meissner, *Life and Faith: Psychological Perspectives on Religious Experience* (Washington DC: Georgetown University Press, 1987).

J. Miles, *God: A Biography* (London: Simon & Shuster, 1995).

A. T. Möller, *Inleiding tot die Persoonlikheidsielkunde* (Durban: Butterworth, 1980).

J. Moltmann, *Mensch: Christliche Anthropologie in den Konflikten der Gegenwort*, Themen der Theologie, Band 2 (Stuttgart: Kreuz, 1971).

J. Moltmann, *God in Creation: A New Theology of Creation and the Spirit of God* (Minneapolis: Fortress, 1993).

J. Moltmann, "Theologie im Projekt der Moderne," *Evangelische Theologie* 55, no. 5 (1995) 402-415.

Monk of the Eastern Church, *Orthodox Spirituality: An Outline of the Orthodox Ascetical and Mystical Tradition* (London: SPCK, 1980[2]).

K. Müller, *Wenn Ich "Ich" Sage: Studien zur Fundamentaltheologie. Sehen, Relevanz, Selbstbewusster Subjektivität* (Frankfurt: Peter Lang, 1994).

H. Müller-Pozzi, *Psychologie des Glaubens: Versuch einer Verhältnisbestimmung von Theologie und Psychologie* (München: Kaiser, 1975).

O. Noordmans, *Versamelde Werken*, deel 2. Dogmatische peilingen rondom Schrift en Belijdenis (Kampen: Kok, 1979).

J. C. Noordzij, *Religieus Concept en Religieuze Ervaring in de Christelijke Tradisie: Proeve van een Psychologie van de Spirituele Ontwikkeling* (Kampen: Kok, 1994).

W. E. Oates, *The Presence of God in Pastoral Counseling* (Waco: Word, 1986).

C. E. Osgood, "The Nature and Measurement of Meaning," *Semantic Differential Technique*, eds. J. G. Snider & C. E. Osgood (Chicago: Aldine, 1969).

C. E. Osgood & G. J. Suci, "Factor Analysis of Meaning," *Semantic Differential Technique*, eds. J. G. Snider & C. E. Osgood (Chicago: Aldine, 1969).

J. Overduin, *Worden als een Man* (Wageningen: Zomer & Keunings, 1967).

W. Pannenberg, *Anthropologie in Theologischer Perspektive* (Göttingen: Vanderhoeck & Ruprecht, 1983).

G. E. Pence, "Recent Works on Virtues," *American Philosophical Quarterly* 21, no. 4 (1984) 281-295.

O. H. Pesch, *Frei Sein aus Gnade: Theologische Anthropologie* (Freiburg: Herder, 1983).

T. Peters, *God — The World's Future: Systemic Theology for a Postmodern Era* (Minneapolis: Fortress Press, 1992).

G. Peterson, *Conscience and Caring* (Philadelphia: Fortress, 1982).

J. Pieper, *The Four Cardinal Virtues* (Notre Dame, Indiana: University of Notre Dame Press, 1966).

P. W. Pruyser, *The Minister as Diagnostician: Personal Problems in Pastoral Perspective* (Philadelphia: Westminister, 1976).

P. W. Pruyser, "Psychopathology and Religion," *Dictionary of Pastoral Care and Counseling*, ed. R. J. Hunter (Nashville: Abingdon, 1990) 1014-1016.

E. Rayner, *Human Development: An Introduction to the Psychodynamics of Growth, Maturity and Ageing* (London: George Allen & Unwin, 1978²).

J. J. Rebel, *Pastoraat in Pneumatologisch Perspektief: Een Theologische Verantwoording vanuit het Denken van A. A. van Ruler* (Kampen: Kok, 1981).

J. J. Rebel, "De Pneumatologische Dimensie in het Pastoraat," *Ervaren Waarheid: Opstellen Aangeboden aan Dr. H. Jonker* (Nijkerk: Callenbach, 1984).

J. J. Rebel, "Klinische Pastorale Vorming — in Discussie met Orthodoxe Theologen," *Ontginningswerk: Klinische Pastorale Vorming — een Overzicht* (Kampen: Kok, 1985) 137-141.

W. Rebell, *Psychologisches Grundwissen für Theologen* (München: Kaiser, 1988).

L. A. Richards, *A Practical Theology of Spirituality* (Grand Rapids: Academic, 1987).

H. Ridderbos, *Paulus: Ontwerp van zijn Theologie* (Kampen: Kok, 1966).

R. Riess, *Seelsorge* (Göttingen: Vandenhoeck & Ruprecht, 1973).

A-M. Rizzuto, *The Birth of the Living God: A Psychoanalytic Study* (University of Chicago Press, 1979).

P. J. Roscam Abbing, *Psychologie van de Religie: Godsdienstpsychologie in verband met Filosofie en Theologie* (Assen: Van Gorcum, 1981).

G. S. Roux, *'n Psigo-opleidingsmodel om Teologiestudente tot Psigiese Volwassenheid te Begelei* (Bloemfontein: Universiteit van die Oranje Vrystaat, s.a.).

D. N. Ruble *et al.*, *The Social Psychology of Mental Health* (New York: Guilford, 1992).

G. Ruhbach, *Theologie und Spiritualität* (Göttingen: Vandenhoeck & Ruprecht, 1987).

W. Russel, "The Apostle Paul's View of the 'Sin Nature'/'New Nature' Struggle," *Christian Perspectives on Being Human: A Multidisciplinary Approach to Integration,* eds. J. P. Moreland & D. M. Ciocchi (Grand Rapids: Baker Book House, 1993).

M. Sarot, "Pastoral Counseling and the Compassionate God," *Pastoral Psychology* 43, no.3 (1995) 185-190.

R. L. Saucy, "Theology of Human Nature," *Christian Perspectives on Being Human: A Multidisciplinary Approach to Integration,* eds. J. P. Moreland & D. M. Ciocchi (Grand Rapids: Baker Book House, 1993).

Von L. Scheffczyk,"Die Frage nach der Gottenebenbildlichkeit in der Modernen Theologie: Eine Einführung," *Der Mensch als Bild Gottes*, Hrsg. Von L. Scheffczyk (Darmstadt: Wissenschaftliche Buchgesellschaft, 1969).

R. Schippers, "Telos," *The New International Dictionary of the New Testament* vol. 2, ed. C. Brown (Exeter: Paternoster, 1976) 59-65.

B. Sieland, "Emotion," *Handbuch der Psychologie für die Seelsorge,* Band I: Psychologische Grundlage, Hrsg. J. Blattner *et al.* (Düsseldorf: Patmos, 1992).

D. J. Smit, "Wat is Gereformeerde Spiritualiteit?," *Ned Geref Teologiese Tydskrif* 29, no. 2 (1988) 182-193.

W. A. Smit, *Pastoraal-Psigologiese Verkenning van die Client-Centered Terapie van Carl Rogers* (Kampen: Kok, 1960).

R. Sons, *Seelsorge zwischen Bibel und Psychotherapie* (Stuttgart: Calwer, 1995).

K. Stock, *Grundlegung der Protestantischen Tugendlehre* (Gütersloh: Chr. Kaiser, 1995).

S. Strasser, *Fenomenologie en Empirische Menskunde* (Arnhem: Van Loghum Slaterus, 1965²).

C. T. Taylor, *The Ethics of Authenticity* (Cambridge: Harvard University Press, 1991).

N. Ter Linden, *Het Verhaal Gaat* (Amsterdam: Balans, 1996).

S. Terrien, *Till the Heart Sings: A Biblical Theology of Manhood and Womanhood* (Philadelphia: Fortress, 1985).

N. S. T. Thayer, *Spirituality and Pastoral Care* (London: Sheldon, 1985).

G. Theissen, *Psychologische Aspekte Paulinischer Theologie* (Göttingen: Vandenhoeck & Ruprecht, 1983).

P. Thevénaz, *What is Phenomenology?* (Chicago: Quadrangle Books, 1962²).

H. Thielicke, *Mensch Sein — Mensch Werden: Entwurf einer Christlichen Anthropologie* (München: Piper, 1978²).

H-J. Thilo, *Beratende Seelsorge* (Göttingen: Vandenhoeck & Ruprecht, 1971).

D. Tieleman, *Geloofscrisis als Gezichtsbedrog: Spiritualiteit in een Postmoderne Cultuur* (Kampen: Kok, 1995²).

D. Tieleman, "De Pastor als Grenzganger: Pastoraat in een Post-Moderne Context Voorbij Restouratie en Secularisatie," *Praktische Theologie* 1 (1996) 3-23.

E. Todt, & S. Heils, "Denken," *Handbuch der Psychologie für die Seelsorge,* Band I: Psychologische Grundlage, Hrsg. J. Blattner *et al.* (Düsseldorf: Patmos, 1992).

D. Tracy, "The Foundations of Practical Theology," *Practical Theology,* ed. D. Browning (San Francisco: Harper & Row, 1983).

D. Tracy, *On Naming the Present: Reflections on God, Hermeneutics, and Church* (New York: SCM Press, 1994).

G. Trianosky, "What is Virtue Ethics all About?" *American Quarterly* 27, no.4 (1990) 335-344.

A. van de Beek, *De Adem van God: De Heilige Geest in Kerk en Kosmos* (Nijkerk: Callenbach, 1987).

A. van de Beek, *Schepping: De Wereld als Voorspel voor de Eeuwigheid* (Nijkerk: Callenbach, 1996).

G. van den Brink & M. Sarot (red.), *Hoe is uw Naam? Opstellen over de Eigenschappen van God* (Kampen: Kok, 1995).

J. van der Lans, "Voorwoord," *Spiritualiteit: Sociaalwetenschappelijke en Theologische Beschouwingen*, ed. J. M. van der Lans (Baarn: Amboboeken, 1984).

J. A. van der Ven, *Entwurf Einer Empirischen Theologie* (Kampen: Kok, 1990).

J. A. van der Ven, "De Structuur van het Religieuze Bewustzijn," *Tijdschrift voor Theologie* 36 (1996) 39-60.

J. A. van der Ven, "Autonom vor Gott?," *Autonomie und Glaube: Festschrift Herman Häring*, Hrsg. H. Küng (Kampen: Kok, 1997).

F. O. van Gennep, *De Terugkeer van de Verloren Vader* (Baarn: Ten Have, 1990⁴).

C. A. van Peursen, *Lichaam-Ziel-Geest* (Utrecht: Bijleveld, 1961²).

P. J. van Strien & N. C. A. Meyer, "Semantisch onderzoek van religieuze begrippen", *Nederlands Tijdschrift voor de Psychologie en haar Grensgebieden* XXIV, no. 8 (Sept. 1969) 541-550.

W. van 't Spijker, "Tussenbalans," *Spiritualiteit*, ed. W. van 't Spijker (Kampen: De Groot Goudriaan, 1993).

P. Vardy, *Het Raadsel van God* (Baarn: Callenbach, 1997).

J. Veenhof, "Spiritualiteit in de Gereformeerde Kerken," *Gereformeerd Theologisch Tijdschrift* 92, no. 3 (1992) 157-171.

W. H. Velema, *Nieuw Zicht op Gereformeerde Spiritualiteit* (Kampen: Kok, 1990).

A. Vergote, *Religie, Geloof en Ongeloof: Psychologische Studie* (Antwerpen/ Amsterdam: De Nederlandsche Boekhandel, 1984).

A. Vergote, "Psychology of Religion as the Study of the Conflict Between Belief and Unbelief," *Advances in the Psychology of Religion*, ed. L. B. Brown (Oxford: Pergamon, 1985), 52-61.

M. Viau, *Perspectives on Practical Theologies and Methodologies*, Unpublished paper read at the International Academy of Practical Theology, Seoul, Korea (April 1997) 22-26.

J. M. Waliggo et al. (eds.), *Inculturation: Its Meaning and Urgency* (Kampala: St Paul Publications).

G. D. Weaver, "Psychology of Religion," *Psychology and the Christian Faith*, ed. S. L. Jones (Grand Rapids: Baker, 1986).

O. Weber, *Grundlagen der Dogmatik I* (Neukirchen-Vluyn: Neukirchener Verlag, 1972⁴).

H. Weder, "Exegese und Psychologie: Zu Gerd Theissens Analyse Paulinischer Theologie," *Verkündigung und Forschung* 33, no. 1 (1988) 57-63.

J. Weima, *Reiken naar Oneindigheid: Inleiding tot de Psychologie van de Religieuze Ervaring* (Ambo: Baarn, 1988).

M. Welker, *God the Spirit* (Minneapolis: Fortress Press, 1994).

B. Wentsel, *God en Mens Verzoend*, Dogmatiek Deel 3a (Kampen: Kok, 1987).

H. Wiersinga, *Verzoening als Verandering: Een Gegeven voor Menslijk Handelen* (Baarn: Bosch & Keuning, 1972).

H. R. Wijngaarden, *Hoofdproblemen der Volwassenheid* (Utrecht: Bijleveld, 1952).

C. Wilson, *Lord of the Underworld: Jung and the Twentieth Century* (Wellingborough: Aquarian, 1984).

E. Wolff, *Anthropologie des Alten Testaments* (München: Kaiser, 1973).

K. M. Woschitz, *De Homine: Existenzweisen Spiegelungen, Konturen, Metamorphosen des Antiken Menschenbildes* (Graz: Verlag Styria, 1984).

E. Yarnold, "The Theology of Christian Spirituality," *The Study of Spirituality*, eds. C. Jones & G. Wainwright (London: SPCK, 1986).

A. Zegveld, *Tot Vrijheid Bestemd: Spiritualiteit en Geloofsbelijdenis* (Baarn: Gooi & Sticht, 1994).

W. Zijlstra, *Op Zoek naar een Nieuwe Horizon: Handboek voor Klinische Pastorale Vorming* (Nijkerk: Callenbach, 1989).

PRINTED ON PERMANENT PAPER • IMPRIME SUR PAPIER PERMANENT • GEDRUKT OP DUURZAAM PAPIER - ISO 9706

ORIENTALISTE, KLEIN DALENSTRAAT 42, B-3020 HERENT